OUTDOOR EDUCATION

OUTDOOR EDUCATION

second edition

JULIAN W. SMITH
Professor of Education
Michigan State University

REYNOLD EDGAR CARLSON
Department of Recreation and Park Administration
Indiana University

GEORGE W. DONALDSON
Professor, Taft Field Campus
Northern Illinois University

HUGH B. MASTERS
Director Emeritus
Georgia Center for Continuing Education
University of Georgia

PRENTICE-HALL, INC., ENGLEWOOD CLIFFS, NEW JERSEY

PHOTO CREDITS: *title page, Part I, Part III* and *Part IV*, courtesy of World Wide Photos; *Part II*, courtesy of Wendy Holmes, photographer; *Part V*, courtesy of Bloomfield Hills (Michigan) Public Schools

LB
1047
.S58
1972

1972, 1963

ISBN: 0-13-644997-2

Library of Congress Catalog Card Number: 70-37638

10 9 8 7 6 5 4 3 2 1

PRINTED IN THE UNITED STATES OF AMERICA

Prentice-Hall International, Inc., London
Prentice-Hall of Australia, Pty. Ltd., Sydney
Prentice-Hall of Canada, Ltd., Toronto
Prentice-Hall of India Private Limited, New Delhi
Prentice-Hall of Japan, Inc., Tokyo

contents

v

3   outdoor education and the learning process 38

II
outdoor education in schools and colleges

4   education in the outdoors 53

5   outdoor education in camp settings 104

6   education for the outdoors 146

III
outdoor education through public, professional, and private agencies

7   outdoor education through park and recreation agencies 177

IV
resources and leadership for outdoor education

V
planning for outdoor education

preface

This book is designed as a guide for providing learning experiences in the outdoors and for teaching the skills necessary to successful outdoor living. It is directed toward those who would use this environment to supplement and enhance the educational process and toward those who desire to help people find satisfaction in a wide variety of outdoor interests and pursuits. No new body of knowledge is being proposed. Rather, it is the aim of this text to show how known principles of learning can apply to education *in* and *for* the outdoors.

Outdoor education, as conceived by the authors, is multidisciplinary in character. The term is used in its broadest sense to include schools, colleges, and public and voluntary agencies. In the following pages the authors attempt to show the application of outdoor experiences to the broad education of people, young and old. It is our thought that this will add freshness and vitality to learning. There is discussion of the role of state, federal, and voluntary agencies which provide leadership, land, and facilities. Suggestions are given for personnel and leadership preparation and for the initiation of outdoor education programs in schools, colleges, park and recreation departments, camps, and community agencies. Many illustrations are provided of successful outdoor programs now in operation throughout the country.

It is hoped that this book will serve as a guide to administrators, teachers, and community leaders for initiating outdoor education in the school or college curriculum or in agency programs. In this way the full value of the outdoors can be brought within the reach of millions of people who might otherwise be deprived of these experiences. There is a wealth of available resources that will help make outdoor education a reality in every community. These resources, as well as why and how they should be used, are examined in this book.

The authors are indebted to many people whose inspiration and leadership have helped to direct professional efforts in outdoor education. We are especially grateful to those who have given counsel and encouragement in the preparation of this book. The limitations of space will not permit mention of the names of those whom we would like to recognize, but we do wish to pay special tribute to our parents, who first taught us to love the outdoors.

JULIAN W. SMITH
REYNOLD E. CARLSON
GEORGE W. DONALDSON
HUGH B. MASTERS

OUTDOOR EDUCATION

I

philosophy
and development

1

the societal setting
for outdoor education

A new urgency in the need for outdoor education pervades America today. Never before have humans faced the kind of crisis now menacing the world. A population increasing at a rate that threatens to overwhelm the earth has brought overcrowding, erosion of soil, pollution of air and water, and unprecedented pressures on resources. Open space has become more and more difficult to hold. Ugliness and noise have intruded on our sensibilities. Wildlife habitats have disappeared, and some species have vanished irretrievably. The social evils of the ghetto, poverty, and crime may be attributed in large part to overpopulation.

Environmental quality and the general quality of living are intimately related: only as we provide for one can we have the other. Among the many things the quality of living is dependent on are food, air, water, and living space; it is also dependent upon such nonmaterial things as opportunities for self-achievement, social relationships, mental and emotional stimulation, and love and beauty.

Technology may solve many of the problems of the environment, but it cannot do so without the understanding and support of people. In democratic countries, informed and concerned people are essential in making political decisions affecting the environment. The United States is dedicated as no other country in the world to the idea of education for all; it is now in the midst of a renewed and expanded effort to educate all ages and all segments of society, to bring about an understanding of environmental problems, and to stimulate popular participation in their solution. Since the United States is also the world's greatest consumer of nonrenewable resources and the greatest polluter of air and water, the country has a moral responsibility to lead the world in education for improving environmental quality.

Outdoor education is concerned with that segment of man's natural environment which might be termed biophysical—air, water, land, and living things. It is concerned with ecology—man's dependence on his natural environment and the interrelationships within it. Too often man has stood aside in the belief that he was an observer of the natural world. Today we recognize that man is not merely an observer but an integral part of the community, nourished and buffeted like other living things by the wind, sun, rain, and all other natural phenomena.

Many young people today are concerned with "relevance" in education. Nothing is more relevant to human life than understanding man's relationship to and dependence upon the world of nature. In this period of crisis, however, knowledge is not enough. From knowledge there must develop convictions and actions to make possible solutions of the problems that beset us. A positive activism must result, with each individual recognizing that his own actions have contributed to the problem, and that changes in individual actions may be even more important than the collective actions we must take.

Outdoor education is based on an assumption that many things about the natural environment are learned best in direct contact with that environment. Such learning makes the deepest impact and endures the longest. Teacher and student become partners in the outdoor experience as this learning is planned and organized.

During most of man's existence, the outdoors has been his home. In the open spaces he has sought food and shelter, enjoyed what leisure time was available, and taught his offspring how to live. Now, in the twentieth century, and in one of the world's greatest materialist cultures, modern man turns to outdoor living to spend some of his newly acquired free time. Most people would immediately agree that it is good for man to spend time in the outdoors, to participate in activities that will help him enjoy, understand, and appreciate nature's phenomena. The outdoors is, after all, man's earliest and most natural home.

But modern living has removed much of the population from close contact with the land, and has created a need for man to learn about his physical universe and to acquire the skills and appreciations necessary to enjoy fully some of the values of his original habitat. To meet these present-day needs, a broad educational program will be required—one which has implications for all the institutions, organizations, and agencies that impinge on the educative process. Such a program must encompass all ages and include all the planned and contrived learning experiences available in the community.

the societal setting

Outdoor education should be viewed in relation to the needs of the society in which it originates. Far-reaching changes are taking place in America, and these changes must be reflected in the schools supported by that society. A number of contemporary societal influences have given impetus to outdoor education.

1. Deterioration of the natural environment has brought us to such a crisis that without drastic changes in the management and use of resources, extremely serious consequences to mankind will result.

2. Increasing urbanization has deprived many children and youth of contact with the land.

3. The tempo of modern living is frenzied and much of man's work is specialized and meaningless, depriving him of the opportunities for creative expression formerly associated with work.

4. Automation, mechanization, and computerization, paradoxically, have increased the amount of time available for off-the-job living, while offering little opportunity for the development of knowledge, skills, and attitudes necessary for the worthy use of leisure time.

5. Industry and automation imposed on age-old biological patterns of humans have suddenly removed many of the opportunities for physical exercise, making it necessary to find additional ways of keeping fit.

6. The cumulative effect of the industrial age has created a world of abstractions, words, and spectators—thus producing a need for real and firsthand experiences in the educative process.

7. Materialism has come to dominate the life style of many Americans, and its threat to the human spirit makes it necessary to reassess the qualities that make a good life.

In order to better understand the influences which have created the need for learning and living in the outdoors, it is necessary to examine some characteristics of modern society more closely.

1. *Deterioration of the environment.* For years voices crying in the wilderness have warned of a coming crisis, but only recently has there been serious realization that the course of our so-called progress would have to be turned—if it was not already too late—from its certain path to ruin. The loss of excellence in the environment makes excellence of living impossible. Water and air are polluted. Soil washes away. Forests and range lands are debilitated. Wetlands disappear. Wildlife is decimated. Open lands are covered by highways, shopping centers, housing developments—urban sprawl. Litter is everywhere.

Deterioration of the environment has reached such drastic proportions that fundamental changes in our way of life are critically necessary. Not the least of these changes must come in education.

If excellence of living is a legitimate objective, and no one disputes it, then degrading the environment is intolerable. Educated, thinking people will do something about the ecological problem. They will seek to establish a working relationship between man and nature; they will make rational choices when deciding on problems of land and water use; in short, they will respect and restore the delicate balance necessary for excellence of life.

2. *Urbanization.* Industrialization is the key to most of the great changes, current and past, in our society. Industrial plants, often employing thousands of people, have taken the place of the small, family owned and operated business of the past. Even agriculture, considered by some as our most efficient industry, has become industrialized. Urbanization has been a direct result of industrialization: larger and more specialized industry requires more workers; workers require goods and services, which are furnished by still more people drawn into the population complex. Recent years have witnessed what has been called a "flight from the great cities," even if this flight has only been to suburbia or "exurbia." America has a tradition—authentic and real—of small town and rural living. It may be that the retreat from the great cities is motivated by a subconscious urge to return to the simpler life of a past era. But, like all of man's yearnings to reverse the tides of modern life, this one, too, is doomed to only partial success. Modern man, in the mass, can no more return to rural living than he can reverse the course of history, as indeed he would have to do to become rural.

3. *The frenzied tempo of modern living.* One needs only to view the traffic going into a large city on a weekday morning, or to watch the rush onto a subway train, to be convinced that the tempo of modern living is frantic. The visible experiences of a typical day

for millions of people would indicate mechanical behavior. If the inner workings of the mind could be seen as easily, there would be frustration and confusion for too many people. The attempts to escape from all of these disturbing influences are portrayed in the great exodus from the cities during weekends and on holidays.

The fact that much of man's work is meaningless, depriving him of many of the opportunities for creative expression, is one of the causes of the rapid tempo of living and the restlessness that accompanies it. Specialization of vocation is essential to the industrial society. Assembly line production methods call for a high degree of expertness in a fragmented operation. Even industrial planners, whose primary concern must be mechanical efficiency, have expressed concern about the worker whose job seems unimportant to him because he is unable to visualize his role in—and importance to—the productive process. Specialization has manifested itself, not only in the factory, but throughout American life; even the farm has become a place of machines and of relatively specialized workers. This trend has many implications for those interested in education and personality development.

4. *Mechanization, automation, and computerization.* Beginning with the Industrial Revolution, man's work has been more and more accomplished by machines, which themselves have become more and more automatic. Now computers are programming the machines. In a very real sense, the working day of many Americans is spent in serving a machine.

Reduction of work, both in amount and difficulty, is another of the concomitants of industrialization which may be a mixed blessing. Although he has reduced his work day and week, as well as the physical toil involved, man has, by and large, failed to make good and creative use of the time and energy saved. This is becoming a critical issue in a society which gives so much more time for leisure but offers little help in how to use it. Education generally has not stepped into this breach in American life. A deplorable number of Americans actually search for ways to kill time. Work gives dignity and meaning to life; likewise, leisure must fulfill the need for creativity and recreation.

Thus modern living denies people many desirable experiences that were the heritage of their forebears. With most of the adult population two generations removed from the land, there is a noticeable lack of skills, appreciations, and attitudes about the land and the outdoors. These changes in living have significant implications for education, with special implications for health and recreation. Since people are not born with the skills and knowledge for using natural resources of the land wisely, children and adults of this day must have educational experiences in the outdoors before they can make the greatest use of the natural physical endowments of the land.

5. *Sedentary living.* Industrialization and automation are creating a style of living that affects the functioning of the human body. Imposed on old physiological patterns of humans, the forces that have eliminated many of the hardships and ills of rugged frontier life have also removed most of the opportunities for normal physical exercise. All too many of man's ills and diseases are being traced directly or indirectly to soft living with its lack of exercise. There is, and has been, considerable national concern for fitness, partially due to the high number of rejections from military service which occurred in World Wars I and II. In the early 1940s an office of physical fitness was established in Washington, D.C., starting a trend continued in the Eisenhower, Kennedy and later administrations. John F. Kennedy, in an article entitled "The Soft American," said:

> For physical fitness is not only one of the most important keys to a healthy body; it is the basis of dynamic and creative intellectual activity. The relationship between the soundness of the body and the activities of the mind is subtle and complex. Much is not yet understood. But we do know what the Greeks knew: that intelligence and skill can only function at the peak of their capacity when the body is healthy and strong; that hardy spirits and tough minds usually inhabit sound bodies.
>
> In this sense, physical fitness is the basis of all the activities of our society. And if our bodies grow soft and inactive, if we fail to encourage physical development and prowess, we will undermine our capacity for thought, for work and for the use of those skills vital to an expanding and complex America.
>
> Thus the physical fitness of our citizens is a vital prerequisite to America's realization of its full potential as a nation, and to the opportunity of each individual citizen to make full and fruitful use of his capacities.[1]

Outdoor experiences make an important contribution to fitness. The escape from routine, the demand for physical exertion inherent in many outdoor activities, and the lift to the spirit that comes to many participants all contribute to a healthy mind and body. Through their variety, ranging from the most contemplative to the most strenuous,

---

[1] From "The Soft American," by President-elect John F. Kennedy (*Sports Illustrated*, December 26, 1960). By special permission of *Sports Illustrated*, Time, Inc.

outdoor experiences can meet the needs of all age groups and numerous personal interests and inclinations. Dr. George D. Stoddard, Chancellor of New York University, in addressing a Conference of the State Inter-Agency Committees for Recreation said:

Outdoors we are more likely to remember that man, a glorious animal, is still an animal. Under a heavy veneer of culture, he responds to differentials in food, digestion, exercise, and disease resistance—to organic fitness, if you will—in a world that is highly artificial. In the past, plague and hunger brought him close to annihilation. In the future, the deadliness is not there, nor is old-style killing; it is in new-style radiation that can poison the very air we breathe. If my remarks were to focus upon the adult population, they would be somewhat gloomy. Having gone from good specimens of animals—as a naturalist would rate them—to rather weak, pale, unexercised, dependent creatures—all in order to achieve the higher virtues of speech, history, and technology—man is now, through notable defects in social and spiritual quality, in danger of losing this new life. If he does lose what has been painfully built up in the last ten thousand years, he will become at once a poor brute and a pitiable personality. Unable to return to the caves and the woods, where he would starve, he would, I suppose, clutter up the roads that lead to mass institutional care.[2]

6. *Abstractions.* Much of man's living in western culture is surrounded by abstractions and words. The absence of some of the realness and simplicity of rural and pioneer days is most evident in the so-called middle class—skilled labor, management, and the professions. One of the obvious symptoms of these excessive abstractions is the return to do-it-yourself activities and other pursuits of a tangible nature. One can observe in any suburban area the afternoon rush from the office to the backyard, the workshop in the basement, or the favorite stream or field, where words give way to solitude and abstractions are crowded out by reality. The Bermuda-clad adult male operating his power lawnmower on a small lot is perhaps more concerned with the therapy of the power-drawn machine than the cutting of the grass. Psychologists call this an escape, which in this instance is probably a search for freedom from the tensions and abstractions of the workaday world. Outdoor education helps fill the gap created by city living. The return to the outdoors, the life of the trail and the camp,

[2] George D. Stoddard, "Educating People for Outdoor Recreation," presented to the Conference of State Inter-Agency Committees on Recreation, Bear Mountain, New York, May 23, 1961.

is exciting and challenging to people if only for a brief time and under simulated conditions. To hordes of Americans these ventures into the open spaces represent the life that the human race once knew—so intimately, in fact, that much of his physical and neural structure is designed for it.

7. *Materialism.*   Many critics of modern society deplore the preoccupation with the technological gadgets of today. Selectively used, these developments can certainly give increased comfort and convenience, and can enrich the possibilities for entertainment and education. Too often, however, they have so preempted attention and time that people have lost more basic satisfactions. For example, the American "love affair" with the automobile has made it a dominant force in our economy and in our daily lives; yet it is a mixed blessing. It has brought air pollution, usurpation of valuable land and money for highways, violent death from accidents, frenetic restlessness of many, failure to exercise, and the decrease in interest in simple pleasures and pursuits.

Television addiction can likewise be a danger, substituting vicariousness for real experiences and passivity for activity. To be bound to things—be they automobiles, television sets, boats, planes, extravagant homes, or the countless other material developments of our age —may distract us from the consideration of values important to both youth and adults.

society's needs

Modern society, with its improvement of the standard of living, has created certain basic human needs which can in part be met by outdoor education. They include (1) the need for creative living; (2) the need for physical and mental fitness; (3) the need for roots in the soil; (4) the need for broader and deeper ecological understandings; and (5) the need for spiritual satisfactions. A close examination of these needs will offer some clues for better educational programs that relate to the use of the outdoors.

The Need for Creative Living.   The phenomenal interest and increased participation in a wide variety of free-time activities, including those that occur in the outdoors, is not only due to the greater availability of free time, but also is an indication of the need for creative living. Dr. Harold H. Anderson, Research Professor of Psychology at Michigan State University, says, "Creativity is to be aware of one's world of things and of persons, to encounter, respond, commune, communicate with the world about one." [3] It expresses itself in poetry, art, music and numberless other ways. Young and old alike seek outlets for their inner feelings.

It is axiomatic that every human being has a spark of creativity that needs to find expression. It is what Dr. Jay B. Nash called "mother wit" or a "sixth sense." The change in the amount and nature of work has removed many of the opportunities for expression of creativity which in earlier days was exhibited in craftsmanship and ingenuity. Leisure-time must take on the more important function of providing an outlet for this need. Outdoor learning and living have a most significant role in supplying wholesome interests and pursuits of lifelong value.

The Need for Physical and Mental Fitness.   Industrialization and the resultant vicarious nature of present-day life have been responsible for restlessness, boredom, and tension—all of which affect the fitness of the individual. The need for physical fitness created by sedentary living is also closely related to the mental and emotional needs of people.

Living in crowded cities is fraught with the potentials for maladjustment, crime, and delinquency. There are few places in metropolitan areas where anything which resembles a child's community can be found outside the school environment, other than the occasional park and camp. It has been observed that when city children are transported to day camps or other outdoor areas, the first overt act outside the crowded bus is to roll down the grassy slopes or climb nearby trees. Children's reactions such as these should provide some clues to the physical and emotional needs of human beings who now live under conditions for which their minds and bodies are unprepared. The value of outdoor education in this regard will be discussed further, and programs will be suggested that will meet some of the needs.

The Need for Roots in the Soil.   Increasing attention is being given to the interdependence of living things and their relationship to the land. Conservationists are warning the public that more concern must be given to the wise use, care, and protection of natural resources. In a society which is becoming increasingly urban, ways must be found to create attitudes and an appreciation of man's relationship to the land. Psychiatrists, psychologists, sociologists, and others are also expressing concern over people's lack of contact with

---

[3] Harold M. Anderson, Introduction to *Creativity and Education* (mimeo.), 1961.

the physical world which supports them; too many are now so removed from the land that they have no knowledge or concern about the sources of food, shelter, and clothing. Those interested in the growth and development of human beings deplore the lack of opportunities for children to take part in the growing of living things—a garden, farm animals, or a pet. Many believe that contact with the land is essential in the normal growth of the individual.

The Need for Deeper and Broader Ecological Understandings. Closely related to the need for roots in the soil is society's need to understand the totality and interrelatedness of the environment in which it exists. Ecological crises have made Americans keenly aware of their environmental problems. New programs are mounted to meet these crises and we are told that mankind must mend his ways or perish.

Outdoor education, taking place as it does *in* the environment and using outdoor resources for educational purposes, is in a unique position to influence both understanding of and feelings about the environment. Indeed, outdoor educators were among the earliest practitioners of what has come to be called environmental education, because their outdoor education programs have usually stressed the need to understand, to appreciate, and to protect the environment.

The Need for Spiritual Satisfaction.   The spiritual needs of man are difficult to describe, and impossible to separate completely from the emotional, social, and physical aspects of life. However, the potential contribution of outdoor education to moral and spiritual values warrants a special emphasis here. Few would deny that outdoor experiences offer unusual opportunities for perceiving the why and how of the universe. Quiet and solitude in the open spaces, free from the noise and distractions of city living, are conducive to meditation, appreciation of natural beauty, and worship. Since outdoor settings, particularly camps, offer opportunities for developing appreciations that contribute to spiritual satisfaction, those planning outdoor education programs should not overlook these possibilities. Free from sectarianism and creed, the outdoors is rich in opportunities for finding what Henry James has called "the great good place."[4] This increasing awareness of the value of outdoor experiences, of the need for skills to enjoy the outdoors, is a significant factor in the recent interest in outdoor education on the part of schools.

[4] Quoted in V. Pullias, "Woods, Streams, and Unobstructed Sky," *NEA Journal* (May 1959): 48.

the need for outdoor education

The characteristics and trends of today's mechanized society call for outdoor education. The outdoors can serve many of the present-day needs of people—physical, emotional, and spiritual. Machines insure production; education must provide for the creative and wise use of increased free time. It has been predicted that automation will change our lives as much as did the Industrial Revolution. An enormous task lies ahead in upgrading the activities of a sizable proportion of our population, to swing them away from the frivolous to the constructive use of their leisure hours, and to insure an environment fit for living.

Outdoor education is needed to enrich and vitalize education. Succeeding chapters will describe what can be done to provide learning and living experiences in America's outdoors.

SUGGESTIONS FOR FURTHER STUDY AND RESEARCH

1. What changes in the last fifty years in your own community have implications for outdoor education?
2. Examine a modern sociology textbook for predictions of conditions in the future which may influence outdoor education.
3. Analyze your own leisure-time activities during the past year and estimate the percentage of time spent in outdoor pursuits. What were the types of activities: passive or active? appreciation arts or manipulative skills?
4. Learn about the organizations and agencies in your community which focus on environmental problems. What relation do they have to outdoor education? What relation can you see them having?
5. What are your state's procedures for dealing with environmental problems? Are there implications here for outdoor education?

REFERENCES

American Association for Health, Physical Education and Recreation. *Outdoor Education for American Youth.* Washington, D. C.: AAHPER, 1957.

Brightbill, Charles K. *Man and Leisure*. Englewood Cliffs, N. J.: Prentice-Hall, 1961.

Freeberg, William H., and Taylor, Loren E. *Philosophy of Outdoor Education*. Minneapolis, Minn.: Burgess Publishing Company, 1961.

Outdoor Recreation for America. A Report to the President and to the Congress by the Outdoor Recreation Resources Review Commission. Washington, D. C.: U. S. Government Printing Office, January 1962.

2

the development of outdoor education in the american educational system

Learning from nature has always been a part of the developmental process of man. It is not surprising in an industrialized and materialistic culture which has created the current environmental crisis, that society seeks to rediscover the link between man and the earth from which he sprang. A thread of the concept of learning in and for the outdoors has run through the public's belief about education for generations. Wordsworth put the thought into these words:

> And hark! how blithe the throstle sings!
> He, too, is no mean preacher:
> Come forth into the light of things,
> Let Nature be your Teacher.
>
> She has a world of ready wealth,
> Our minds and hearts to bless—
> Spontaneous wisdom breathed by health,
> Truth breathed by cheerfulness.
>
> One impulse from a vernal wood
> May teach you more of man,

Of moral evil and of good
Than all the sages can.[1]

In *Education for All American Youth*, published by the Educational Policies Commission in 1952, several references were made to the need for education in outdoor settings.[2] The late Dr. Earl Kelley, formerly Professor of Secondary Education at Wayne State University, in his refreshing and delightful book entitled *Education For What Is Real*, says:

Part of the education of urban children should take place in rural settings. City life is very artificial. Milk comes in bottles. Pieces of paper are the medium of exchange. There are many possibilities for education in a large city, but man grievously needs to have a chance to make contact somewhere with the good earth from which he sprang. He cannot forever deny this heritage. In the country, life springs up all around. The mysteries of the earth itself, of plant and animal husbandry, of procreation and of decay, teach the lessons of life as no city pavement can do.[3]

One of the chief characteristics of modern education is its seemingly changing nature. This is particularly noticeable when "new" terms appear to give special emphasis to existing parts of the general curriculum. Illustrative of this procedure are terms such as health education, physical education, driver education, and home and family living.

Modern educational philosophers generally agree that the function of American education is to help build a society where the good life is within reach of all. Applying this to the individual, a broad rational basis for making choices must be developed. In this connection, the Educational Policies Commission, in a publication entitled *The Central Purposes of American Education*, says:

The worthy use of leisure is related to the individual's knowledge, understanding, and capacity to choose, from among all the activities to which his time can be devoted, those which contribute to the achievement of his purposes and to the satisfaction of his needs. On these bases, the individual can become aware of the external pressures which compete for his attention, moderate the influence of

[1] William Wordsworth, "The Tables Turned" (1798), lines 13-24.
[2] Educational Policies Commission, *Education For All American Youth* (Washington, D.C.: The National Education Association, 1952).
[3] Earl C. Kelley, *Education For What Is Real* (New York: Harper & Row, 1947).

these pressures, and make wise choices for himself. His recreation, ranging from hobbies to sports to intellectual activity pursued for its own sake, can conform to his own concepts of constructive use of time.[4]

Outdoor education is the term currently used for the learning experiences in and for the outdoors; one of the puposes of this chapter is to place it in its proper setting in general education.

HISTORICAL DEVELOPMENT

Let us examine some of the historical developments in education which have influenced those working to regain their heritage of outdoor learning and living. A concept of learning in and from nature will be found early in education literature, although the term "outdoor education" is of a more recent origin. Colonial schools, such as Latin grammar schools and academies, were established to serve the select few who were preparing for the learned professions. Reading, writing, arithmetic, and Latin were the main academic offerings of that period. Sports, games, and social events were outside the limited curriculum, but were available to the more favored as extracurricular activities in private schools or within the home and neighborhood of those who could afford the "luxury."

The nature and purpose of early American schools restricted formal education to a small segment of the children and youth—10 to 15 per cent at the most.

The founding fathers' belief in education was evident in the official documents of that day and in the federal Constitution itself. They felt the success of the new democracy depended on the education of all the people. This belief in education, accompanied by a demand for schooling for more children and youth, opened the way for a system of free public education. Universal education brought changes in the scope and content of the schools' offerings. As could be expected, the curriculum did not keep pace with the rapid growth of free public schools, which eventually became available to all children. The famous Kalamazoo Case of 1871, which established the twelve years of free public education, signaled the beginning of an educational system which became increasingly more sensitive to the needs and desires of the people, even though it was several decades before

[4] Educational Policies Commission, *The Central Purpose of American Education* (Washington, D.C.: National Education Association, 1961).

OUTDOOR EDUCATION IN THE CURRICULUM

OUTDOOR EDUCATION

EDUCATION **IN** THE OUTDOORS ———— and ———— EDUCATION **FOR** THE OUTDOORS

Use of outdoor settings as laboratories for classroom-related field experiences, study, observation, and research

Teaching manipulative skills for outdoor interests and outdoor recreation

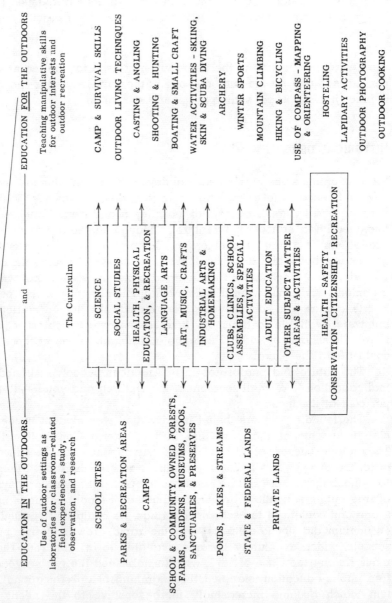

The Curriculum

| SCIENCE | CAMP & SURVIVAL SKILLS |

SCHOOL SITES

PARKS & RECREATION AREAS

CAMPS

SCHOOL & COMMUNITY OWNED FORESTS, FARMS, GARDENS, MUSEUMS, ZOOS, SANCTUARIES, & PRESERVES

PONDS, LAKES, & STREAMS

STATE & FEDERAL LANDS

PRIVATE LANDS

SCIENCE

SOCIAL STUDIES

HEALTH, PHYSICAL EDUCATION, & RECREATION

LANGUAGE ARTS

ART, MUSIC, CRAFTS

INDUSTRIAL ARTS & HOMEMAKING

CLUBS, CLINICS, SCHOOL ASSEMBLIES, & SPECIAL ACTIVITIES

ADULT EDUCATION

OTHER SUBJECT MATTER AREAS & ACTIVITIES

HEALTH - SAFETY
CONSERVATION - CITIZENSHIP - RECREATION

CAMP & SURVIVAL SKILLS

OUTDOOR LIVING TECHNIQUES

CASTING & ANGLING

SHOOTING & HUNTING

BOATING & SMALL CRAFT

WATER ACTIVITIES - SKIING, SKIN & SCUBA DIVING

ARCHERY

WINTER SPORTS

MOUNTAIN CLIMBING

HIKING & BICYCLING

USE OF COMPASS - MAPPING & ORIENTEERING

HOSTELING

LAPIDARY ACTIVITIES

OUTDOOR PHOTOGRAPHY

OUTDOOR COOKING

OTHERS

many school systems established a program sufficiently broad to meet the varied needs of the greater numbers attending schools.

In the early part of the twentieth century, with the rapid growth of industrialization, the Smith-Hughes Act stimulated the development of vocational education. During the same period, there was an expansion of the schools' offerings in general education, with emphases on citizenship, home and family living, music, guidance, art, and other areas of learning which had significance for community living. What has been termed "progressive education," stimulated by the Eight-Year Study,[5] made marked changes in teaching methods and content in many schools. Despite criticism during and after the so-called progressive education movement, it was in this period that the newer philosophy and concept of learning made headway, resulting in adaptations of the curriculum which would more nearly meet the needs of a greater percentage of students.

MAJOR INFLUENCES IN CURRICULUM CHANGE AFFECTING OUTDOOR EDUCATION

Two major forces on American education that had significant implications for outdoor education were industrialization and the newer views on the nature of learning. In 1917, the Educational Policies Commission set forth the famous seven cardinal objectives of education; of these, health and the wise use of leisure were important influences on the early beginnings of outdoor education. In a book entitled *Leisure and the Schools*, a significant statement concerning the relationship of the curriculum to leisure-time interests is made:

> The entire school curriculum must be conceived as a tool for developing attitudes, understandings, knowledges and skills required for leisure literacy.[6]

Another historical incident affecting the growth of outdoor education was the public concern over physical fitness following World War I. The widely publicized statistics regarding rejections from military service due to the lack of fitness and the presence of a large number of physical defects were responsible for drawing much attention to health and physical education. Mandatory legislation regarding health and physical education was enacted in many states,

---

[5] Wilford M. Aikin, *The Story of the Eight-Year Study* (New York: Harper & Row, 1942).

[6] *Leisure and the Schools* (Washington, D.C.: American Association for Health, Physical Education and Recreation, 1961).

while directors and supervisors were appointed to state departments of education to give leadership to school districts. Most of the earlier efforts in outdoor education and camping can be traced to health, physical education, and recreation departments in colleges, universities, and state departments of education.

WHAT IS OUTDOOR EDUCATION?

Outdoor education means learning *in* and *for* the outdoors. It is a means of curriculum extension and enrichment through outdoor experiences. It is not a separate discipline with prescribed objectives, like science and mathematics; it is simply a learning climate offering opportunities for direct laboratory experiences in identifying and resolving real-life problems, for acquiring skills with which to enjoy a lifetime of creative living, for building concepts and developing concern about man and his natural environment, and for getting us back in touch with those aspects of living where our roots were once firm and deep.

This concept of outdoor education brings it within reach of every school, college, and educational agency in the land. Most teachers and youth leaders will find outdoor resources which they can use to enhance learning and to provide opportunities for acquiring knowledge and skills necessary for wholesome outdoor pursuits.

EDUCATION IN THE OUTDOORS

It is fortunate that outdoor education is not regarded as a specialized or circumscribed area of learning. Its most distinguishing characteristics are its boundlessness and abundance. Learning outdoors is unique in that it makes use of the natural environment in the educative process, and offers opportunities for solving many of the real problems that are found there. The outdoors may be described, therefore, as a laboratory that offers an opportunity for direct experiences leading to a greater appreciation, a clearer interpretation, and a wiser use of the natural environment in achieving the purposes of education. This phase of outdoor education might well be called the appreciation arts.

The late L. B. Sharp described the principal thesis underlying outdoor education:

That which can best be learned inside the classroom should be learned there. That which can best be learned in the out-of-doors

OUTDOOR EDUCATION

IN THE SCHOOL

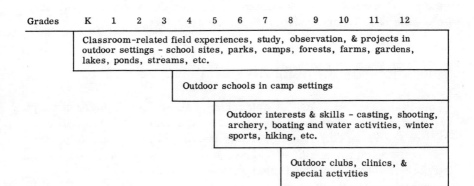

Grades	K	1	2	3	4	5	6	7	8	9	10	11	12

Classroom-related field experiences, study, observation, & projects in outdoor settings - school sites, parks, camps, forests, farms, gardens, lakes, ponds, streams, etc.

Outdoor schools in camp settings

Outdoor interests & skills - casting, shooting, archery, boating and water activities, winter sports, hiking, etc.

Outdoor clubs, clinics, & special activities

IN SUBJECT MATTER DISCIPLINES

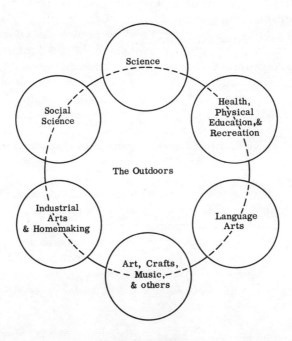

Science

Social Science

Health, Physical Education, & Recreation

The Outdoors

Industrial Arts & Homemaking

Language Arts

Art, Crafts, Music, & others

through direct experience, dealing with native materials and life situations, should there be learned.[7]

If one accepts the premise that the outdoors is a good place for achieving some of the accepted goals of education more effectively than can be done in the classroom alone, then educational experiences outdoors become an integral part of general education.

EDUCATION FOR THE OUTDOORS

This is the second phase of outdoor education. This broader concept of outdoor education was developed by the Outdoor Education Project of the American Association for Health, Physical Education and Recreation, and has added greater dimension to outdoor education programs throughout the United States.

The skills, attitudes, and appreciations necessary for the intelligent use of the outdoors are integral parts of a good educational program and constitute an important phase of outdoor education. While many of the skills necessary for outdoor pursuits are often considered a part of physical education and recreation programs, they have significance in science, conservation, health, safety, citizenship, and other subjects which cut across all areas of the curriculum.

The development of attitudes concerning conservation is an important part of learning outdoor sports such as camping, casting and angling, shooting, and hunting. Relating casting activities to a class in biology, or including game management in a program of shooting, are simple illustrations of how outdoor education may vitalize classroom learnings. Outdoor skills and appreciations, while usually considered an important part of a well-rounded program, have often been neglected in favor of gymnastics and team sports and games.

Today's needs call for more emphasis on the teaching of greater numbers of skills that involve individual participation. Many outdoor activities, such as the ones described in this book, are appropriate for all ages.

One needs only to look at the current scene to realize how Americans are engaging in a great variety of outdoor activities. Millions of people, often without adequate skills, are surging into woods and onto lakes and streams. They crowd into parks; they camp everywhere; they move around the country in search of adventure and relief from crowded areas. These people, young and old, come from all walks of life.[8] It is estimated that by the year 2000 A.D. there will be ten times as many people participating in outdoor activities as there are now. There never was a more dramatic time for schools and communities to revamp their programs to provide better education for living.

OUTDOOR EDUCATION AND RELATED TERMINOLOGY

Educational labels tend to be confusing. One of the difficulties encountered by students is the fragmentation of education with its creation of various bodies to administer community educational programs. The "pigeon hole" approach used in many instructional programs often presents unnecessary obstacles in the learning process.

The effectiveness of outdoor education will depend upon a broad interpretation of its meaning by all the educational disciplines and organizations that administer outdoor programs and facilities.

The relationship of outdoor education to such terms as recreation and conservation education needs careful clarification and interpretation. The confusion and wasted energy, for example, in trying to differentiate between education and recreation is a good illustration of what should *not* happen in outdoor education. Most of the difficulties arise in the administration of various types of programs by organizations and agencies. Many involved in these activities tend to separate and fragment disciplines and learning activities in order to obtain identification and status. The term "education" is often delimited and misunderstood, and in the minds of many connotes only "formal schooling." This was the concept of a limited curriculum in grades one through twelve in the schools at the beginning of the century. The modern community school, however, makes available to all age levels many activities and services. Some programs bear such labels as recreation, conservation education, and health education. To say that an activity is recreation or education, or to determine the difference between outdoor education and outdoor recreation, is unnecessary if the focus of the community's educational program is on human growth and community improvement.

Outdoor education. As stated, *outdoor education* applies to a wide variety of learning experiences that take place in an outdoor

[8] Marion Clawson, "The Crisis in Outdoor Recreation," *American Forests* (March 1959 and April 1959), Reprint No. 13, Resources for the Future, Inc.

setting, and to the skills, appreciations, and attitudes needed for maximum satisfaction in outdoor recreation and activities. Some of these may relate to subject matter areas, educational disciplines and activities, while others contribute more specifically to physical and mental fitness. In outdoor settings, rich in nature's resources, outdoor education provides many opportunities to develop conservation concepts, and, more importantly, to bring about behavioral changes for the improvement of the environment and man's life in it. Outdoor education also provides opportunities for acquiring skills and interests in outdoor pursuits.

Re-creation. The greatest contribution of outdoor education may be in the re-creation of mind and body of millions who must find release from the tensions and complexities of modern living. The outdoors offers countless opportunities for individuals to seek activities in which they can participate and find maximum satisfaction. Unorganized and unregimented, millions can enjoy outdoor living if they have some preparation for it. The term recreation, which so often has only the connotation of organized activities, hardly describes most of the wholesome free-time pursuits, many of which are related to the outdoors.

Although outdoor education as described in this book makes many specific references to the curriculum of schools and colleges, the application and use of the knowledge acquired in and for the outdoors is often labeled outdoor recreation. The meaning of recreation in this context is more aptly described as *re-creation* and applies to what man does with himself in the time spared from obtaining the necessities of life. The words *recreation* and *leisure*, with the current scene as a backdrop, mean much more than the Puritanical concept which implied idleness. Recreation involves basic human values. It has been said that most of the good and evil of society emanates from the time which is not spent in working or sleeping. Creative living involves improving the quality of this extra time.

Dr. Jay B. Nash conceives of recreation as an outlet to creativity.[9] Thus defined, it describes the potential for man's endeavors during the newly acquired time at his disposal. While some may find opportunity for self-expression and creativity in their work, most will seek creation and re-creation during the nonworking hours.

The scope of activities that could be labeled "recreational" is as broad as life itself. What is, or has been, considered work for some is recreation for others. The range of pursuits may vary from quiet med-

[9] Jay B. Nash, *Philosophy of Recreation and Leisure* (Dubuque, Iowa: William C. Brown, 1953).

itation and reading to mountain climbing and vigorous sports. Relatively few of life's most satisfying activities require being led or being regimented. On the contrary, the desire, motivation, and performance coming from within the individual will be expressed through the hand, mind, and heart. Unfortunately, recreation has come to mean only *organized* activities to many people; this fact may account for part of the lag in good leadership and adequate facilities for such organized activities.

Recreation has an added challenge and responsibility in this day of sedentary living: *fitness*. It is obvious that the American adult more likely to keep fit does so by participating in self-directed activities of his choosing, provided his education has included a wide variety of lifelong interests and skills. Decades before industrialization reached its full stride, when the work week was long and the time for recreation short, the job of earning a living required more physical energy. It was during this time that passive recreation and organized activities constituted a major portion of the program sponsored by public and private recreation agencies. Coming off the farms, up from the mines, and away from the trades, many people sought rest and relaxation in organized sports and games and social forms of recreation. Today, with longer periods of free time and paid vacations, neither passive diversion nor organized activities can meet all of man's recreational needs. The tensions and complexities of city and suburban living and routinization of much of work create a great demand for self-propelled and self-directed recreational activities. The great surge of interest in all forms of outdoor activities illustrates the desire to escape from mechanized living and return to open spaces.

Recreation and outdoor education are inseparable when educational experiences occur and men find full expression through creative living.

Environmental and conservation education.   Aldo Leopold's definition of conservation as "a state of harmony between men and land" [10] is accepted generally by conservationists. The development of concepts and attitudes in humans as reflected in their behavior toward their physical environment has been labeled *conservation education*. The term *environmental education* is used by some as an alternative. Both refer to the man-land ethic or the "ecological conscience" of which Aldo Leopold spoke so impressively.

Environmental education seeks to broaden the concept of ecological relationships of the physical environment which hindered the

[10] Aldo Leopold, *A Sand County Almanac*, with other essays on conservation from *Round River* (New York: Oxford University Press, 1966), p. 222.

cause of conservationists. It attempts to see man as a part of the total environment rather than as an organism on the outside looking in. It sees man as the major educable, decision-making factor in the ecological mix. Environmental education, however, like conservation education, suffers by being a little of everything poured into an educational pot, and thus means many things to many people. There are many educational experiences that inspire humans to seek behavior promoting an improvement in the quality of the physical environment. Some of these experiences are associated with subject areas such as science and social studies; others are concomitants of skills and outdoor sports such as angling and hunting. Many concepts and attitudes are developed in the classroom; others are achieved more effectively in the presence of natural resources. When an individual realizes the need for a better environment for himself, he becomes more aware of its importance for society—even to prolonging man's existence on the earth. Food, clothing, shelter, and outdoor recreation relate him directly to the physical environment. The millions that seek outdoor pursuits today are the greatest potential students of the outdoor environment, for they have an immediate stake in natural resources. Outdoor education has great possibilities for children and youth, especially those who are developing interests in outdoor activities. It is to the credit of leaders in outdoor education that an appreciation of and a concern for the improvement of the environment has always been one of the major objectives of outdoor education.

The development of attitudes toward a quality environment is accomplished best when the learner has satisfying experiences with the resources involved, as in outdoor programs described in this book. Schools report that when children have experiences in the improvement of their environment, whether it be planting trees or helping to prevent erosion and pollution, they feel a greater responsibility for the care and wise use of natural resources. They have a stake in the land. The young adult who learns the skills and finds satisfaction in angling, hunting, boating, hiking, camping, and nature activities will have more concern about the care and management of the natural assets that contribute to his recreation. Direct experiences, followed by study in the classroom, constitute a complete learning circle in a given phase of outdoor education. Similar results occur in the care and planning of school sites when children have had a part in beautification and landscaping. In the Civilian Conservation Corps of the 1930s young men had the opportunity to improve the land and develop attitudes toward its wise use. In sections of the country where there have been good programs of outdoor education young citizens not only seek more recreation in the outdoors, but tend to use the resources more wisely.

Terms such as outdoor education, recreation, environmental education, and conservation education have common characteristics and are interrelated. None of them can be regarded as disciplines, for they have no basic content of their own. The content is in the long-established disciplines, and the identity of the terms is dependent upon the setting of the activities involved, the grouping of the experiences, and their applications.

Resident outdoor education or school camping.   The term *school camping*, and its relationship to outdoor education has caused some confusion. Historically, school camping described the educational experiences that took place when a school used a resident camp for a period af several days. The term *outdoor education* includes such school programs in camp settings and is the more appropriate description, differentiating the experience from organized camping. A week in a camp, planned by a classroom and involving children and their teachers, differs in many ways from the more extended summer camping programs under the auspices of public or private agencies. More recently, the term *resident outdoor education* has been used. It is generally accepted now that a school program in a camp setting, regardless of its name, is one mode of outdoor education—and a very successful one.

The term *outdoor education* is being used by educators and by many conservationists, park and recreation leaders, and others involved with community agencies, to describe outdoor experiences which contribute to the well-being of people and to the wise use of natural resources. To this end, it will vitalize and enrich the programs of institutions, organizations, and agencies designed to improve the quality of living.

IMPLICATIONS OF OUTDOOR EDUCATION FOR THE CURRICULUM

One of the best ways to ascertain the nature and validity of outdoor education in the curriculum of schools and colleges is to examine the underlying principles. The following were formulated by George W. Donaldson and Oswald H. Goering:

1. Outdoor education is a method or process utilizing the outdoors.
2. Outdoor education is not a separate discipline; it has no subject matter of its own.
3. Direct experiences in the outdoors are essential to the understanding of one's environment and, thus, to general education.

4. Useful outdoor experiences may be as brief as a few minutes or as long as several days or weeks.

5. A comprehensive outdoor education program provides direct experiences in the outdoors for all children at all grade levels.

6. Outdoor education involves the learner, emphasizes the exploratory approach, and utilizes multisensory experiences.

7. Outdoor experiences should be an integral part of modern education.

8. Outdoor education can be utilized to develop the understandings and skills necessary for the wise use of leisure time.[11]

Some principles, particularly relating to elementary schools, are described in the booklet *Outdoor Education*, published by the American Association for Health, Physical Education, and Recreation.[12]

OUTDOOR EDUCATION AND THE OBJECTIVES OF EDUCATION

Most of the specific objectives of various subject areas lie within the goals of general education. The best known and most widely accepted listing of the aims of education are those set forth by the Educational Policies Commission.[13] The preservation and development of both the individual and society demand that every normal individual develop the abilities and characteristics essential to effective social living in a democracy. These abilities and characteristics translated into aims may be stated as:

1. the objectives of Self-Realization
2. the objectives of Human Relationship
3. the objectives of Economic Efficiency
4. the objectives of Civic Responsibility.

The testimony of those conducting outdoor programs and a perusal of the literature describing activities under way in many schools indicate how various outdoor activities, related to the aims mentioned above, can contribute to the broad purposes of education. A brief outline will illustrate.

[11] George W. Donaldson and Oswald H. Goering, *Outdoor Education: A Synthesis* (Las Cruces, N.M.: Educational Resources Information Center/Clearinghouse on Rural Education and Small Schools, New Mexico State University, 1970), p. 2.

[12] Julian W. Smith, *Outdoor Education*, rev. ed. (Washington, D.C.: AAHPER, 1970).

[13] Educational Policies Commission, *The Purposes of Education in American Democracy* (Washington, D.C.: National Education Association, 1938).

1. *Self-Realization.*   Children and youth have a basic need for individual and group experiences in the natural outdoor environment. Camps and other outdoor settings offer a variety of social situations. Examples:

a. Living in groups and associating with people in informal situations.

b. Facing experiences that center around the basic physical needs for food, clothing, and shelter.

c. Performing community and group service activities.

d. Gaining an understanding of man's relation to plants, animals, and the total universe.

e. Exploring new avenues for individual creativity that are stimulated by beauty and the outdoor setting.

f. Acquiring skills in outdoor living in connection with satisfying experiences.

g. Applying school subjects such as science or mathematics to life situations in the outdoors.

h. Enjoying good physical and mental health through outdoor living.

i. Providing for status needs and feelings of self-dependence.

j. Sensing spiritual thoughts and feelings through contact with nature.

2. *Human Relationships.*   Through democratic processes, the individual is free to choose his activities and participate in decisions that affect his way of living. This develops his personal dignity. The friendliness and informal nature of many outdoor activities is conducive to good social living and better human relationships. Examples:

a. A variety of social settings are provided where people can be themselves and where the group relationships and individual feeling are in proper balance.

b. Camp can be a miniature community where most community problems have their counterparts.

c. Many outdoor activities are possible only through teamwork and group action.

d. Outdoor and camping experiences offer opportunities for developing new friendships.

e. Living in the outdoors is informal and simple. There is little adherence to social or economic status or other barriers to real understanding.

f. In outdoor school activities the teacher can more easily occupy the friend or pal role, thus establishing better rapport for guidance.

3. *Economic Efficiency.*   Outdoor adventures widen the horizons and present opportunities to see new fields of endeavor and other skills necessary in the total economy. Examples:

a. There is pay and satisfaction in performing a job that shows pride in good workmanship—for example, making use of trail skills, setting up camp, and engaging in good conservation practices —which will improve the natural environment.
b. More opportunities are available for planning, executing and completing a project, thus there is satisfaction in the dignity of purposeful work.
c. New professions and vocations are seen, such as forestry, park management, and agriculture.
d. Tools involving new skills are used. They may be useful in a hobby, trade, or vocation.
e. Youth can perform useful community service in improving lands, building needed facilities, and preventing pollution.

4. *Civic Responsibility.*   The development of good citizenship is a major aim of good outdoor programs. There are situations where people can gain a better understanding of the use of natural resources and realize a civic responsibility toward them. Examples:

a. Purposeful work experience for the good of the group and the larger community is an important part of many outdoor programs.
b. Sharing and cooperative planning are basic in most outdoor programs.
c. Planning committees and camp councils exemplify citizenship rights and responsibilities.
d. Outdoor programs are conducive to a maximum amount of freedom and permissiveness, accompanied by orderly planning.

GOALS OF OUTDOOR EDUCATION

Since outdoor education, as conceived by the authors of this book, is an approach to teaching, and a setting and process whereby learning is facilitated, outdoor education becomes a means rather than an end. Since outdoor education has no identifiable content of its own, it has no goals other than those of general education. A task force of the

Council on Outdoor Education and Camping of the American Association for Health, Physical Education, and Recreation, after much study, identified the relationship between some goals of general education and the means by which they might be achieved through outdoor education. In an interim report, submitted in 1971 for further consideration by the Council, a number of goals and means to achieve them were listed. Some of these appear in the chart below.

EDUCATIONAL GOALS AND MEANS IN THE OUTDOORS

Goal	Means in the outdoors
To develop the full potential of the individual	through optimum exposure to and involvement with the natural environment
To develop knowledge, skills, attitudes and appreciations for the constructive and creative use of leisure time	through exposure to outdoor interests and instruction in outdoor sports and component skills
To promote the development of social relations and individual responsibility	through group living experiences, particularly in resident outdoor education, where there are unique opportunities for student-teacher planning and participation in the camp community
To promote the development of civic responsibility	through active participation and problem-solving situations in: the community, the improvement of the physical environment, and the development of good human relationships through cooperative projects and activities
To promote the development of aesthetic interests and appreciations	through participation in positive experiences in the natural environment which contribute to the creative expression of talents and interests
To help the individual become more self-reliant and secure	through adventuresome and challenging outdoor pursuits and skills

EDUCATIONAL GOALS AND MEANS IN THE OUTDOORS (Cont.)

goal	means in the outdoors
	which require initiative and active participation in solving problems related to comfort, safety and survival
To provide opportunities for the individual to strengthen his self-concept	through achieving success and accomplishments in activities which are meaningful to the learner

Other general goals of education relate to the link between man and the world of nature about him; outdoor education contributes to the achievement of such goals. Examples:

To develop awareness, appreciation, understanding and respect for man's relationship and stewardship responsibility to the natural environment	through opportunities for exploration and problem solving in the outdoors

THE SCHOOL-COMMUNITY SETTING FOR OUTDOOR EDUCATION

Developments in American education preceding the recent emphasis on education in and for the outdoors have been recounted. The community school constitutes the modern version of the school as a service agency in an educative community. It is the most effective setting for outdoor education in its broadest sense. Since the nature and operation of a true community school is relatively new, considerable attention is devoted to it in the remaining pages of this chapter.

During the past quarter of a century, a new concept of the relationship between the school and society has developed. The idea of a school whose curriculum is responsive to the throbbing life of new communities laid the foundations of the idea of the community school. This concept furthers the realization of the goals and purposes of education by meeting individual growth needs while providing social training for democracy.

The American school aims to be a locally controlled, dynamic institution maintained by the community and delegated by the citizenry to meet basic educational needs of children, youth, and adults.

The community school is this institution in action. Its scope includes instruction and services. The school thus instituted operates within the community structure, with all the agencies interested in education, through the community curriculum. These broad offerings of educational opportunities include all of the planned and contrived learning experiences of the community, the impact of natural and manmade resources, and the supervised educational, recreational, and group work activities therein.

Characteristics of this new American institution as contrasted to the early formal school of colonial days include: general education; teaching processes; planning processes; community services; supplemental services to meet educational needs not provided by other agencies; school activities of a developmental nature; and service to people throughout their lifetime, with special attention to those of compulsory school age.

The translation of community school principles into action has definite possibilities for outdoor education. Some of these principles, and their application to outdoor education, will serve as illustrations.

1. **The community school functions as an important unit in the family of agencies serving the common purpose of improving community living.** It is therefore in a strategic position in relation to the physical environment and the outdoors. There are many local agencies, as well as state and national organizations with counterparts in the community, that have responsibilities for facilities, lands, and programs for the improvement of living. This is particularly true of those organizations concerned with the wise use of natural resources, whether for improving the soil, for better agriculture, or for providing recreational opportunities for all. There are also youth-serving agencies and social organizations concerned with providing wholesome educational and recreational programs; many include outdoor activities in their program offerings. Sharing a common interest in the outdoors are other operations of government such as park and recreation departments. Thus the community school, in seeking to enrich life through the various means related to the outdoors, should be regarded as an important resource. It often serves as a mobilizing force for concerted action, as when schools and city government cooperate in the development of a park-school, or join with other agencies in securing adequate camp facilities for the entire community.

2. **The community school acts as a service agency through which citizens assume continuing responsibility for the identification of community needs and the development of action programs to meet these needs.** The natural projects for it to undertake are those

OUTDOOR EDUCATION IN THE COMMUNITY

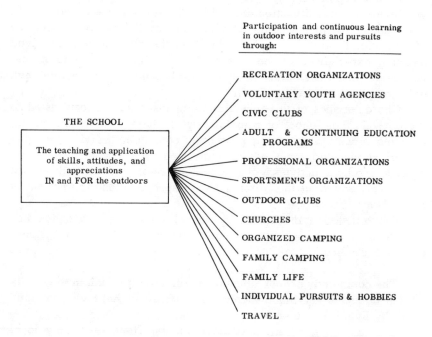

relating to the outdoors. Obviously the improvement of living is often directly or indirectly related to the physical environment and land use. The beautification of the landscape, the prevention of water pollution, and the improvement of agriculture are all practical illustrations of improvement projects that should be a part of the school's instructional and service programs.

3. **The community school assumes its responsibility for better living by beginning with the immediate school environment in designing a curriculum sufficiently comprehensive and flexible to achieve this purpose.** One of the newer ideas in building a local school curriculum is to begin with local community problems. This procedure fits well into the generally accepted principle of developing learning experiences in accordance with the interests and purposes of the classroom group. Consequently, when problems arise in any of the school subjects, such as the physical and social sciences and communication arts, it is logical to focus attention on solving local problems first, then consider state, national, and world affairs. With this approach, which is fundamental in the development of a community school curriculum, outdoor education occupies a logical and natural place. Physical science courses might focus on problems of reforestation, water

and air pollution, and game management in some sections of the country. In other places, land considered marginal in terms of agricultural use might more profitably be developed into park and recreation areas. The utilization of outdoor areas for physical education and recreation in some communities would make for a curriculum richer than the traditional programs in gymnasiums and playfields.

4. **The community school makes full use of all community resources for learning experiences.** The use of the outdoors as a resource for learning is a natural development. Playgrounds, parks, camps, recreation areas, and other available facilities and lands are laboratories for many activities which are included in the usual school program. They provide a multitude of informal educational and recreational opportunities in which children, youth, and adults are interested. A community with a bird sanctuary or museum of natural history could ill afford to use classroom space for mounted specimens. A school district would be foolish to spend tax money in purchasing a large tract of land for a playground site, with an adequate park in the same neighborhood. Community planning is concerned with the complete utilization of all natural resources of an area for educational purposes.

5. **The community school is a dynamic, constantly changing social institution which stands ready to serve the learning needs of all in accordance with the responsibilities assigned to it by the citizens.** A school located in a suburban area, where people sought fresh air and open spaces, would miss its calling not to be involved in land use planning, beautification, experiences in gardening, solving problems of water supply, sewage disposal, and pollution. Likewise, schools of inner cities and ghettos can use limited space and green areas as laboratories to help solve problems relating to the improvement of the environment.

6. **The community school service program is cooperatively planned with the people. The professional staff of the school serves in a consultant relationship.** Staff members thus have unique opportunities to give a new kind of educational leadership. The teacher is a guide to children enrolled in the school; the administrators and teachers become consultants in the improvement of community living. The science teacher may be of invaluable assistance in the development of a sanctuary; the agriculture instructor may be the most competent of the community's consultants in the improvement of agriculture; or the teacher in physical education may be a key figure in the development of recreational facilities such as parks or winter sport areas. All too often, the best trained lead-

ers and consultants—the school staff—are overlooked in the zeal of securing experts from afar. The improvement of the environment, whether it be the control of pollution or the beautification of the landscape, might well stem from the community school curriculum.

It is in the community school setting that the functioning of other educational agencies comes into focus. Recreation departments, youth-serving agencies, and community organizations of various types have a significant role in supplementing the school's program and, in this instance, outdoor education. Adult and continuing education, usually a part of the public school system, are important in extending outdoor education for the population beyond the senior high school or college levels.

Many of the outdoor programs and activities described in this book have applications for community agencies and recreation programs. While it is the responsibility of the school to provide basic instruction in a variety of outdoor sports and skills, other agencies need to provide additional opportunities for participation in a wide range of activities. A nearly ideal situation is the community school which assumes its full responsibility for a broad educational program by offering outdoor education, and by working with all other agencies in the community to insure outdoor experiences for all.

SUGGESTIONS FOR FURTHER STUDY AND RESEARCH

1. Examine various statements dealing with the purposes of education in light of our present concept of outdoor education.
2. Examine earlier concepts of education as stated by educational philosophers, such as Spencer, Pestalozzi, and Froebel, for parallels with present thought about outdoor education.
3. Make an analysis of some of the new movements in education and indicate the changes in society which have brought them about.
4. Develop the structure of a community campus, including schools and agencies, from your readings or from a situation with which you are familiar.
5. Describe your concept of a community school as gained from your readings or a community with which you are familiar.
6. How does the concept of outdoor education fit into the report of the Educational Policies Commission entitled **The Central Purpose**

of **American Education** (Washington, D.C.: National Education Association, 1961)?

REFERENCES

Aikin, Wilford M. *The Story of the Eight-Year Study.* New York: Harper & Row, 1942.

American Association for Health, Physical Education and Recreation. *Leisure and the Schools.* Washington, D. C.: AAHPER, 1961.

_____. *Outdoor Education for American Youth.* Washington, D. C.: AAHPER, 1957.

Association for Supervision and Curriculum Development. *Balance in the Curriculum.* 1961 Yearbook. Washington, D. C.: National Education Association, 1961.

Donaldson, George W., and Goering, Oswald H. *Outdoor Education: A Synthesis.* Las Cruces, N.M.: Educational Resources Information Center (ERIC), Clearinghouse on Rural Education and Small Schools (CRESS), 1970.

Educational Policies Commission. *The Central Purpose of American Education.* Washington, D. C.: National Education Association, 1961.

_____. *Education For All American Youth.* Washington, D. C.: National Education Association, 1952.

_____. *The Purposes of Education in American Democracy.* Washington, D. C.: National Education Association, 1938.

Hammerman, Donald R., and Hammerman, William M., eds. *Outdoor Education: A Book of Readings.* Minneapolis, Minn.: Burgess Publishing, 1968.

Kelley, Earl C. *Education for What is Real.* New York: Harper & Row, 1947.

_____. *In Defense of Youth.* Englewood Cliffs, N.J.: Prentice-Hall, 1962.

Mand, Charles L. *Outdoor Education.* New York: J. Lowell Pratt, 1967.

Nash, Jay B. *Philosophy of Recreation and Leisure.* Dubuque, Iowa: William C. Brown, 1953.

Seay, Maurice F., and Crawford, Ferris N. *The Community School and Community Self Improvement.* Lansing, Mich.: Clair L. Taylor, Superintendent of Public Instruction, 1954.

Smith, Julian W. *Outdoor Education.* Rev. ed. Washington, D. C.: AAHPER, 1970.

3

outdoor education and the learning process

Outdoor education, like other kinds of education, came about in response to (1) the needs of the society in which it originated and (2) the nature and needs of the learners in that society. The first has been discussed in the previous chapter. The impact of societal changes on mankind generally, and childhood particularly, is enormous. Its significance is apparent when one considers child rearing of a few generations ago. Not too long ago, most Americans were born into a society characterized by:

1. Rural or semirural settings;
2. Relative lack of mechanization;
3. Parents who were vocationally nonspecialists;
4. A family which was truly an economic unit, every member contributing to making a living;
5. A family very likely to stay put in a community in which it had deep roots; and
6. A family and community which provided most, if not all, of its simple recreation.

Today's youth grow up in a radically different environment. Disintegration of the family as a social and educative force came as an indirect result of the Industrial Revolution. But it most certainly came. Despite recent emphasis on "togetherness" and some of the more encouraging developments in family recreation, the family simply does not exercise the educative role it once did. Population mobility is another requirement of the industrial society. While it was once commonplace for a person to live out his life at or near his place of birth, the modern American family moves freely, sometimes almost casually.

This is not to suggest that the latter half of the twentieth century is completely bad for youngsters. Far from it! But industrialization has created gaps in the experiences by which man rears his young. A brief look at the nature of learning, and at the person to be educated, will document these gaps.

THE NATURE OF LEARNING

What is now known about the nature of learning has importance for outdoor education. Much of the current theory of learning can be traced to John Dewey's philosophy. While there has been, and still is, controversy over some of his ideas, the importance of direct experience and problem solving persists in the theory of learning and in educational methods. According to Professor John L. Childs, "Dewey developed the conception that experience is not primarily a process in which a detached spectator passively beholds an external world; it is rather an active process of providing for interests through creative interaction with life surroundings." [1] Learning, which includes the acquisition of habits, skills, and perceptions, is a function in the process of doing, undergoing, and testing. In all statements from Thorndike to Dewey to contemporary educational philosophies, it is apparent that thinking and doing cannot be separated, that together they form the whole man. According to Stoddard, "We think what we learn." [2] Outdoor education thus becomes an important set of stimuli for learning and growth. The outdoors, as a climate for learning, encompasses both academic and skilled types of experiences. The learner can ob-

[1] John L. Childs, "Enduring Elements in the Educational Thought of John Dewey," *School of Education Bulletin*, University of Michigan, Vol. 31, No. 2 (November 1959), p. 23.

[2] George D. Stoddard, "Educating People for Outdoor Recreation," presented to the Conference of State Inter-Agency Committees on Recreation, Bear Mountain, New York, May 23, 1961.

serve, search, study, and compare, trying many theories. At the same time he can acquire skills and perceptions that contribute to his personal happiness and satisfaction. These two general types of experiences constitute the foundation of outdoor education.

In reference to the outdoor experience, Stoddard says, "It is educational only if the experience is progressively structured into an intellectual whole that is perceived by the participant." [3]

CHARACTERISTICS OF HUMAN GROWTH AND LEARNING

The young are active and energetic.   The restrictions placed upon youth by an industrial, urban society are unnatural. Nature has equipped youth for a highly active growing-up period.

The young are adventurous.   The urge to be adventurous, to explore and discover, is inborn. Youth constantly seeks new experiences. Wholesome outlets for this desire are fewer and fewer as our society becomes more complicated.

Achieving independence is a primary developmental task of children and youth.   The ultimate goal of childhood and youth is to grow up. Constantly increasing independent behavior is an important means toward that end. Yet many forces in today's world impose frustrating delays in the natural step-by-step achievement of independence.

Youth is curious.   Casual observation of the young documents this urge. Children and youth constantly seek to experience, to learn, to know. Too many ready-made answers dull the edge of curiosity. The child is a "natural" scientist who seeks to learn by a rough equivalent of the scientific process, which always proceeds from the specific to the general, from experiences to words. Yet too much of the process by which a child is educated begins and ends with words alone. This is unfortunately as true in the sciences as in other curriculum areas.

Sensory experience is an important aspect of learning.   Each sense complements and reinforces the others. Good outdoor teaching employs every possible avenue to learning—looking, listening, tasting, feeling, and smelling.

People need fun.   The era is past when fun was looked upon as undesirable, even sinful. Everyone needs diversion—especially

[3] Ibid.

the young. For youth, it may be an end; for educators it may be a means to many desirable ends. The outdoors is generally regarded as a place to have fun.

Man needs identification with something larger than self. One of the serious problems of our times is the essential rootlessness of man. It is unfortunate that this has occurred in the midst of material plenty, when the potential for true richness of living is at its greatest. Man, with all his gadgets, his superhighways, his supermarkets, with his civilization which might be called "super" in all material respects, is restless and afraid. His actions reveal his need for things that are rooted and enduring.

The surge of mankind from the cities on weekends and holidays suggests that he instinctively knows where he can go to satisfy this need. "Getting away from it all" at the seashore, the park, or the mountain lake, is actually a much more positive reaction than the words indicate. Although his cave man ancestors lived in a world of constancy, man's present environment is transient. He seems to find in the changelessness of the mountains, forests, and deserts the experiences of an almost forgotten permanence and stability.

The spiritual values of the outdoors remain largely unexplored. The means by which these values can be had by all are well stated by René Dubos:

> Our genetic makeup and therefore our most basic needs are still essentially the same as those of the Paleolithic hunters from whom all originated. Those hunters moved freely among trees and grass, streams and rocks, tame and wild animals. They engaged in occupations which were at times dangerous and which always sharpened their wits. They had to make decisions on their own, rather than being entirely programed for a limited social role. The maintenance of biological and mental health requires that technological societies provide in some form the biological freedom enjoyed by our Paleolithic ancestors.
>
> Survival is not enough. Seeing the Milky Way, experiencing the fragrance of spring and observing other forms of life continue to play an immense role in the development of humanness. Man can use many different aspects of reality to make his life, not by imposing himself as a conqueror on nature, but by participating in the continuous act of creation in which all living things are engaged. Otherwise, man may be doomed to survive as something less than human.[4]

[4] René Dubos, "Mere Survival is Not Enough for Man," *Life,* Vol. 69, no. 4 (July 24, 1970), p. 2; reprinted by special permission of the author.

Modern man has essentially the same basic drives and needs as his primitive forebears. But most of today's youth are growing up in environments which restrict or frustrate their natural development. Today's adults—products, too, of an industrial society—need educative experiences in the outdoors if they are to make full and creative use of our great outdoor heritage.

Outdoor education is truly an interdisciplinary field, cutting across many curricular areas. It possesses no subject matter of its own; its major contributions are ways of learning. Eight characteristics distinguish outdoor education, all of them relating to the methodology of learning.

1. **Direct experience.** Probably the key characteristic of outdoor education is the direct exposure to learning experiences. Without depreciating the values of vicarious experience—lectures, books, visual aids—outdoor education holds that much learning is best achieved when the materials of learning are experienced directly.

2. **Discovery, exploration, adventure.** Although students in the outdoors may never make a truly original discovery, the excitement of exploring can be theirs. Good teaching in the outdoors will seek to employ the methods of science, working from the specific to the general.

3. **Sensory learning.** Good outdoor teaching will employ every applicable sense to the learning experience. The feel and the smell of rich soil adds depth to the learner's appreciation; the sound of birds singing adds new perspective.

4. **Activities natural to childhood and youth.** Because outdoor activities are lively, exciting, even thrilling, they have an inherent appeal for youngsters. None of the gimmicks of artificial motivation are needed.

5. **Intense interest.** Interest is high when learners are totally involved in learning experiences. Because of the natural appeal of the outdoors to most children and youth, it is a relatively simple matter to secure total involvement and intense interest.

6. **Reality.** Problems in the outdoors are real to learners. They are not problems of words, pictures, charts, or diagrams. An eroded hillside is stark reality. The colors in a real sunrise have only been approximated by artists and photographers.

7. **Problems in context.** Problems encountered by learners in the outdoors exist in a real setting. In many instances, the setting is as significant as the problem itself. A problem of soil erosion in a little-used wilderness area suggests certain treatment. The same

issue in a city park or camp site requires a quite different solution. The context makes the difference.

8. **Learners most active.** It is almost a truism in educational theory that purposeful activity educates. The outdoors provides many real challenges of such character as to stimulate the learner—not just the teacher. Learners become truly active in the learning process.

OUTDOOR EDUCATION
FOR CURRICULUM ENRICHMENT

Reference has been made to outdoor education as a climate for learning and as a means of curriculum enrichment. Dean D. Willard Zahn, College of Education, Temple University, in speaking on curriculum enrichment through outdoor education, said:

It seems, therefore, correct to accept outdoor education in its present perspective as an integral part of total education, as no longer haphazard and almost whimsical, as having no real relation to status interests either within or without education per se, but rather as a means of extending interests, increasing scope, providing important means of developing creative power, in fact, aiding in meeting more effectively the total objectives of the educative process.[5]

Throughout this book, it will be shown that outdoor education is a means of curriculum enrichment, and many illustrations will be given to document this point of view. It is important, therefore, to determine which of the objectives of education and the purposes of classroom experiences can be achieved most effectively through outdoor education. Some of the unique contributions of the outdoor setting to learning are briefly described:

1. *Increases the power of observation.* The use of all the senses is important in the learning process. The outdoors provides a wealth of opportunities to see, hear, touch, taste, and smell. The classroom and the outdoor experience must be linked together. Much of the effectiveness of outdoor education will depend on the development of attitudes, activities, and response to stimuli, which should be cooperatively planned by the teacher and students.

[5] D. Willard Zahn, "Educational Enrichment Through Outdoor Education," a presentation to the Pennsylvania Regional Leadership Conference on Outdoor Education, Marshalls Creek, Pennsylvania, May 10, 1961.

2. *Stimulates interest and improves the quality of experience.* The outdoors, with its lore and attractions, serves to develop new interests and extend those which have already been partially developed. The quality of the experience is enhanced by the realism of the outdoor setting and is developed at the level of the child's experience.

3. *Provides materials for learning.* The outdoors, as one of the important community resources for learning, is nature's best equipped laboratory. It has a multitude of living and colorful materials which promote direct experiences. It is important in outdoor education that the physical world is not taken apart, but that the child sees nature first in its wholeness. Science, for example, should help children see forests, then trees, then leaves, and then the more finite life structures. The synthesis of experiences previously learned is one of the potential values of the outdoor classroom.

4. *Provides opportunities to acquire outdoor skills.* The acquisition of outdoor skills and interests for lifelong enjoyment are among the most important and unique contributions of outdoor education. The teaching of the skills for outdoor pursuits may be done directly through specialized areas such as health, physical education, and recreation, or as components of science, conservation, social studies and other phases of the curriculum that lend themselves to the use of the outdoor laboratory. This contribution of outdoor education to learning is within the broader area of creative living, which has often been called education for the wise use of leisure.

5. *Extends the classroom beyond the four walls.* Someone has said that outdoor education is a painless method of curriculum revision. Going outside the classroom, whether on the school site, to the park, or to the camp, is a logical and natural way to make more complete use of community resources. It may be the first step in utilizing the broader environment which surrounds the learner. Outdoor education opens the way for some important aspects of what many call resource-use education.

6. *Offers opportunities for exploration and research.* The outdoor laboratory is conducive to exploration and research, if the teacher, in the role of guide and learner herself, can participate in outdoor experiences and refrain from "telling" the students or giving the answers. There is no place in the school curriculum where real adventure and exploration can take place more effectively. All too often, the so-called "field trip" is a conducted tour. It has been said that some field trip leaders in an unfamiliar area find it necessary to case the woods in advance and pull up all the unknown species.

Outdoor education should be an exciting adventure that will utilize instruction through discussion and individual research. Follow-up in the classroom and research will compound the value of the period spent in the outdoors.

7. *Helps verbalizing and communication.* The permissiveness and naturalness of the outdoor environment, with careful preparation and teaching, provides unique opportunities for children to communicate, react, and to verbalize their experiences. The late Dr. Donald C. Randall, Director of the Clear Lake Camp of the Battle Creek Public Schools, often stated that the most important value of the educational experience in the camp setting is to help children communicate. In this setting particularly, inhibitions caused by classroom procedures disappear and give way to more free and creative expression.

8. *Helps supply knowledge and adds mastery.* In all too many instances the classroom does not go beyond abstractions. Many community resources, including the outdoors, not only increase the opportunities for concrete learning but also help change abstractions into meaningful life situations. In the biological sciences, for example, the learning experience may progress from the field trip to the study of ecology and then back to the outdoors for more observation.

9. *Helps extend the teacher.* Educational experiences in outdoor settings offer new and effective opportunities for teaching. Too much of the preservice preparation of teachers deals with fixed content in books and in methods classes. In contrast, the outdoor laboratory has an infinite variety of potential knowledge, often unsuspected by both teacher and children, which challenges their best efforts and demands increased study and better planning.

10. *Encourages better human relationships.* Some types of outdoor educational experiences, such as those that occur in camp settings and other group activities, offer valuable opportunities to develop better human relationships. The simplicity and wholesomeness of outdoor living encourage close personal relationships, informal associations with people, and cooperation with other members of the group. This is well illustrated when a class goes to a camp for a week. Camping and outdoor activities, especially, may restore to children a sense of belonging. The development of family camping may have possibilities for reestablishing some of the values of family living that were more evident in former days. It has often been said that outdoor living removes the shackles of sophistication and the veneer of class rank and creed. Outdoor education offers some of the best situations for good student-teacher relationships. It also helps develop

sound practices of interpersonal relations when students work and plan together.

SPECIAL EMPHASES IN OUTDOOR EDUCATION

Outdoor education as portrayed in this book is an integral part of the education continuum from preschool to the upper limits of continuing education. The underlying principles, philosophy, and program designs are generally applicable to all learners in all agencies, according to individual interests and needs, socioeconomic status, and geographic location.

There are, however, some special areas in outdoor education that deserve mention and recognition. Since program activities and facilities, with appropriate modifications, apply to all those involved in the regular educational system, two special emphases are treated briefly.

outdoor education for the handicapped

It is a generally accepted principle that insofar as possible, the physically handicapped and the mentally retarded are included in the general education continuum. Special education programs, however, are offered to supplement or, in some cases, to supplant the regular education program. Outdoor education has great meaning for the handicapped. An increasing number of programs are being designed for those who cannot participate successfully in all regular activities utilizing the outdoors as a laboratory for learning or the teaching of outdoor skills and interests. Outdoors, as in the classroom, handicapped children may excel those classed as normal in various kinds of sensory learning. The blind or partially sighted, for example, have a potential for perceiving and understanding through the senses of touch, taste, and smell superior to those who have a better sense of vision. Likewise, those with hearing difficulties may be more perceptive in the other senses. The physically handicapped may have unusual success in some individual outdoor skills that require special instruction and persistence. Mentally retarded children also find satisfaction and accomplishments in outdoor skills that may be impossible to achieve in the home or classroom.

Examples of rewarding and successful outdoor activities for those whose handicaps prevent them from participating in more complete programs include: nature trails especially designed for those who do not have vision; ramps, trails and camp facilities for wheel chairs;

archery, casting and angling, shooting sports, and other outdoor sports for those unable to participate in more active outdoor pursuits; and arts and crafts from native materials for many who have limited physical abilities.

Federal and state funds are available for the handicapped—often in proportionately larger amounts than for regular programs. Many unusual and successful programs could be described if space permitted. Information about such programs is available from the U. S. Office of Education and special education departments in local school districts.

outdoor education for inner cities

In the earlier stages of the growth of outdoor education, most developments took place in suburban, middle class, and smaller school districts. The administrative difficulties in transportation, the lack of open spaces near cities, and the larger number of children presented more difficulties in developing outdoor education programs in large cities. History will probably evaluate the move of outdoor education into the cities as its most significant gain during the 1960s. Spurred largely by federal funding, programs serving inner city children and youth sprang up in many cities, including Chicago, Detroit, Trenton, Indianapolis, Cleveland, and Seattle. Most of the programs to date for inner city children have been one-week resident ventures serving homogeneous population. However, a heartening development has been the beginning of cross-cultural programs, such as one in which Bellevue, Washington schools invited inner city children from Seattle to join Bellevue children in two resident outdoor education programs in camp settings.

Most of the outdoor education programs and activities described in this book are appropriate to, and within the reach of all schools. These include programs that require the open spaces and facilities of camps, large parks and recreation areas, as well as those activities which can occur in small areas, playgrounds, and mini-parks. Resident outdoor education programs and trips to larger outdoor areas and centers outside crowded cities are as important, if not more so, for inner city and ghetto children as for those fortunate enough to live close to the outdoors. To say that a brief experience in a resident outdoor education program is only a tantalizing and futile venture when followed by the return to the old environs of the inner city, is poor justification for not providing such experiences for inner city children. How else will a child ever know what lies beyond—or how can the desire be created within him for what the outdoors can offer

—if he never has a satisfying experience in an outdoor environment?

Changes in attitude, behavior, and the deepening of perceptions may be attained in short, intensive, and emotional experiences such as those to be had in resident outdoor education. At the same time, there can be more frequent outdoor-related learnings within the inner cities. Environmental consciousness may be acquired when children can contrast the conditions in deprived areas with the more abundant outdoor resources beyond the city. Much can be done through urban renewal and planning of green areas in the center of crowded housing and concrete jungles. While the problems of designing outdoor education programs within and without crowded metropolitan areas for inner city children may take more planning, more funds, and greater administrative flexibility in the school structure, the needs of those to be served are proportionately greater. The priorities in the objectives of outdoor education may also be different since outdoor education should make its contribution in terms of the needs of those to be served.

OUTDOOR EDUCATION AS A CHANGE AGENT

Using the outdoors as a learning environment has great potential for change in the classroom. In observing outdoor education programs that are now in operation, and in reading reports from schools that have had long experience with various outdoor learning activities, it is evident that one of the major contributions of outdoor education to the curriculum is its potential as a change agent. In recent years much has become known about effecting change. Research has helped identify the components of the change process and the role of change agents. One doctoral dissertation made a significant contribution by identifying specific strategy agents, many of which apply to outdoor education.[6] In an article entitled "Outdoor Education —Curriculum Change Agent," Miller states that outdoor education affects three major areas: people, process, and program.

Outdoor education changes people. It can help students, teachers, administrators, and parents gain new perceptions of themselves and of others. Outdoor education, because it takes place in real life situations, can provide opportunities to build better human relationships between people of diverse races, cultural backgrounds, and

[6] Peggy L. Miller, "Change Agent Strategies: A Study of the Michigan-Ohio Regional Educational Laboratory" (doctoral dissertation, Michigan State University, 1968).

experiences. It can be one of the most effective forces in the community to prevent human erosion as well as land erosion; it can be one means of saving youngsters from the education scrap heap, of reducing human diminution. Through experiences in the outdoors young and old may gain self-renewal, and become aware of their oneness with the earth, the universe, and their Creator. Outdoor education can help establish a better relationship between man and his environment by making him aware of the responsibilities for maintaining and restoring harmony between man, the land, the sky, and the oceans.

Outdoor education changes process. Outdoor education can change the methods which teachers use to help youngsters learn. Outdoor education's emphases on learning by doing, problem solving, direct experience, working with concretes instead of abstracts, and "involvement of the total organism" have been cited by educational leaders. An outdoor setting seems to demand that a teacher apply teaching and learning theories to practical situations.

Outdoor education changes program. Outdoor education can help teachers, students, and administrators look at subject matter in new ways. Outdoor education often results in the revision and reorganization of disciplines, and in the integration of various areas of the curriculum. Outdoor education dramatically points up the disparity between those learning experiences which are meaningless and artificial and those which are real and have importance for youngsters. Outdoor education often extends the rigid periods of the school day into longer blocks of time, so teachers and youngsters can explore issues and solve problems without interruption by bells.[7]

The foregoing pages described some conditions of modern society which affect the learning process. A number of characteristics of the learner have been noted. The unique contributions of outdoor education to the learning process have been briefly mentioned. The following chapters will be devoted to ways and means of improving the curriculum through outdoor education.

SUGGESTIONS FOR FURTHER STUDY AND RESEARCH

1. Write an imaginary sketch of a day in a child's life 75 years ago and compare it with today's.

[7] Peggy L. Miller, "Outdoor Education: Curriculum Change Agent," *Journal of Outdoor Education* 4, no. 1 (Fall 1969): 4.

2. Identify some outdoor learning experiences which illustrate each of the ten contributions of outdoor education to curriculum enrichment as stated in this chapter.

REFERENCES

American Association for Health, Physical Education and Recreation. *Children in Focus.* 1954 Yearbook. Washington, D. C.: AAHPER, 1954.

_____. *Outdoor Education for American Youth.* Washington, D. C.: AAHPER, 1957.

Educational Policies Commission. *The Purposes of Education in American Democracy.* Washington, D. C.: National Education Association, 1938.

Journal of Outdoor Education. Oregon, Ill.: Lorado Taft Field Campus of Northern Illinois University.

Kelley, Earl C. *Education For What Is Real.* New York: Harper & Row, 1947.

Perceiving, Behaving, Becoming. 1962 Yearbook. Washington, D. C.: Association for Supervision and Curriculum Development, 1962.

Smith, Julian W. *Outdoor Education.* Rev. ed. Washington, D. C.: AAHPER, 1970.

_____. *Outdoor Education: An Overview.* Las Cruces: New Mexico State University, Educational Resources Information Center, Clearinghouse on Rural Education and Small Schools (ERIC/CRESS), 1969.

II

outdoor education
in schools
and colleges

4

education in the outdoors

Education in the outdoors is concerned with all those experiences that bring the learner into direct relationship with the outdoor environment. Such experiences are offered on the assumption that the outdoors is a setting for learning, and that direct experiences give reality to the educative process and contribute to the enrichment of classroom learning. Education outdoors is based on the principle that some things are learned most effectively through direct experiences and that such learning is in harmony with accepted objectives of education.

It is the purpose of this chapter to describe some of the techniques and settings for using the outdoors as an educational medium. The variety of outdoor learning experiences is infinite. Only the ingenuity of the teacher, leader, or students limits the possibilities.

Outdoor experiences run the gamut from field trips, explorations, and area studies to practical projects. They may range from simple observations by kindergarten children to sophisticated investigations by college students. They may be related to a particular subject area or may cut across several areas. They may also involve bringing into the classroom and the laboratory materials to enrich indoor learning experiences. The careful selecting, planning, and evaluating of outdoor activities related directly to the classroom program will add interest and help motivate students.

Tools and equipment of many kinds may be used as aids. Among them are rulers, tape measures, thermometers, field glasses, magnifying glasses, microscopes, telescopes, levels, surveying instruments, triangles, weather instruments, soil testing kits, timing devices, turbidity recorders, increment borers, tree-measuring sticks, compasses, collecting jars, insect nets, notebooks for observations, and a library of natural science books.

Although isolated outdoor education experiences have significance, their greatest value lies in their integration into the total program. Outdoor education makes its contribution at varying grade levels and in numerous subjects of the school curriculum. Every school system should discover how outdoor experiences best contribute to its established goals.

A teacher should consider the following objectives in planning outdoor experiences.

1. They should provide direct experiences that will lead to clarifying and understanding abstractions of the classroom.
2. They should illustrate concepts related to man's dependence upon, use of, and responsibility for his environment.
3. They should reinforce the idea that the quality of living and man's very survival are dependent upon the solution of environmental problems.
4. They should contribute to an understanding of the active citizen's role in his community's handling of environmental problems.
5. They should develop an awareness and appreciation of the natural environment as a lifelong source of leisure satisfactions.

The following kinds of educational experiences are illustrative of many ways to employ the outdoors in the learning process.

EXPLORATIONS, FIELD INVESTIGATIONS, AND FIELD TRIPS

Of all outdoor learning experiences, the most common is the field trip or exploration. It may consist of a few minutes spent in a school yard or be an extended visit to a forest or farm. The value of any field trip depends upon the extent to which it is a real learning experience. To the participant it should be interesting and adventurous.

Educationally it should relate to the total program of the classroom or to that of the sponsoring agency.

The field trip generally consists of three parts:

1. The preplanning, including discussion of principles which will be illustrated by the field trip. Research indicates that learning increases markedly when proper preplanning has been done.
2. The trip itself. The trip should be well organized with the objectives in mind. Participants should understand that the trip is to be an educational experience.
3. The follow-up. After a trip is over, there should be a review of what has been done and the principles that have been learned.

There are various types of field trips. Ont type might be called ecological and might involve an intense study of a particular area such as a desert, marsh, or woodland. It would be concerned with the relations of living things to each other and to the physical environment. A second trip might be designed to illustrate certain important concepts, such as the dependence of man on plants and animals, the formation of soil, or the preparation of living things for winter. While these concepts are ecological, they may be illustrated in different types of ecological areas. A third type of trip might be centered around some particular science, such as geology or botany. While field identification is important, more important is an understanding of relationships, human uses, and life histories. A fourth type of field trip might be a free discovery exploration to learn how the seasons and other factors effect change in the environment; such a trip has ecological significance. A fifth trip might be designed to develop aesthetic appreciation and be related to writing, reading, music, and art. On such a trip students would be encouraged to write, draw, or otherwise express themselves concerning the outdoors.

A few reminders for teachers conducting outdoor explorations follow:

- Remember that there is no magic in just taking a field trip. There must be planning and purpose in the experience.
- There is no one way of conducting the trip. Each teacher must do it according to his own knowledge and inclination.
- Have a plan for each trip but be willing to improvise when opportunities present themselves.
- Know the area of the field trip. Each area has its own story to tell, and background is helpful.

- Do not expect to know all the answers to students' questions. Suggest, "Let's find out," and "Let's see if we can come up with a logical answer." Be willing to learn with the group.
- Encourage the learner to speculate on the basis of his own observations and reasoning. Exercise caution, however; inferences may be wrong, and research may be needed to verify an answer.
- Generalizations may be drawn, although doing so may be postponed until the return to the classroom.
- Field identification is important but has little value by itself. Supplement it with studies of relationships, life histories, human uses, and significance for humans, with attempts to explain the "hows" and "whys." Concepts may sometimes be demonstrated even when the name of a natural object is not known.
- Try to develop perception and arouse interest and enthusiasm. These may be more important than specific knowledge.
- Encourage full use of the senses in observation. Look, listen, smell, and, where possible, touch and taste.
- Sometimes it is wise to divide a large group into small groups to work on solving problems.
- Beware of talking too much yourself. Curb the temptation to give immediate answers. Telling has its place but must not be the basic approach to outdoor learning.
- Stimulate learners' participation through questions and problem-solving approaches. Have them observe characteristics of things observed, looking for differences and similarities, comparing with known things, examining the environmental settings, and looking for explanations of existing circumstances.
- Communication is an essential part of the experience. Use oral and written accounts, graphs, charts, and pictures.

field trips in specific science areas

In the following kinds of natural science field trips we are concerned primarily with becoming acquainted with the world of nature through direct experience.

Botany. General botanical trips may be taken, or there may be emphasis on special areas such as flowering plants, fungi, trees, lichens, or mosses and their relation to their particular setting. A textbook acquaintance may be strengthened through direct knowledge of the plant itself.

Forestry. Forest trees, their relationship to each other, forest succession, value of the forest, and the relation of forests to wildlife, soil, and water might be studied.

Geology. Rock formations, glacial action, and identification of local rocks and minerals might be foremost in a geology field trip. Small samples may usually be collected freely. The relationship of rocks and minerals to soil, plants, and animals is a significant study.

Zoology. This study may range from insects, amphibians, and reptiles to the higher forms of mammals. The variety of animal life, the struggle for existence, adaptations to environment, life histories, and habits of behavior are among the things to be observed.

Some particular area of zoology, such as ornithology, might receive emphasis. With young children, a simple acquaintance with the common birds might suffice. More advanced groups might try to determine habitats, territoriality, nesting habits, patterns of bird song, and seasonal appearances.

General science. The observation of seasonal changes, weather and the adaptations to weather, and other subjects related to major science fields might form the basis of a trip.

SUGGESTIONS FOR NATURAL SCIENCE FIELD TRIPS

The example given here is a field trip to study trees, inasmuch as there are few areas in the United States which do not have some trees. The trip may be adapted to any school age level, though only two levels are illustrated.

Fifth or sixth grade level. A great deal can be gained by students of this age group if the three parts of the trip are geared to their abilities and interests.

In the *preplanning stage* the class should secure a simple book on the common trees of the state and how to identify them. Most state conservation departments publish such books. The children should become acquainted with certain terms, including *deciduous, evergreen,* and should know something about typical leaf shapes, tree flowers, seeds, plant succession, climax vegetation, and plant communities. Classroom preparation for the trip should also include reading and discussing the value of trees as lumber, aids to wildlife, watershed control, soil formation. The Department of Agriculture's chart, "How a Tree Grows," might be posted and discussed. There are many suitable movies on forests which might be shown. Certain topics and questions for observation and discussion might be prepared before the class goes afield.

The trip itself may consist of a half-day excursion to a nearby forest or a shorter trip to a schoolyard or camp. A forester or other specialist might accompany the group. The teacher should, however, assume major responsibility. The following things might be done:

- Learning to recognize common trees by leaf shape, leaf arrangement, bark, tree shape, and location of growth.
- Making a leaf or seed collection to bring back to the classroom. Leaves may be pressed between sheets of a soft-pulp magazine to preserve them for classroom use.
- Keeping a list of trees seen.
- Recording observations and indicating conclusions reached as a result of the observations.

The following are suggestions for topics of observation and discussion.

- Competition of plants for light, moisture, and growing room.
- Trees and their relation to soil holding and soil formation.
- Micro-world of a rotting log and its relation to water, soil, and wildlife.
- Plant communities: What are they? What is a climax forest? What is forest succession?
- Growth characteristics of trees. An increment borer would be helpful here. The cross-section of a stump can reveal the age of a tree when cut, injuries, and climatic conditions.
- Wildlife relationships and provisions for food, shelter and protection.
- Relation of trees to water runoff.
- Differences in air and soil temperatures as determined by a thermometer.
- Problems of forest management.
- Man's dependence upon forests.
- Aesthetic and recreational values of forests.

Many other topics might be added to this list. Any single topic might occupy the attention of any one outdoor experience.

Full value from the trip will not be realized without a *follow-up*. Review in the classroom might include developing a composite list of the trees seen, organizing and identifying the leaves or seeds collected, making ink prints of some of the leaves, discussing what was learned on the trip, writing about local trees and their values, and carrying on individual projects with trees. The economic, aesthetic, and recreational values of forests might be considered.

High school level. Preplanning and follow-up are desirable at this level as well as at other levels. Discussion and observation might include problems of forest communities, plant succession, forest conservation problems, and forestry practices. Detailed classification of trees and identification through the use of keys might be undertaken. Trips would have particular application for classes in biology.

field trips to study conservation practices

For the purpose of witnessing both wise and unwise practices in the use of land and the results of these practices, trips might be taken to the following places:

Eroded and devastated areas. Most parts of the United States have some land that has been gullied, with soil washed away as a result of overgrazing, fire, unwise farming methods, or other causes. Trips to see such land provide opportunities for discussions of land use and changes that are taking place, either through natural forces or man's intervention.

Farms and forests with good conservation practices. Farming and forestry where there is production without damage to the land.

Deserted farms. Such farms offer opportunities to delve into the history of the land and to project its future through observation of the succession of plants on the area.

Fire lookout stations. Visiting these stations gives a chance to study the need for fire control in forest regions and to emphasize individual responsibility and governmental authority.

Reforestation projects. Principles of the growth and value of forests can be emphasized through visits to reforestation projects.

Fish and game hatcheries. The production of wildlife for fishermen and hunters and the need for adherence to fish and game laws could form the basis of a valuable trip.

Wildlife sanctuaries. An understanding of the needs of wildlife and the value of encouraging and preserving it can be emphasized in a trip to a wildlife sanctuary.

Parks or natural areas. A consideration of land use problems, city beautification, and the protection of natural resources could develop from this trip.

Water supply systems. A visit here could result in probing into water quality and the difficulty of maintaining a clean and adequate water supply.

City or camp sewage systems. Problems of handling human and industrial waste may be discussed as a result of a visit here.

City dumps. The dump provides another setting in which to discover the difficulties of solid waste disposal.

Flood plain areas. An investigation of a flood plain area could serve as a basis for a study of land use and planning.

other trips

Visits to sites of local or national significance in history and archeology provide opportunities for a better understanding of primitive life and historical events. Places visited might include battlefields, Indian village sites, old graveyards, deserted towns, and early settlements.

Educational trips might also be made to lumber mills, quarries, mines, reservoirs, filtering plants, nature preserves, nature centers, trailside museums, nature trails, and parks with scenic and scientific significance. Areas where local food products are processed are also of interest, such as making maple sugar and apple cider.

plot and area studies

Studies of specific areas may be either intensive or extensive. By intensive studies we mean studies of small areas—perhaps a square yard of forest floor, an ant hill, a decaying log, a soil profile, or a rock covered with lichens, mosses, and grasses. Extensive studies would include large ecological communities such as marshes, meadows, or forests. All studies would be concerned with the relationships of living and nonliving things to changes taking place in the areas.

INTENSIVE STUDIES

In an intensive study, one might seek answers to questions such as the following:

What living things are found here? (A magnifying glass is of considerable help in discerning the various types of plants and animals. Microscopic forms may be detected sometimes by odor and color in the absence of a microscope.)

How are the living things related to each other?

How do the living things affect the soil, rocks, and minerals? Lichens, mosses, and grasses growing in a rock illustrate how soil is formed so that larger plants may eventually be accommodated.

How much moisture is available and how long is it held? Run-off, absorption, and evaporation may be studied.

What is the effect of sunshine, shade, and wind on this plot?

Even a square yard of forest floor or other land contains a surprisingly wide variety of life. Comparisons of small plots of forest, meadow, lake shore, eroded areas, or roadsides can provide an understanding of the varied habitat requirements of living things.

EXTENSIVE STUDIES

The kinds of areas available for study vary from community to community. Though deserts and seashores are available to only a small percentage of children, there are woodlands, ponds, streams, lakes, or meadows available in most communities. Regardless of the area, the following activities may usually be carried on:

Mapping the area, determining the acreage and topographic features.

Recording resources—plant, animal, soil, and mineral.

Taking soil profiles and soil testing where possible.

Learning the geological history.

Studying the types of living things and their relationships to other living and nonliving things, and finding evidences of the food chain.

Learning the human history of the area and how man has modified the environment through his economic and recreational uses.

Analyzing the area from the point of view of conservation practices used or needed.

Some examples of extensive area studies are as follows:

Woods or forests. Possibilities for study in woods and forests include man's modification of the natural community through cutting, grazing, killing of wildlife, and replanting; effect of seasonal variations in rainfall, sunlight, and temperature (if it is possible to visit the area during different seasons); human uses—economic and recreational—of the forest or woods; the layers of living things from the subsoil to the canopy of trees; evidence of the struggle for existence; evidence of animal life; the number of board feet of timber available and its value.

Lakes or ponds. To the geologist, a lake or pond is a temporary feature. As soon as it forms, it begins to disappear. Water at varying depths has its own zones of plant and animal life. The shoreline, too, is modified by the waters so that certain plants and animals are to be found on its borders that are not found in drier areas. Following are a few of the many activities that might be pursued in a pond or lake study.

The depth of the water at various spots may be determined by using a cord, knotted at five-foot intervals, with a weight at the end. A profile of the lake bottom may be made from information thus gathered.

The distance across the lake in various directions may be computed mathematically or by the use of maps.

The character of the water may be studied. Water differs tremendously from one body of water to another. Temperature readings may be taken at different levels. A thermometer dropped to lower depths should be drawn quickly through the upper part so that the reading will not change appreciably. The clarity of the water may be measured by dropping a metal disk, such as the top of a tin can which is weighted, into the water to determine the depth at which it can no longer be seen.

The life at different depths or along the shore line may be observed. A small but deep net may be used to collect specimens. If placed in a shallow pan, these may be studied and identified. There are many forms of very small living things that can be secured only with a fine mesh cloth net.

Plankton, insects on the surface of the water as well as within the water, water plants, shoreline plants, amphibians, and fish all offer opportunities for study. One of the most fascinating topics to discuss is the balance of living things within and surrounding the water area. Evidences of the "chain of life" should be uncovered. If fish are caught, the food in their stomachs should be examined for evidences of this chain of life.

Rivers or streams. Many of the activities suitable to lakes or ponds are applicable to rivers and streams. One might note the sorting action of water, by which sand is deposited in one place and large gravel in another, with the finer materials settling in the quiet pools. Measuring the speed and quantity of water flowing past a particular point is an interesting mathematical project. Various forms of water life may be found under boulders, or rock ledges, in quiet water, and in rapidly flowing water. Gravel bars and the beds of fast flowing streams are good collecting spots for rocks and minerals.

Meadows. By a meadow we mean an open grassy area. A moist meadow or a dry, treeless area may differ markedly. Things to do include determining whether particular meadows are natural or the result of the elimination of the original forest; finding out what kinds of plants and animals prefer the meadow; getting acquainted with soils and how they are formed (the meadow is an especially good place for the study of soil); and finding out what animals live in the soil and how they affect soil formation.

Swamps or *bogs.* Like a lake, most swamps and bogs are temporary and become drier as years pass. A class may look for evidence of changes through the years. Some very interesting plants are peculiar to bog communities. Sometimes insectivorous plants may be found, and the reasons for their location in bogs may be studied. Swamps and bogs, and the plants therein, differ greatly in various parts of the country.

Deserted farms. Many parts of America have farms which have been abandoned for a few to as many as a hundred years. A study of such farms is extremely revealing in terms of the local history, problems of conservation, and natural science. Some of the things to look for, speculate about, study, and read about include: What was this land like when the first settlers came? Where did the settlers come from? Why? When? What were the problems of clearing the land and making it usable for agriculture? What did the people who lived here raise? Where did the people get fuel and water? How did they take care of food through hot and cold weather? Were they good or poor farmers in the way they cared for the land? Where were the fields and gardens? When was the land last farmed? Why was the farm abandoned? What is happening to the abandoned fields? What plants are now growing there? If the land is left untouched, what will eventually be its condition? (This question provides an opportunity for the study of plant succession.) How could man speed the recovery of the land? What was the effect of the farm on the wildlife of the area?

Where you live. A study of one's own home environment, whether farm, city, small town, or suburban area, can be very rewarding. Trees, soil, natural beauty, water supply and waste disposal, industries dependent upon local resources, and the like may be studied. Science here may be coordinated with social studies.

Other areas. Every section of the country has its characteristic areas worthy of extensive study. Even within a desert there are communities which differ from one another in moisture, types of soil, and other factors. Along the seashore the communities studied may range from sandy beaches and dunes to rock cliffs and tide pools, and from warm to cold climates. If one can find a piece of original prairie that has not been grazed too much or plowed, it would make an interesting study. The life zones found at different elevations in the mountains provide distinct communities for study. The effect of exposure to sun and wind on plants and animals affords an opportunity for observation.

bringing the outdoors indoors for study and observation

The study of living things in their natural habitat contributes far more to understanding them than study in an artificial setting. If outdoors time is limited, there are many things that can be taken indoors for continued study. In such cases collectors should adhere strictly to sound conservation principles.

COLLECTIONS

Collecting excursions properly conducted may be fruitful learning experiences in themselves. They provide strong incentive to look, hunt, and observe. Fall is usually a good time to collect, since leaves, seeds, and abandoned bird nests may be taken without harm to the environment. Certain things may be collected freely. Others, if needed for further study and discussion, may be taken with discretion. Still others should never be removed from their natural environment. One determining factor may be the location. In parks and in-town areas it is usually unwise or even illegal to collect any plants. In other areas, certain plants may be so abundant that the removal of specimens may have little or no effect on the character of the environment. The collector should always ask himself, "What effect does my taking this material have? Does it leave the area less usable and enjoyable for others? Does it adversely affect the biological community?" Generally the following may be collected: rocks, minerals, and fossils; tree leaves, insects, driftwood, fallen seeds, abundant weeds, winter twigs, abandoned bird nests, animal tracks (collected by means of plaster of Paris casts). Photographs or sketches are excellent things to collect from the point of view of conserving the environment.

Some states publish lists of flowers which may be collected freely, sparingly, or not at all. The use of such lists presupposes a knowledge of flower species. Generally speaking, flowers that grow in tremendous abundance in waste areas, such as Queen Anne's lace, yarrow, and goldenrod, may be picked.

Another principle to observe in collecting is that the materials should serve an educational function. Unless they do, they might be better left outdoors. Some things which might be taken for study by a class or as part of a school collection might not be collected for individual use.

Identifying the specimens and mounting them for display are important parts of the activity.

Wildlife. Sometimes various forms of wildlife, such as snakes, turtles, frogs, and small mammals, may be caught and kept alive for study purposes. Animals should be kept for only short periods of time and should then be released unharmed in their natural habitat. While kept, they must be cared for properly. Lack of care is miseducation of the worst kind. If animals must be killed for study purposes, they should be killed as quickly and painlessly as possible.

Vivariums, terrariums, and aquariums. A properly stocked and managed terrarium can be of great interest. Children might bring back from field trips the necessary materials such as gravel, soil, lichens, mosses, certain fungi, and other small plants. A suitably constructed terrarium might serve as a home for insects, amphibians, small turtles, and similar creatures.

An aquarium may consist of a large balanced environment or a mere jar of pollywogs. Trips to ponds, streams, and lakes will provide materials.

Soil samples. Soil profiles may be brought indoors for adequate labeling and study.

Collecting insects. Collecting insects requires collecting nets and killing jars. Care should be taken with killing jars, as the poisons used may be extremely dangerous to use around children. Carbon tetrachloride is somewhat safer than cyanide but must be handled with caution.

Insect varieties are so numerous that identification may be extremely difficult. However, classification into major families and identification of the most common forms may be undertaken by children in the upper elementary grades. The collection may be displayed in insect-mounting cases or in cigar or hosiery boxes.

SPECIAL PROJECTS

conservation projects

Every school and community offers many possibilities for participation in conservation projects which should add to the understanding and appreciation of conservation. The following are some of these.

School ground improvement.   There are places in many school grounds for plantings to beautify the grounds, for the relocation of walks and paths to prevent or halt undue wear, and for the construction of walls to support steep areas.

Soil erosion control.   In school camps, forests, and farms, there are often areas in need of erosion control. Measures to be applied may include the construction of diversion dams, the piling of brush, and plantings to reduce erosion.

Stream and pond improvement.   The actual building of a farm pond is not beyond the capabilities of older youth, with some help from parents or other adults. Stream improvements through cleaning, construction of small dams, piling up brush for fish, planting of fish, and control of bank erosion are possible in some areas.

Forest improvement.   Thinning, pruning, removing of undesirable species, and tree planting are possible on school lands or government-owned land.

Fire protection.   Proper fire-building spots may be established in picnic and camp areas. Fire lanes may be developed. In areas of high fire hazard, fire-fighting stations with Indian fire pumps, rakes, and flappers might be set up. Probably only older youth should participate in actual fire fighting, but certainly children of all ages should be acquainted with fire prevention.

Cleanliness.   One of the most fundamental conservation projects is keeping outdoor areas clean. Pollution by human wastes should be prevented. Prompt removal of garbage and cleanliness in cooking and eating areas will help to keep insects and rodents away.

Planting for wildlife.   Plants which will provide both food and shelter are needed to attract wildlife.

Development of a wildlife sanctuary. In many camps, a special area is set aside for protection of wildlife, both plant and animal. Boundaries should be clearly marked. Protective measures, augmented by plantings for wildlife food and cover, may make it possible for wildlife to increase. The area may offer opportunities for excellent observation and study.

weather stations

A simple weather station can be maintained either at a school camp or on school grounds. Making regular weather observations and learning to read and interpret weather instruments relate to school science programs. Young people enjoy making weather predictions and waiting in suspense to see if their predictions are accurate.

Excellent instruments can be purchased from any science supply house. Simple instruments may be made by the children themselves. A weather station commonly requires a thermometer, high-low thermometer (recording high and low temperatures for each day), hygrometer (for the measurement of humidity), barometer (for the measurement of air pressure), rain gauge, weather flags, weather vane, and a shelter for the instruments. Daily weather maps may be secured from the U. S. Weather Bureau at a nominal cost.

Weather observations of older school children may include temperature, temperature changes, barometric readings (changes and trends), relative humidity, wind direction, wind velocity, cloud formations, and character of the atmosphere. The observer should follow his observations with predictions for the next few hours.

The keeping of weather records over an extended period of time is an impetus to outdoor observation. The records may be accompanied by records of the flowering of plants, the leafing of trees, the appearance of fall colors, the migration of birds, correct times for plantings, and other seasonal events.

scenic improvement

Many communities today are making a special effort to eliminate unsightly areas and to improve the appearance of streets, homes, school grounds, and public areas, many of which have never been adequately landscaped. A visitor often judges a community by its concern for aesthetic values.

If school grounds are to be improved, a master plan should be drawn. Help in preparing the plan may be secured from a landscape architect, forester, or nurseryman. Various sections of the country require different plants and different care, and local conditions must determine the selection of the plants. There should be provision for shade, open areas, grass, and windbreaks. Care must be taken to preserve play areas and other special developments.

Such projects may be cooperative, involving school authorities, local park and recreation authorities, and representatives of private or voluntary agencies. Local garden clubs are often willing to assist.

If school groups make use of camp areas, a landscaping plan should be developed which will give consideration to protecting areas subject to overuse and to developing utilization. Many of the suggestions for school grounds pertain also to camp grounds and to individual back yards.

Several large school systems offer classes in horticulture in which special plots are developed for instructional purposes, teaching proper planting and care of home grounds, including lawns and horticultural plants.

construction projects

Young people differ greatly in their ability to learn vicariously. Work experiences, though they may be of value to all youth, are of particular value to those who learn best through direct experience involving physical activity. Success in construction work not only gives a feeling of pride in accomplishment, but also creates a desire to use properly the thing constructed.

There are many kinds of work projects through which young people may learn. Many of these can be carried on outside of school, while some may justifiably be included in the regular school instruction. The following might be developed on school grounds or outdoor education areas if adequate space is available.

Nature Trails. Unless a previously established trail is used, the building of the trail itself will involve physical labor. The chief educational value of the trail lies in the gathering of information about the natural features along the trail and the preparation of the labels or guide books. In general, nature trails are of three types. First is the unlabeled nature trail in a rich natural area, along which leaders may conduct groups. Second is the labeled nature trail, with short, concise labels placed alongside the objects of interest. Such a trail is an excellent educational tool for the users, although the greatest value comes to those who develop the trail and the labels. Leaders who are not confident of their knowledge of the outdoors appreciate the opportunity to use such trails for instructional purposes. Sometimes labels are merely temporary, so that succeeding groups of children may prepare new labels for their own trails. Ordinary shipping tags make excellent temporary labels. More permanent markers may be printed on wood, plastic, or metal, and may be weather-proofed. A third type of trail is one in which the trail itself is un-labeled, but for which a booklet is mimeographed or printed containing information to be given to those using the trail. Sometimes numbered markers are placed at points of interest to correspond with numbered explanations in the booklet.

Questions and suggestions of things to look for should be used to stimulate observations along the nature trail. Local resource people may be enlisted to assist in the preparation of a nature trail. Natural-ists, foresters, and science teachers may help identify objects seen along the trail and prepare interesting materials for labels or book-lets.

Trail Development and Maintenance. The development of trails through camp and forest areas can be a desireable work project. Plan-ning for such developments must be based on the wishes and desires of the owners and managers of the lands as well as on the needs of the users.

Outdoor Meeting Place. A place where groups may work on projects, hold discussion sessions, and engage in recreation may be built. A small amphitheatre, a campfire circle, a picnic area, or a shelter house are among the possibilities.

Outdoor Cooking Areas. Spots for outdoor cooking, including outdoor fireplaces, trash cans, picnic tables, and shelters in case of bad weather, are useful developments.

Special Projects. Other projects might include the establishment of bog gardens, rock gardens, fish ponds, or turtle pits. Many of the conservation projects previously listed are suitable work experiences.

SCHOOL AND COMMUNITY SETTINGS FOR OUTDOOR EDUCATION

An important part of the education of every child is achieving an understanding of the problems of growing the world's food, fiber, and timber. This understanding is as fundamental as the three Rs. Some of this education can be attained in the classroom, but real under-standing requires direct experience with domestic animals and grow-ing plants.

The role of the school in providing experiences with plants and animals is growing as our population becomes urbanized. It is estimated that by the year 2000, less than 3 per cent of the population will be engaged in producing our nation's food. The remaining 97 per cent will be consumers. More than 80 per cent of our population will live in communities of over 2500 population. Coming generations will therefore have little direct contact with the soil except as society, through its educational agencies, provides such contact.

Many schools and communities provide, particularly for urban children, experiences with gardening, farming, forestry, and animal care. Sometimes the school operates farms, forests, or gardens. In other instances, the school and community cooperate in such ventures.

There are a variety of other excellent settings for outdoor education that will be found in many communities and which may be used by schools and other agencies. In larger cities, especially, community owned and operated museums, nature centers, and zoos should be regarded as educational laboratories and used extensively for educational experiences. Park-schools, which are becoming more prevalent, constitute a near ideal arrangement for outdoor education. A number of school and community settings are described in the succeeding pages.

school and community gardens

In the United States today several hundred communities, through schools or community agencies, provide gardening for children. However, many communities have not recognized gardening as a part of education.

In the early history of our country, most people lived on farms or in small towns, where access to growing things was the common right of every child. The urbanization of American life divorced the population from the land. The movement to the suburbs from our large cities, which counteracts the growth of cities to some extent, may be explained in part by the desire of people to reestablish their contact with growing things. Today the family garden is primarily maintained not for economic reasons, but for the satisfaction that comes from partnership with nature. The desire to grow things is one of the strongest urges of human beings.

What should be the responsibility of the community and the school in providing knowledge and experience in the culture of vegetables and flowers? Certainly gardens provide one of the most practical situations for learning some aspects of science. They combine knowledge and theory with practice, involving working with soil, seeds, and plants and learning about their relationship to insects, water, and weather.

Because a successful children's garden must be cared for through the vacation, such a project provides an excellent opportunity for cooperation between schools and park and recreation departments or voluntary agencies. The garden program can be offered as part of the school science program or the vocational agriculture program. It may also be part of the school's extracurricular and vacation activities.

This program needs no justification, as its value is self-evident. Yet following are some of the reasons for a school to assume responsibility for gardening.

- Gardening is a learning experience. Many of the principles of science and conservation that are part of the school program are both taught and practiced in a garden project.
- Because young people may some day have their own homes with lawns, shrubs, flowers, and vegetable gardens, some instruction should be given so that they will be successful in caring for them.
- Gardening is a meaningful work experience. "As ye sow, so shall ye reap" is demonstrated. The child who plants and cares for a garden will receive a return largely commensurate with the effort expended and knowledge applied.
- Growing a garden provides an understanding of the problems involved in supplying the world's food. Lessons are learned about man's dependence upon weather and the hazards of insect pests and plant diseases. The need to care for our soil resources is effectively demonstrated.
- Understanding the economic value of food should come from the garden experience. In some garden projects, the prices of truck garden produce are posted daily during the summer, and gardeners carefully weigh their produce and keep a record of its commercial value.

TYPES OF GARDENING PROJECTS

In some communities, the park and recreation departments cooperate with the schools in presenting the program. The gardens are planted during the spring months, at which time much of the instruction is given in the schools. During the summer leadership may be provided by the park and recreation departments. In other communities, the summer program may be organized by private groups such as botanical gardens or garden clubs. Elsewhere, cooperative programs may be organized by the schools, the city, and voluntary youth organizations such as the Scouts.

A community may have two or three types of organization in

operation at one time. For example, Cleveland, Ohio has a garden department within the school system. The children participate in different kinds of garden projects according to their age level. Potted plants, window boxes, and seeds for classroom experiments are supplied to younger children. The schools also maintain tract gardens for children who do not have space at home for gardening. In addition, the schools sponsor an extensive home garden project, whereby children plant gardens in their own yards which are visited at least twice during the summer by teachers or members of the garden staff. Finally, older boys and girls with an interest in horticulture learn how to care for lawns and plants as part of the school vocational education program.

Tract gardens. Tract gardens are usually areas of land broken into small plots for individuals or two children working together. The plots may range in size from about four by eight feet to about twenty by fifty feet. Small plots are used if land is scarce or the children are small, whereas large plots are used if land is abundant or the children are older.

The gardeners begin by preparing the soil, planting, and learning to care for garden tools. This part of the program must take place in the spring before the end of the school year. The care of the plot and the harvesting generally take place during the summer. The gardeners usually work through the summer on a definite schedule—two or three times a week—for periods ranging from one hour to half a day. When school is in session, gardeners may work after school or on Saturdays, although sometimes school time is used.

Plots are usually planted according to definite plans; seeds and fertilizer are offered to gardeners at a minimum charge. It is common practice to plan a garden so that the crops will not all mature at the same time.

The success of the tract garden depends upon good land and, even more important, good leadership. Leaders must have good backgrounds not only in gardening, but also in working with children and in organizing programs. During the summer, it is generally desirable to provide special programs from time to time to maintain interest and make the endeavor more valuable. These may include trips, evening picnics, or parents' visiting days. In some tracts the gardens that are carefully kept are marked with special stakes.

The tract garden is particularly suitable in those communities in which children do not have space at home and in which there may be particular value in having a large group work together.

Home gardens. Many children may have garden plots at home. Their incentive to work in these gardens is increased if they are made part of a home garden project sponsored by the school or other community agencies. The school usually offers instruction and provides seed and fertilizer. A definite planting plan, probably similar to that of the tract garden plot, is desirable, particularly for beginners. Home garden visits by teachers or garden directors are very important to assure success. In one large city, teachers are paid two days' extra salary for visiting home gardens during the summer vacation. In other cities, gardens may be visited every two weeks by a member of the garden staff. In communities where a garden show or festival is presented at the end of the season, home gardeners participate and may receive certificates if they have successfully completed their projects.

Group gardens. A children's garden club or a school class may plant a garden on a group basis. A school class must make some provision for the care of the garden through the summer months.

Most commonly these group gardens are flower gardens. If vegetables are planted, some system of dividing the harvest is usually worked out ahead of time.

In some sections of the country, gardens may be planned so that the produce may be harvested before school is dismissed for the summer.

Indoor gardens. Indoor groups in schools, community centers, and even hospitals may carry on gardening projects, using potted plants and window boxes. In one city school greenhouses provide plants for schoolroom use. An outdoor garden may be started indoors through the use of flats. These projects may often be related to the school science program.

Cleveland school garden program. The school garden program of the city of Cleveland, Ohio is generally considered one of the best and most extensive in the United States. Special lesson units in gardening are taught in science classes in all grades from the third through the ninth. The instructional units are prepared by the Garden Division, which is administratively an auxiliary agency of the schools. There are eight garden teachers employed on a twelve-month basis. In addition, many regular teachers are employed on a part-time basis during the summer.

The Cleveland program involves nine tract gardens and teaching centers. These centers provide mateials for the classrooms but they are primarily places where children may engage in gardening. In these tracts, over two thousand children have plots which they care for and from which they reap a substantial amount of produce.

Enrollment takes place through the schools, and a small fee is collected from each participant. Work in the garden during the school day takes place during time allotted to science. Children who do not have individual plots still participate in the garden project during the school year. During the summer, children attend for an hour and a half two days a week. The summer program is entirely voluntary; should some child fail to care for his garden, it is turned over to another child on the waiting list. Less than 5 per cent of the children fail to care for their garden plots.

There is also a home garden project as part of the school program. Children having their own space at home plant gardens in accordance with specific plans furnished by the Garden Division. Home gardens are visited by teachers who give assistance and encouragement.

Gardeners who complete projects are given certificates. Special recognition is given for special achievement. During the summer, picnics and parties are held for those who are successfully caring for their garden plots.

Children's gardens have important contributions to make, not only in learnings and understandings related to the out-of-doors, but also in the personal development of the gardener through participation in cooperative work and healthful physical exercise. The activity should have a carry-over value into adult life far above that of many activities.

school forests

A school forest constitutes an excellent laboratory for outdoor education. Many of the educational experiences described in this chapter could take place in forest settings such as are found in many communities.

Many of the school forests now in existence grew out of the period when the need for reforestation was beginning to be evident. A consciousness about the fate of the cut-over lands where great forests had been and the development of a concept of proper land use impelled agriculture and conservation leaders to educate the public about the need for conservation and wise use of natural resources. Farming had followed the great timber slash with little or no attention to the ability of the land to raise farm crops; the result was often a bare existence for those who moved out on the land, and finally properties reverted to the state government due to tax delinquency. It was during this period that the practice of deeding land to counties, townships, cities, villages, and schools developed. Although the original purpose was to get the land replanted with trees and to demonstrate the need for better reforestation and land use, it was hoped by many that the forests would help serve the educational and recreational needs of the communities, particularly the schools.

Legislation was enacted in several states, permitting the establishment of county, township, village, city, and school district forests. In most instances the properties were deeded by the state agency holding the lands, such as the Department of Conservation, with provisions that reforestation and timber management practices be carried out.

A law was enacted in Wisconsin in 1927 (revised in 1949), which reads as follows: "Sec. 28.20. Any city, village, town or school district may acquire land, engage in forestry and appropriate funds for such purposes. In the case of a city or village or school forest, the forest property may be located outside the city or village limits."

As a result of state laws, many hundreds of parcels of land varying in size from a few acres to several hundred were deeded to Michigan schools. In districts where there were high schools, the Agriculture Department usually took the lead in carrying out the reforestation program. Trees were furnished by the State Department of Conservation, and most of the land was soon planted with trees which were appropriate to the soil and location.

During the time of low-priced land and available tax-reverted tracts, many schools purchased land for forest purposes. The major use was at first tree planting, but in many instances farsighted administrators and teachers saw in the school forest new opportunities for outdoor education, related to the school's instructional program.

PURPOSES OF THE SCHOOL FOREST

The school forest has two major purposes:

1. To develop an understanding of the growth and wise use of the forest through reforestation and management of the plot.
2. To provide an outdoor laboratory for learning activities that can take place best in a forest environment.

Forestation and management. The first of these purposes is concerned primarily with getting proper land use of the specific plot and developing public concepts and attitudes about good conservation practices. It also demonstrates the social and economic benefits accruing from proper land use, develops an appreciation of the importance of woodlands, and encourages those who own property to carry out good woodland management. If the school forest was made possible by a land grant, the school has specific responsibilities in carrying out the original purposes. Periodic reporting is necessary, and there should be working relationships with local, state, and national units of government for achieving the greatest results and providing channels for communicating with the public.

A sample form for reporting is suggested in a publication on school forests by Michigan State University.[1]

Developing the school forest to satisfy the purposes of the land grant requires careful and technical management. Some of the activities included may be:

1. Mapping and establishing boundary lines.
2. Making a master plan.
3. Tree planting.
   a. Areas to plant.
   b. Choice of stock and obtaining trees.
   c. Ground preparation.
   d. How to plant.
4. Care of plantations.
5. Christmas tree production.
6. Tree protection; disease and insect control.
7. Thinning and pruning.
8. Harvesting.
   b. Marking and scaling.
   b. Sale.

All of these activities can be of great value to adult participants and those who may observe the process over the years. It is sometimes difficult for a community to keep a substantial interest in the program over a period of years unless there is constant use of the forest for school and community activities. More effort and planning are required for the less spectacular process of management. In an effort to improve school forest practices a number of excellent publications have been prepared such as those from Michigan and Wisconsin.[2]

General educational use of the forest. The use of the school forest in the educational program of the community school is almost unlim-

---

[1] Michigan State College Cooperative Extension Service, *School Forests—Their Educational Use* (East Lansing, Mich.: Michigan State College, 1954).

[2] Ibid.; University of Wisconsin Extension Service, *School Forests—A Handbook*, Circular 387, Conservation Department Publication 614 (Madison: University of Wisconsin, March 1950); and State of Wisconsin Conservation Department, *Forest Planting Handbook* (Madison: State of Wisconsin, 1937).

ited. There is an increasing trend for school districts to purchase parcels of land, often located near the central school buildings, that can be developed into forests. In many communities there are pieces of marginal lands, often barren and unsightly, that could be purchased at a reasonable cost. In some cases, plots are given to schools by private individuals or industries. Sometimes these areas are wooded and well developed; in other instances the site may be an abandoned farm or deserted real estate subdivision. In either situation, there is a great opportunity for a unique educational program which will pay big dividends in community education, often with some financial profit.

Witness, for example, some of the beautiful pines now growing on what were denuded and eroded hillsides before planting in the late thirties or early forties by the Civilian Conservation Corps. In some sections of the country, roadside signs will be seen pointing to a school forest or a public recreation area which was once a barren piece of land.

One of the greatest values of a school forest is found in the selection, purchase, planning, and development of the site. Youth having a part in the development of land may well be the school's greatest contribution to citizenship and social responsibility. Many state and local subdivisions now have maps, aerial photographs, and descriptive material of lands. Whether a school obtains its forest from public authorities or purchases it from private owners, the project should be, as much as possible, a whole school affair. In contemplating such an event, school-community planning committees should be formed. Many resources are available for help, such as the county agricultural agent; the Soil Conservation Service; national, regional, and state forest offices; conservation and parks departments; and colleges. Much literature is available, such as school forestry publications and conservation department materials.

SCHOOL FOREST PROGRAMS

Many of the outdoor education activities available in parks, camps, and farms are available in the school forest. Forests usually are the habitat of more wild animals and birds than would normally be found in a smaller, more domesticated area, thus creating more opportunities to study trees and observe the interrelationships that exist among plants, animals, soil, and water.

Some of the more common uses of the forest include:

1. A laboratory for elementary classroom activities, such as science, social studies, music, art, and conservation.

2. Learning opportunities for school groups with special interests such as forestry, agriculture, conservation, botany and zoology, history, and shop.
3. Opportunities for development of skills and hobbies, such as use of native materials, simple shelter construction, fire protection, archery, and camp crafts.
4. An outpost facility where camp shelters may be constructed for day or resident camping.
5. A recreation resource for the community for picnics, hikes, and other outdoor activities appropriate to the environment and the property.

A brief example of a school forest program will illustrate its versatile use for outdoor education.

Nels P. Evjue Memorial Forest, Merrill (Wisconsin) Public Schools. The land, located ten miles from the city and on the banks of the historic Wisconsin River, was puchased in 1944 by W. T. Evjue as a memorial to his father. The forest, now made up of 732 acres, is an all-school project and is a center for resource-use education of the Merrill Schools. Through community planning and extensive participation by children, youth, and adults, the property was developed from the standpoint of good conservation practices. Seventy-five thousand trees were planted, and trout and beaver have been supplied.

As a basis for using the forest in the educational program of the community, the following principles were set forth:

1. All teachers should be well oriented with the program and have opportunities to discuss it thoroughly.
2. The Board of Education must be kept informed of the program and have an active interest in it.
3. The community should be involved in the program and be kept informed.
4. All plans and procedures should be carefully documented to provide for constant evaluation.
5. Adequate instructional material, equipment, and professional assistance should be made available to all teachers.

The school forest has been widely used by the various school departments. Specific projects and activities are determined in part by the age level of the students.

In the elementary schools, for example, frequent trips have been made to the forest by classroom groups. Science-centered activities are carried out. Communication skills are developed by describing experiences, orally and in writing. Mathematics is used in lumbering calculations, and the social sciences study the history of the area.

The junior high school has taken a conservation approach through field trips and camping experiences involving the social sciences, communications, industry, and the practical application of English. Homemaking is involved in the preparation of outdoor meals and living together.

The approach in senior high school has been largely through the agricultural and forest management aspects of the program. The varied and real activities include the use of simple power tools, bookkeeping practices, and marketing. Another significant development in the program is the construction of shelters which can be used as outdoor schools in grades six through twelve. Several excellent publications relating to the use of the forest have been developed.[3]

school farms

School farms have great promise in the development of comprehensive outdoor education programs. They should serve two major purposes: (1) providing opportunities for direct agricultural experiences for students specifically interested in agriculture; and (2) furnishing a variety of learning situations centered around rural living for the whole school and community.

In the past, school farms were acquired largely for the vocational agriculture program of the school. The land is usually purchased, leased, or rented by the school district, the agriculture department, or the F.F.A. club. In a study by George P. Deyoe,[4] in 14 of 29 agriculture departments reporting school farms the land was owned by the schools or some department or organization therein, and in the other instances the land was rented. As schools acquire larger acreages of land, master plans will be developed for broad outdoor education programs which include agriculture. While the two indicated purposes of school farms are closely related and in some instances analogous, a discussion of program activities will follow for each of the two major purposes.

---

[3] Guidepost for Projecting the School Forest into the Classroom, survey made by Trees for Tomorrow, Inc., Merrill, Wisconsin, July 1952; and "An Approach to Resource Education" from the Annual Report of the Superintendent of Schools, Merrill, Wisconsin, 1954.

[4] George P. Deyoe, The Use of School Land by Departments of Vocational Agriculture in Illinois Schools (Urbana: University of Illinois, College of Education, Division of Agriculture Education, 1951).

SCHOOL FARM PROGRAMS FOR TEACHING AGRICULTURE

One of the most significant aspects of vocational agriculture in schools is the relation of theory and practice. Originally, nearly all of the students studying agriculture in schools came from farms. It was usually a requirement of the course that each student have a project which would be carried out on the home farm. Depending on the type of agriculture in the community, the interest of the students and parents, and the type of land, the projects ranged from field crops and horticulture to livestock and poultry. These projects, planned and initiated by the students, were closely related to the school program, with the agriculture teacher serving as a helpful consultant and supervisor. The farm projects also served as laboratories and observation centers for field experiences in the various agricultural subjects and occasionally in other subjects such as science.

The value of the farm projects and the needs to be served gave rise to the development of school farms in some communities. In communities that became more urban, increasing numbers of students interested in agriculture had no access to land for their projects; in other cases, a school-managed farm suited needs of the school's agriculture program. School farms serve a variety of needs; part or all of the following purposes apply to various programs observed.

1. To provide actual field experiences in agriculture, which relate theory and practice.
2. To demonstrate and initiate good agricultural practices in the community by making the school farm an observation center, and to provide some services such as the introduction of certified seed and registered breeding stock.
3. To conduct experimental programs in land use, crop varieties, fertilizers, or breeding stock.
4. To provide experiences in community cooperation for students and adults.
5. To furnish opportunities for agricultural projects for students who do not have access to land and facilities.
6. To make opportunities available for project activities, finance, and interpretation of the school's agriculture departments and farm clubs.

Some of these purposes can be partially achieved through home projects, but the school farm idea tends to make the experiences available to other students in the school in addition to those studying agriculture. The number of school farms reported in various states fluctuates over the years. Some of the causes leading to the discontinuation of school-managed farms are change of agriculture teachers, lack of stability, insufficient farm income, and the overemphasis on money-making projects as compared to educational values. In Michigan, there is a decided trend toward and interest in developing school farms, and reports from other parts of the country would indicate the same to be true. The lasting and most successful ventures are those that serve the purposes of both vocational agriculture and general education.

USE OF THE SCHOOL FARM FOR A BROAD OUTDOOR EDUCATION PROGRAM

A school farm with varied land resources, well located and skillfully administered, could be the foundation of an outdoor education program for a community school. If typical of the land of the area and suitable for the existing agricultural pattern, the farm could serve as a center for field experiences in vocational agriculture and, at the same time, present unique opportunities for a broad and varied instructional program. A school farm might combine the possibilities of a forest, a camp, gardens, recreation areas, and thus become an outdoor education center for the community. In urban communities, farm animals and wildlife would add many of the features of a children's museum and zoo. In areas where the land is of a prairie type and suitable for general farming, it would be logical to combine farm and camp ideas.

Many of the potential program activities of a school farm are obvious, and the following outline suggests a few of the possibilities:

1. A center for all types of nature and field activities for all age groups, involving plants, animals, birds, and other living creatures indigenous to the area.
2. Conservation projects involving land use, game management, timber management, park development, and similar activities.
3. All appropriate types of gardening.
4. Care and observation of farm animals; milk production, poultry raising, bee raising; raising pets.
5. Outdoor recreation activities such as winter sports, hunting, fishing, and archery.
6. Living experiences for children and teachers in the farm residence.
7. Care, processing, and consumption of farm produce.
8. Home management activities, landscaping, and general improvement of the farm.
9. Agricultural folklore, such as sugar-making, weaving, making

apple butter, corn husking bees, and a variety of other social activities.

10. The use and care of farm machinery.
11. A center for community service activities. This would include farm organizations, discussion groups, city-rural relationships, and other activities appropriate to the community life.

Tyler (Texas) School farm.   The school farm, adjacent to the resident outdoor education center and used by the schools, is under the supervision of the Department of Vocational Agriculture. In addition to its use for vocational agriculture, the farm provides an excellent instructional laboratory where children learn about and care for farm animals, observe good practices in land management, and get some appreciation of rural living. Farm experiences are among the most popular in the school program. Teachers report that city children develop new interests and appreciations in the outdoors as a result of excursions to the farm.

Battle Creek (Michigan) Farm and Garden Program.   The Battle Creek Public Schools own and operate a complete year-round outdoor education facility in the midst of a rural agricultural community, on a 140-acre site, 12 miles north of the city. Each year approximately 5000 boys and girls, grades one through six have a variety of educational experiences at the Outdoor Center.

The Outdoor Center is the setting for four major programs: a 34-week resident outdoor education program for fifth and sixth grade students; a 26-week farm-garden program for third and fourth grade students; an eight-week barnyard experience program for first grade boys and girls; and a social studies unit built around a restored pioneer log cabin.

The unique educational experiences offered Battle Creek boys and girls at the Outdoor Education Center enrich and extend the entire elementary school curriculum and also contribute to education for environmental awareness. This awareness must ally itself with man's ability to provide a quality existence for this generation and generations to come.

museums

There are many types of museums, only some of which are related directly to the out-of-doors. Originally, museums were places for the preservation and study of collections. In recent years, however, there has been a tendency to use materials that arouse interest and tell a story.

Although there are no hard and fast lines between the various types of museums, they may be placed in the following general categories:

1. **Large, comprehensive museums,** which may contain exhibits from all parts of the world and may cover everything from natural science to history, industry, and art. Such museums, though extremely valuable educationally, are not primarily related to the outdoors.
2. **Special museums,** such as natural history museums, art museums, archeological museums, history museums, and museums of science and industry.
3. **Children's museums,** which are both display centers and activity centers. These museums, which have been developed in several hundred communities in the United States, usually function through clubs, classes, and work groups. Some of them carry on extensive outdoor programs, with field trips and explorations.

The children's museums are commonly financed and administered in three different ways: under private auspices; by schools; or by community park and recreation agencies. Many of the older museums of the eastern United States are directed by private boards of directors and financed by private sponsors. Where the schools operate the museums, the museums serve as meeting places for school groups and act as sources of leadership and materials for the classrooms. Museums operated and maintained by community park and recreation agencies are common on the west coast. Many of the general museums have children's divisions which perform many of the functions of the children's museums.

nature centers

A nature center is an outdoor focus of first-hand study, appreciation and enjoyment of the environment by all ages. Usually included is a sample of the landscape, in as natural a state as possible, with its features protected. It is at its best when the terrain is varied and the plants and wildlife abundant. Woods, marshes, ponds, streams, and open meadows present dazzling challenges to would-be learners.

Developments in the nature center may be diverse, but only those that enhance the outdoor education program should be included. Some centers may contain only simple trails, although the term "nature center" is generally restricted to areas that have buildings, have meeting space and displays and serve as focal points of outdoor programs.

Individuals or supervised groups may use the center. The setting encourages an ecological approach to the world of nature and is a source of outdoor enjoyment for its own sake.

Some nature centers maintain professional leadership. Such leaders have the primary responsibility for conducting field trips and preparing displays. Other times the principal job of the staff lies in training teachers and youth leaders on the use of the outdoors, thereby expanding leadership resources for the center.

In many communities visits to a nature center have become a major part of the school outdoor education program. Classes from kindergarten through high school use the center for outdoor studies under the guidance of their own teachers or the center's own staff. The center may also offer special aids for teachers, including field experiences and materials prepared for classroom or field use.

The Natural Science for Youth Foundation is engaged in the promotion of children's nature centers. The Nature Centers Division of the National Audubon Society encourages the establishment of such centers by providing technical and consulting services.

The Little Red Schoolhouse in the Cook County Forest Preserve on the outskirts of Chicago is an illustration of a nature center. Here an old schoolhouse has been transformed into a nature museum, and various trails radiate from the building into the adjoining meadows and woods. During the school year, children come with their teachers to the center, where a professional naturalist staff assists with an interpretive program. Groups go on field trips, walk on the nature trail, observe the museum exhibits, or visit the wildlife areas. In the summer, the Little Red Schoolhouse is visited by children's groups from day camps operating in the Forest Preserve, other organized groups, and individual children and families. The response to this center has been extremely gratifying. It serves a particularly important function in a large metropolitan area.

trailside museums

In many national, state, metropolitan, and municipal parks, as well as on some private lands, trailside museums have been established. The trailside museum, which usually includes naturalist services, is concerned primarily with the interpretation of the particular natural area in which it is located. It is not an end in itself but rather a device to give meaning to the out-of-doors. In some cases live local animals—reptiles, amphibians, and small mammals—are kept in captivity so they may be observed close at hand. The displays are generally designed to show relationships and tell a story, and assist in identification. Nature trails and other trails usually radiate from the museum. There is commonly a meeting place, sometimes both indoors and out. School groups may spend a half day or a day at the museum and the surrounding area.

zoos

Large zoos generally include animals from all parts of the world. In small communities and outdoor education centers, more modest exhibits are maintained, with local species which children may observe at close hand. Individual animals sometimes become tame enough to be petted and handled by visitors. If a wildlife exhibit is part of a nature center or a trailside museum program, leaders are usually available to explain it.

Interest in living animals runs extremely high in both children and adults, as the large attendance at zoos indicates. However, the educational possibilities of zoos have hardly been explored. Zoo visits taken under leadership and related to classroom work can make a genuine contribution to the school program.

natural areas

Schools, forest and park authorities, and private agencies often own and maintain natural areas that are available to school groups for outdoor education. These areas may bear a variety of designations, but they share the common feature of being as unspoiled as possible. Usually both living and nonliving things are protected. The areas therefore are ideal for school groups concerned with ecology and with studies of an environment relatively undisturbed by man.

the park-school

The park-school constitutes an almost ideal setting for outdoor education. The general plan is to locate the school site and buildings adjacent to parks. This provides greater opportunities for public use, both of the buildings and the site.

The park-school plan makes it possible to have a larger area near the school which can be used as a playground and as an outdoor laboratory. It is discussed in more detail in the chapter entitled "Lands and Facilities."

OUTDOOR EDUCATION THROUGH SUBJECT MATTER AREAS AND ACTIVITIES

One of the most realistic and effective approaches to outdoor education, particularly in secondary schools, is through various subject areas. There are numerous potential experiences relating to the outdoors that are in the disciplines and are associated with school and college curricula. Some secondary schools and colleges have demonstrated their ability to develop and profit by flexible schedules. Teachers and students can move in and out of classrooms wherever the environment is most conducive to learning. In the classroom itself, the groundwork can be laid for extensive observation, discovery, and research in the outdoor laboratory.

A considerable amount of administrative flexibility is needed if there is to be full use of the community as a setting. As one investigates the usual content of subject areas in the curriculum, he will find many opportunities to enrich and vitalize classroom instruction through the use of the outdoors. Some of the implications for outdoor education in a number of disciplines are briefly noted in the following pages. Added examples will be found in the chapter on outdoor education in camp settings.

science education

The methods of classroom science differ from those of the out-of-doors. In the classroom, science is approached as an organized body of knowledge, moving from the simple toward the more complex in logical sequence. In the out-of-doors, on the other hand, one begins with sense perceptions—the things we see, smell, handle, hear, or even taste. These sense perceptions are then placed in the total science context.

Learning to recognize the features of the natural world, and to develop a feeling of friendly familiarity toward it, is important. But it is even more important to become aware of the manifold relationships of all living and nonliving things—soil, air, water, sunlight, plants, animals—and their progress through changing weather and seasons. Such concepts may range from the very elementary ones for the young child to the most complex aspects of ecology. Many of the possibilities for outdoor education through science may be achieved effectively through the conservation approach.

The relationship between natural science and conservation education and outdoor experiences can be very close—many outdoor education experiences are in the fields of natural science and conservation. Some schools consider science and conservation the major learning areas in the use of the outdoors as a laboratory.

Outdoor education makes possible direct experiences in science and conservation which enrich the knowledge gained through the classroom and the textbook. The best pictures, textbooks, or discussions can never give a full appreciation of the size of an acre of land, the evanescence of a spring flower, or the stateliness of a forest tree. The relationship of science, conservation, and outdoor education are discussed in the following pages.

CONSERVATION EDUCATION

Increasingly important in our rapidly growing society is a citizenry with an understanding of the problems of the use of natural resources. It is obvious that conservation knowledge is essential for those who produce food, fiber, and wood; but the percentage of our population who actually grow these essentials is steadily becoming smaller, and by far the great majority of people are consumers. These consumers, as voters, are the people who make the laws upon which conservation of our resources depends. Therefore they must have an understanding of the basic principles of resource use.

It is doubtful whether an understanding of conservation can be developed adequately through discussion and reading. It may well be that only through experiences involving the care and wise use of natural resources themselves can we develop citizens who will in future years properly safeguard these resources. A child who has raised vegetables in a school garden probably appreciates the problems of handling soil and water resources in a way that the child without this experience cannot. A child who knows some of the plants and animals of the woods and their place in the natural scheme is more likely to be concerned with their conservation than the child who has never made their acquaintance. A child who has had many outdoor experiences and who has learned to enjoy without destroying his environment is better equipped as a citizen than one who has not had these opportunities.

Conservation education has three major goals:

1. **Knowledge and understanding of the problems of conservation from the standpoint of a local area, the nation, and the world.**
   A knowledge of our resources, their use and misuse, their present status, and the probable future demands to be made upon them should be part of the goal of conservation education. There

should be an understanding that our resources include not only those of economic value but also those of scenic, scientific, historic, and recreational value. Much of this education may be given in the classroom and through reading. But a large part of it can best be achieved through seeing and studying resources at first hand.

2. **The development of attitudes and appreciations.** There is strong reason to believe that the motivations based upon appreciation of the out-of-doors and the perception of nature in its varied forms are essential to desirable conservation education and action. Each person must attain a sense of personal responsibility and stewardship toward outdoor resources.

3. **The development of desirable practices and skills related to the use of outdoor resources.** Field trip groups that refuse to collect the rare spring wildflowers, picnic groups that leave their picnic spots cleaner than they found them, campers who put out their campfires—dead out—and properly dispose of human wastes, hunters and fishermen who adhere to laws governing their sports, all are practicing good conservation measures.

There are many aspects of these goals that can be vitalized through outdoor education:

1. Becoming acquainted with plants, animals, and birds and developing a sense of being at home in the natural world.
2. Learning about the geological structure of a given area and the characteristics of common rocks and minerals.
3. Developing an understanding of the relationships of living things to each other and to nonliving things.
4. Learning problems of land management, particularly in the growing of food, fiber, and wood.
5. Learning simple principles of weather prediction.
6. Getting acquainted with concepts of area, distance, and direction and learning how to read maps and use a compass.
7. Enjoying the world of nature in its beauty and variety.
8. Learning skills in the wise use of outdoor resources, including care of fires, campsites, picnic areas, forest areas; growing of plants and animals.
9. Understanding man's dependence on natural resources.
10. Understanding that man must work in harmony with the laws of nature and that failure to do so may result in fire, famine, flood, and even the loss of freedom.

11. Realizing that conservation is not merely the saving of resources but also the wise use and replenishment of resources where possible.

Types of experiences in science and conservation in outdoor education programs. Science and conservation experiences in outdoor education programs are generally of two types: (1) Those that are planned specifically for learning science and conservation—field trips, explorations, studies of specific areas, farming and gardening, conservation projects (such as erosion control or pond and forest improvement), operating and conducting weather stations, improvement of school grounds and camp areas, development of nature trails, science displays and collections, and star studies; (2) Experiences in which science and conservation are incidental—crafts using native materials (clay, wood, seeds, etc.), cooking outdoors (involving care of fire, cleaning up the campsite), and travel trips by canoe or afoot. Science and conservation should be a part of all aspects of outdoor living.

There are a few general considerations in science and conservation experiences:

1. Most of the science fields may be enriched and comprehension increased through carefully selected outdoor experiences.
2. Science and conservation experiences outdoors should be related to the purposes of education and the course content of the classroom. Outdoor experiences should be preceded by preclass preparation and followed by evaluation and discussion in the classroom. Outdoor activities should stimulate the student to seek and discover for himself.
3. The local resources will always determine the kinds of science and conservation experiences possible. Each area is unique in some manner, and what the specific area itself has to teach should be emphasized. However, the experience should make diverse areas elsewhere more comprehensive.
4. The age, abilities, and backgrounds of the students will usually determine the ways in which outdoor experiences will be conducted and the possible intellectual level of achievement. All levels from the elementary school through the university may benefit from such experiences.

FIELDS OF SCIENCE IN OUTDOOR EDUCATION

Sciences based on the observation of nature can receive considerable impetus in the outdoor setting. Among the fields which may be enriched through the outdoor program are the following:

Astronomy. Outdoor experiences often include evening star study sessions, through which students become familiar with common constellations and individual stars and planets. The use of the telescope may be an important part of this study.

Botany. Students may become acquainted with common plants and make field studies of families of plants and their adaptation to their environment.

Chemistry. Some of the principles learned in the laboratory may be demonstrated and utilized outdoors, such as the identification of minerals.

Ecology. The study of the relationship of living things to their environment is probably one of the greatest contributions which outdoor education can make to the school program. To a child, this study offers a challenge to his abilities of observation. Ecology presupposes some acquaintance with the features of the environment. A class outdoors can focus its attention on a particular ecological environment, such as a marsh, deserted farm, seashore, pond, woodland, desert, or meadow.

Geology and mineralogy. Firsthand acquaintance with the land features, rock structure, and geological story of a given area is an important part of an outdoor education program. Common rocks and minerals may be collected and studied.

Paleontology. Many settings for outdoor education are rich in the evidences of past life. Fossil remains may be located and sometimes collected.

Physics. Principles of physics may be demonstrated through special experiments or may be related to the study of astronomy, weather, and other outdoor interests.

Zoology. The observation of insects, reptiles, birds, mammals, and other animals in their natural habitat arouses interest in a way that mere reading or laboratory work cannot do.

social studies

The outdoors constitutes a well-equipped laboratory for many learning opportunities in the social sciences. Competent and alert teachers have long used the outdoors for exploration, discovery, and research in the social studies. Trips to abandoned farms, ghost towns, industrial communities, and suburban areas help students develop insights into the changing pattern of society. Gravel pits and excavation sites are effective in portraying the story of civilization as they relate to the quality and quantity of topsoil. Eroded fields, muddy streams, and polluted waters are dramatic examples of the importance of conservation practices. The social studies and outdoor education are basic in the development of attitudes and behavior concerning conservation.

Indian life, mining, and timbering are always made more real when classroom study is supplemented by the use of the outdoor laboratory in areas where these cultures and industries have been present. Nearly every community has bridges between the present and the past which should be employed in bringing realism into learning. In these days of travel and mobility, it is particularly important that the social studies contribute more practical knowledge about the earth and its people.

language arts

There are two general areas where language arts and outdoor education converge: (1) the study of prose and poetry that express appreciations; and (2) the use of outdoor settings in teaching the creative use of language through oral expression and writing. In the first instance, much of the prose and poetry included in high school and college English courses is centered on the outdoors or includes references to it. No field of study can contribute more to the appreciation of art and aesthetics related to the outdoors than a study of literature. There is greater need now than ever before to develop appreciation for the wonder and beauty of the outdoors since the changing pattern of living has removed so many from the rural setting. Consider the prose and poetry which have become a part of classroom offerings, such as the works of Longfellow, Wordsworth, Thoreau, Bryant, and Riley. Such works help develop appreciations and spiritual perceptions related to the physical universe.

Secondly, many outdoor settings may be used for the expression of creativity through the writing of poetry and prose. The following verses were written in a classroom by a child who was fortunate enough to have had experiences with his family in the outdoors.

SPRING

Winter's dying,
Spring is crying
To be free.
Free as we shall be,
When spring is here again.

The flowers then will come to bloom,
And snow will leave the ground.
Leaf buds will come through dark brown skin,
And grass will sprout around.

The birds will soon return again,
And build their nests anew,
Some hidden in the forest land,
And others in plain view.

The children now play marbles,
And fly their kites a-high;
There seems to be an awakening,
Beneath the clear blue sky—
'Tis Spring! [5]

Field trips and camp settings, free from the inhibitions imposed on some children by classroom procedures, are conducive to natural expression. The oral reports of field trips, campfire sessions at camp, and planning meetings under the trees are examples of situations where good communication may be learned effectively. Prior to or following experiences in English in the classroom, one school uses its forest as an outdoor classroom for creative writing, oral expression, and music appreciation.

mathematics

There are many learning situations in mathematics where outdoor education activities may supplement classroom teaching. Follow-up experiences in the outdoors involve surveying, measuring, computing board feet of lumber in logs, map and compass activities, estimating distances, staking out plots of land, and a variety of other situations where students make practical applications of mathematical principles. Field trips and camp experiences may require cost estimates and other practical uses of arithmetic. The chapter dealing with "Outdoor Education in Camp Settings" suggests a number of relationships between mathematics and outdoor education.

homemaking and industrial arts

These curriculum areas have great potential for outdoor education relating to food, clothing, shelter, and outdoor living. Outdoor cooking,

---

[5] Written by 10-year-old Jack J. Blohm, Lansing, Michigan, March 20, 1957.

clothing for outdoor wear, construction of shelters and equipment, family camping, and working with fibers and woods offer unusual opportunities for the development of outdoor interests. Carving and nature crafts and outdoor clubs are often a part of homemaking and industrial arts.

health, physical education, and recreation

This group of curriculum offerings has many relationships to outdoor education, both in leadership and content. Camping and outing activities have traditionally been associated with health, physical education, and recreation, and at the college level most of the existing courses in camping and outdoor education are part of these disciplines. Physical education makes its major contribution to outdoor education through the teaching of motor skills (described in detail in a later chapter). These subjects afford additional opportunities in healthful living, safety and first aid, participation in outdoor recreation activities, outdoor clubs, family camping, and emphasize fitness.

These fields may also contribute to outdoor education through cooperation with other disciplines such as science. Relating casting, shooting, and archery to science, for example, offers opportunities to combine a knowledge of the physical environment with an outdoor recreation interest. Casting and entomology make sense to the would-be fisherman. Likewise, shooting and game management combine to develop concepts and attitudes in conservation. These are only a few examples of how activities in health, physical education, and recreation are related to outdoor living and how they may be correlated to other areas in the curriculum.

arts and crafts

There are many ways in which arts and crafts may be related to outdoor education, particularly if they employ native materials or interpret the outdoors through various techniques. Outdoor-related arts and crafts need not be a major part of the school art program, but should be used when they contribute to both outdoor-related learning and to arts and crafts. High standards of artistry and workmanship should be maintained in all outdoor arts and crafts, whether simple or advanced.

The outdoor-related crafts require ingenuity in the securing of materials and creativeness in the craft activities. There is a special satisfaction in being able to create a useful or decorative article from raw material secured in its natural environment. Since some of these crafts were practiced by the Indian and the pioneer, they can be effectively coordinated with social studies and can help give an understanding of life in early societies.

In gathering native materials one must give consideration to conservation principles. Materials should be taken only if no injury results from the taking. It is well to gather things only in the amount required rather than to gather a surplus which must later be discarded. The selection of materials with conservation of resources in mind is itself a desirable learning experience.

Outdoor-related arts and crafts may be placed in five major categories: those using native materials, those interpreting the out-of-doors, those reproducing outdoor materials (casts and prints), those in which equipment to be used in the outdoor education program is constructed, and those in the form of displays and exhibits. Each category is discussed below.

ARTS AND CRAFTS USING NATIVE MATERIALS

Woods. Basswood, white pine, and cottonwood are good carving woods for the beginner, because they are soft and readily worked and do not split easily. Other woods may be chosen for carving because of greater beauty and durability. Walnut, osage orange, and applewood are examples of woods which have beauty of color and grain but which are somewhat difficult to carve. Many woods, such as the Oregon myrtle, redwood of California, or cypress of the southern swamps, are available in limited sections of the country. Driftwood may often be used creatively.

Fibers. Fibers suitable for making ropes and rough cloth are found in many native plants. A few of these plants are yucca, Indian hemp, stinging nettle, and the inner bark of basswood.

Basket-weaving materials. Basket-weaving materials found growing wild include Japanese honeysuckle, willow, cattail, bulrush, grass, pine needles, and the bark of many trees.

Clay. Native clays, found in many places, may be modeled and dried and, when kilns are at hand, fired for permanency.

Stones. Some stones, such as shale, sandstone, and soapstone, may be readily carved. Semi-precious stones, such as jasper and agate, which are far more common than most people realize, may be collected and polished by older children if lapidary equipment is available.

Seeds. Seeds and cones of various types may be used. Cross sections of nuts such as hickory and black walnut may be made into decorative pins, belts, and earrings.

Shells. Shells are a good craft material, especially for younger children.

Native dyes. Pioneers dyed their homespun materials with colors obtained from native plants, including maple bark, black walnut hulls, and hickory bark. Experimenting with these dyes can afford great satisfaction.

ARTS INTERPRETING THE OUTDOORS

Painting, sketching, modeling, and photography find an infinite variety of subjects out of doors. Results may range from attempts at authentic reproduction to imaginative abstractions. Efforts to interpret the out-of-doors through art forms involve the ability to see, analyze, and understand what is visible in the natural environment.

CASTS AND PRINTS

Plaster of Paris and liquid plastics may be used to make casts of perishable natural forms, such as small fish, amphibians, and fungi. Plaster of Paris may also be employed in reproducing animal tracks and leaves. Prints of botanical materials—ink prints, blueprints, ozalid prints, and others—may be made.

CONSTRUCTION OF EQUIPMENT TO BE USED IN THE OUTDOOR EDUCATION PROGRAM

Devices for measurement. Many expensive and intricate measuring instruments are not procurable for school use. Constructing simple devices makes it possible not only to obtain usable instruments but also to demonstrate forcefully the scientific principles involved. The following are a few examples.

A plane table may be developed for simple mapping and surveying, using only a compass and rulers.

An ordinary carpenter's level, mounted on a five-foot stick, with eye screws for sighting devices, makes a simple surveyor's level for determining contour lines and elevations.

An instrument similar to a sextant may be made by mounting a pointer directed toward the North Star and dropping a plumb line across the pointer. Latitude may be determined with a protractor by the use of this sextant.

A large right-angled isosceles triangle can be used to determine heights of trees, distances across rivers, and other measurements, using the principle of equal triangles.

A long rope, knotted every rod (16½ feet), may be used in land measurements.

Sun dials. A simple large sun dial may be made by directing a pointer toward the North Star, then marking off the hour areas on the ground at points where shadows are cast, using a clock or watch the first day. This device will demonstrate the differences between sun time and clock time.

Other types of equipment useful in the outdoor education program which may be constructed include terrariums, aquariums, vivariums, collecting nets, killing jars, display cases and boards, and weather stations.

DEVELOPING DISPLAYS AND EXHIBITS

Order and meaning may be brought to the things collected by means of exhibits, which may range from simple bulletin board displays to habitat cases and trailside museums. Displays which show relationships, give life histories, and indicate the significance of the material displayed have more value than those which merely identify objects. The chief value accrues to the one who does the preparing.

The following are some types of displays which may be prepared either in the outdoor center or in the schoolroom. If outdoor time is limited, it is better to use indoor time for the actual preparation of displays.

Maps. Maps may be very simple or detailed, depending upon the ages and abilities of the children. Topographic and relief maps may be prepared if the children are capable.

Interpretive displays. These may show geological periods, plant succession, food chains, animal food habits, and life histories.

Exhibits of local materials. Materials may be exhibited for acquaintance and identification. Rocks, fossils, minerals, seeds, leaves, and twigs are among the objects which may be displayed.

"What is it?" shelf. Oddities and unidentified materials picked up out of doors may be displayed on this shelf until identified.

Bulletin boards. The preparation and maintenance of a current bulletin board provide incentive in outdoor education. A typical bulletin board might display pictures of local plants and birds, government posters such as "How a Tree Grows," photographs taken locally, and suggestions of what to look for in the local area. Lists of natural objects seen, with the names of the persons seeing them and the dates, may be placed on the board. Such lists tell when plants flower, when birds migrate, and other subjects of seasonal interest.

outdoor learning through games

Games suitable to outdoor education purposes may provide incentives for learning as well as being enjoyable. The following are among the many types of such games.

Trailing games. "Orienteering" is a sport which has long been popular in north European countries and is growing in popularity in the United States. It involves the use of the map and compass in various types of games. The map and compass game may often be coupled with learning botanical or geological facts to add to the learning value.

Scavenger hunts. A search for a wide variety of natural materials may make up the scavenger hunt. Things which should not be removed from the natural environment must not be included.

Look-listen trips. A long list of things to be seen or heard is checked as the items are found. Lists may be checked on either an individual or a competitive basis. Sometimes the names of the objects to be found may be checked on sheets resembling lotto boards.

Identification games. Many games are based on field identification. Some are competitive.

Hiking games. Games encouraging observation along the trail can stimulate interest. "Hold the Front," in which an individual holds his place in the hiking line if he is able to answer questions posed by the leader, is an example.

co-curricular activities

In addition to the curriculum areas mentioned, there are many opportunities for outdoor education through co-curricular activities, particularly in secondary schools. Many of the newer developments in outdoor education have evolved through what were originally termed extracurricular activities. They were conceived as a way to broaden the offerings of schools without facing the difficulties of departmentalized scheduling and prescribed academic subjects. Many of these activities occur outside the school building, often in outdoor settings.

Currently a large number of schools schedule an activity period during the school day, at which time clubs and organizations may meet. The field activities which involve participation in the outdoors usually occur after school or on weekends, as is often the case with outing clubs and outdoor hobby groups. A partial list of clubs and other co-curricular activities includes hiking, outing activities, bird watching, astronomy, casting and angling, shooting and hunting, archery, conservation, taxidermy, mountain climbing, science, lapidary interests, gardening, forestry, and flower raising.

The nature and scope of club programs in secondary schools are illustrated by the two following examples.

HIGH SCHOOL CONSERVATION CLUB

The club was organized at the request of students, both boys and girls, who had participated in the school camping program. The purposes were: (1) to provide opportunities for study and explanation for those interested in conservation, and (2) to encourage school camping in the school. The size of the club was limited to forty members. Programs for meetings include outside speakers, movies, and demonstrations. Problems such as water pollution of the area, proper clothing for deer hunting, game laws, and safe handling of firearms are discussed.

A highlight of club activities each semester is a three-day camping trip to a state group camp. The school bus transports club members to camp on a Friday afternoon and parents call for them on Sunday afternoon. The program at camp includes cookouts, exploration hikes, and other activities. The sponsor of the club is a high school biology teacher.

HIGH SCHOOL OUTING CLUB

The club began with a small group of teachers and students who met together to discuss the possibilities of outing activities that could be school-sponsored. It was evident almost immediately that group enthusiasm was keen, and that such a club had high potential for providing unlimited opportunities for extended education. As the numbers grew, following a few exploratory trips, the group tentatively decided on several types of membership: (1) a student advisory board; (2) active club members; (3) those attending school activities sponsored by the club and open to the student body; (4) alumni; and (5) an adult advisory board composed of faculty members representing the administration, various departments of the school, and interested community members.

Activities for the weekend are planned by the students who meet on school time during an activity period. Rotating committees, such as for cookouts, are selected at that time, and approval is secured from the administrative office.

Many teachers who lead the activities are selected because of their hobbies as well as their departmental representation. For example, a lesson in fly tying was given by an English teacher; following that, a fishing trip was planned. Photography is the hobby of another teacher in the same department and of one of the administrative officers. At these outings, many good snapshots have been taken, developed at school, and posted on the "Snap of the Month" bulletin board at school. Several of the adult advisory board members have selected bird study as a hobby, so the students are quick to take advantage of this type of leadership when planning a trip.

Activities of such clubs may include recreational skills such as hiking, skiing, ice skating, cookouts, skeet shooting, fly tying, fishing, tobogganing, swimming, riding, canoeing, and cycling; they may include social and physical science studies such as conservation, bird and animal tracking, astronomy, reconstruction of history from landmarks, and a recognition of economic and social development as seen through the immediate locale (for example, determining the principal source of income, which might be from the pine crop, from a mining industry, or from farm or dairy lands).

The educational laboratories for these activities could include the school sites, wildlife sanctuaries, parks and recreation areas, camps, and other public and private lands. Facilities of local organizations such as sportsmen's clubs, youth serving agencies, and conservation groups are frequently made available for such school outdoor education programs. Spontaneity and enthusiasm are keynotes of the program.

travel

In Europe, where there is a tradition of educational travel, school children travel much more as a part of their educational program than do American school children. Some of the trips are taken on weekends or holidays, usually with teachers and parents. In the United States, some schools provide trips, particularly to national and state capitals and to special areas of historical significance. When related to the classroom program and organized in accordance with age interests, such trips have great value. Trips may be taken during holidays and vacations, but the use of school time is justified for some of them. Among the kinds of trips are:

Bus trips. Visits to historical sites, national and state parks, and wildlife sanctuaries may be taken by bus. During certain seasons it is possible to camp out. Many college groups take extensive geological and historical trips as part of their program.

Walking and cycling trips.   Many of the school trips in Europe are walking and cycling trips. The youth hostels provide desirable accommodations within a day's journey of one another. Youth hostels are not as common in this country, although there are a few places where such facilities are adequate. Sometimes arrangements can be made for overnight stops in parks and camps.

Wilderness trips.   Trips by canoe, horseback, burros, or afoot to wilderness areas can provide rich experiences for older boys and girls. Such trips require special preparation, skill, and health on the part of the participants. These trips afford excellent learning opportunities in natural science, outdoor living skills, and survival skills, including personal care and use of natural foods.

SUGGESTIONS FOR FURTHER STUDY AND RESEARCH

1. Plan a field trip. Specify the objectives, age group, techniques of handling the group, length of trip, and nature of experiences to be included.
2. Develop a self-guiding nature trail, using either labels or a printed guide to be made available to groups using the trail.
3. Visit a nature center and observe the reactions of various age groups to the program and exhibits.
4. Make a study of native craft materials and their uses. Indicate cautions necessary in securing and using these materials so as not to violate conservation principles.
5. Evaluate the following techniques in terms of effective teaching in the out-of-doors:
   a. Self-discovery
   b. Group projects
   c. Direct teaching
6. Outline the natural science resources for study in a particular area, such as a lake, forest, bog, or abandoned farm.
7. Visit a children's garden. Endeavor to assess its educational value for participants in the program.
8. Make a study of the school and community forests in your state. Determine how these are being used for educational purposes and suggest ways in which their effectiveness as educational media may be improved.

REFERENCES

books

American Association for Health, Physical Education, and Recreation. *Man and His Environment*. Washington, D.C.: AAHPER, 1970.

————. *Outdoor Education for American Youth*. Washington, D.C.: AAHPER, 1957.

Ashbaugh, Byron, and Beuschlein, Muriel. *Things To Do in Science and Conservation*. Danville, Ill.: Interstate Printers and Publishers, 1960.

Audubon Nature Bulletins. New York: National Audubon Society, various dates.

Bale, R. O. *Stepping Stones to Nature*. Minneapolis, Minn.: Burgess Publishing Company, 1960.

Bates, Marston. *The Forest and the Sea: A Look at the Economy of Nature and the Ecology of Man*. New York: Random House, 1960.

Benton, Allen H., and Wernes, William E., Jr. *Field Biology and Ecology*. New York: McGraw-Hill, 1958.

Board of Education of the City of New York. *Operation New York*. New York: Curriculum Center of the Board of Education, 1960.

Brehm, Shirley A. *A Teacher's Handbook for Study Outside the Classroom*. Columbus, Ohio: Charles E. Merrill, 1969.

Brennan, Matthew J., ed. *People and Their Environment: Teacher's Curriculum Guide to Conservation Education, Grades 4, 5, 6*. Chicago: J. G. Ferguson Publishing Company, 1969.

Brown, Robert E., and Mouser, G. W. *Techniques for Teaching Conservation Education*. Minneapolis, Minn.: Burgess Publishing Company, 1964.

Freeberg, William H., and Taylor, Loren E. *Programs in Outdoor Education*. Minneapolis, Minn.: Burgess Publishing Company, 1963.

Gibbens, George H. *The Pocket Knife*. Milledgeville: The Georgia College Outdoor Education Institute, 1970.

Hammerman, Donald R., and Hammerman, William M. *Outdoor Education: A Book of Readings*. Minneapolis, Minn.: Burgess Publishing Company, 1968.

————. *Teaching in the Outdoors*. Minneapolis, Minn.: Burgess Publishing Company, 1964.

Hug, John W., and Wilson, Phyllis J. *Curriculum Enrichment Outdoors*. New York: Harper & Row, Publishers, 1965.

Mand, Charles L. *Outdoor Education.* New York: J. Lowell Pratt, 1967.

Miller, Peggy L. *School Gardens and Farms: Aspects of Outdoor Education.* Las Cruces: Educational Resources Information Center, Clearinghouse on Rural Education and Small Schools, New Mexico State University, 1970.

Milliken, Margaret; Hamer, Austin; and McDonald, Ernest. *Field Study Manual for Outdoor Learning.* Minneapolis, Minn.: Burgess Publishing Company, 1968.

National Association of Biology Teachers. *The Conservation Handbook,* ed. Richard L. Weaver. Danville, Ill.: Interstate Printers and Publishers, 1955.

Nickelsburg, Janet, *Field Trips.* Minneapolis, Minn.: Burgess Publishing Company, 1966.

Odum, Eugene P. *Fundamentals of Ecology.* Philadelphia, Pa.: W. B. Saunders Company, 1959.

Parson, Ruben L. *Conserving American Resources.* 2nd ed. Englewood Cliffs, N.J.: Prentice-Hall, 1964.

Research Division, National Education Association. *Environmental Education in the Public Schools.* Washington, D. C.: NEA, 1970. (Prepared for the National Park Service.)

Shomon, Joseph J. *Manual of Outdoor Conservation Education.* New York: National Audubon Society, 1964.

—————. *Manual of Outdoor Interpretation.* New York: National Audubon Society, 1968.

Smith, Robert L. *Ecology and Field Biology.* New York: Harper & Row, Publishers, 1966.

Stapp, William B. *Integrating Conservation and Outdoor Education into the Curriculum (K-12).* Minneapolis, Minn.: Burgess Publishing Company, 1965.

Turner, Ralph I. *Conservation in Miniature.* Sacramento: The Resources Agency, State of California.

van der Smissen, Betty and Goering, Oswald H. *A Leader's Guide to Nature-Oriented Activities.* 2nd ed. Ames: Iowa State University Press, 1968.

Watts, May Theilgaard. *Reading the Landscape.* New York: Macmillan, 1957.

periodicals

Environmental Education. Madison, Wisc.: Dembar Educational Research Services, Box 1605. (Quarterly.)

Journal of Outdoor Education. Oregon, Ill.: The Lorado Taft Field Campus of Northern Illinois University.

film

Outdoor Education (16 mm, sound, color, 28½ min.). NEA Sound Studios, 1201 Sixteenth Street, N. W., Washington, D. C. 20036.

5

outdoor education in camp settings

Camping, one of the most popular forms of outdoor activity, is an old and accepted way of living out-of-doors. Organized camping has been in existence in the United States for nearly a century, and for a long time has been regarded as educational in character. It is only in recent years that schools began to use camp settings for learning activities. This more recent development in education is a part of the emerging community school program. Educational leaders, seeking more opportunities to provide real and direct learning experiences for children, have found that many things can be learned best in a camp setting. The acceptance of this principle by educators, coupled with the popularity of outdoor activities, has given impetus to the development of a substantial number of school programs in camps throughout the United States.

A rapidly changing American life has hastened the advent of the school's use of camp facilities. City living, specialized vocations, and automation all accentuate the need for a simple living-learning program close to the earth. Man's concern about the physical environment, the wise use of natural resources, and the need of young people to know and protect those resources have influenced the back-to-earth movement.

The program of outdoor schools in camp settings gives an increasing number of children a short but effective living experience in the out-of-doors as a part of school education. This program in no way duplicates or conflicts with the many excellent programs of organized camping in which less than 20 per cent of the children in the United States participate each year. In fact, experience in a number of communities suggests that agency camping programs benefit from outdoor education experiences conducted by the schools.

THE NATURE OF PROGRAMS IN CAMP SETTINGS

Resident outdoor education, also referred to as school camping, when conceived as an aspect of general education, has many implications for curriculum building and improvement. Living in a camp combines a democratic living experience with adventure in learning in the outdoors. The concept is a simple one. Boys and girls live, work, and play together in a rich and natural outdoor environment. The facility itself, usually separated by considerable distance from the main school campus, is considered to be a regular part of the school district's physical plant and equipment. The activities at the campsite are an integral part of the curriculum as are the educational programs that take place in the classroom, on the campus, or in the community.

Learnings achieved best out-of-doors, or practiced more effectively in 24-hour group living, find their place in the camp program. Many of the learning processes involving children and their teachers can be planned, put into operation, completed, and evaluated in the short time of the school camp. It often would take many weeks to complete these processes in the classroom, and then they would lack the reality and vitality of direct experience.

BEGINNINGS

It is difficult to say when educational experiences in camps began to find their way into the school program. Camping in the United States began with a recreational emphasis, then gradually tended to be educational.

Interested teachers have gone on camping and outing trips with their pupils for many years. Most often, these trips had little or no relationship to the school or its curriculum. In some instances, schools actually operated camps, but largely for recreation. The current pattern of outdoor classrooms, or school camping as it was first termed, can be traced directly to two institutions—Life Camps, Inc. and the W. K. Kellogg Foundation.

With the establishment of Life Camps in the 1930s, L. B. Sharp, Director, began to encourage school camping. It was not until 1940, however, that the first year-round camp went into operation on the assumption that school experiences in a camp should be an integral part of the curriculum. This first program was made possible by the W. K. Kellogg Foundation of Battle Creek, Michigan. The Clear Lake Camp and staff were made available to three Michigan schools. For one year, students from grades 4 through 12 went to the camp for periods of two weeks. The new venture was so successful that the schools of Calhoun County, including Battle Creek, initiated a similar program in 1944 at St. Mary's Lake Camp which was leased from the W. K. Kellogg Foundation. Because of the newness of the project, no one school district was asked to assume administrative responsibility. Instead, a nonprofit corporation, the St. Mary's Lake Camp Association, was formed. A Board of Directors, including the superintendents of several of the school systems in Calhoun County, as well as a number of laymen, became the policy-making body of the Association. A professionally educated staff was employed and a year-round program begun. Although this early program operated at several instructional levels, primary emphasis was on fifth and sixth grades.

The St. Mary's Lake Camp Association was dissolved in September 1947 when the Battle Creek Schools agreed to assume administrative responsibility for the program. At the same time, program and staff were moved to Clear Lake Camp (now the Battle Creek Outdoor Education Center). In addition to providing outdoor education experiences for thousands of children and youth in the local area, the Clear Lake Center has served as a demonstration center on the state and national level. Professional visitors from all over America have studied its facilities and program. Educators who served on its staff have moved out to all parts of the country to assume roles of leadership in new programs.

EARLY DEVELOPMENTS CENTERING AROUND
CLEAR LAKE CAMP

It is important to note how a single new educational program, carefully conceived and under good leadership, may influence the character and design of significant nationwide developments in education. As an illustration, a brief description of a series of events will show the impact of the Clear Lake school camping program in the earlier years. It is believed also that these facts are significant historically in the growth of the outdoor school idea throughout the United States.

When the Clear Lake Camp was made available by the W. K. Kellogg Foundation in 1940 to the three Michigan schools—Lakeview of Battle Creek, Otsego, and Decatur—there was a well-qualified staff already employed at the camp with Edwin Pumala as director. Later, when the city and county schools of San Diego, California, decided to initiate a comparable program and were seeking a director, Edwin Pumala was employed, and his experience with the three Michigan schools for a year helped shape the design of the new program.

In 1945 a director was needed at St. Mary's Lake Camp, then operated by the schools of Calhoun County. George W. Donaldson, Director of the Lanning Demonstration School at State Teachers College in Trenton, New Jersey, was called to take the position. In the meantime, Clear Lake Camp was leased to Western Michigan University for a period of three years. During that time summer workshops were held for teachers, and during the school year a number of nearby schools used the facility. When the lease expired in 1947 the program which had been conducted at St. Mary's Lake was moved to Clear Lake. The administration of the program was assumed by the Battle Creek Public Schools; a number of schools, including those in Calhoun County, used the camp under the new plan. In 1957 Clear Lake Camp was deeded to the Battle Creek Public Schools by the W. K. Kellogg Foundation. Kenneth Pike, Leslie Clark, and the late Archie Potter were members of the staff when the program was moved from St. Mary's Lake. In 1948 Kenneth Pike left Clear Lake to direct the new program which was being initiated in the Long Beach, California school system. He later became responsible for outdoor education in the Department of Health, Physical Education and Recreation of the University of California at Los Angeles.

In 1948 citizens from Tyler, Texas, became interested in outdoor education, and a delegation from that community visited the W. K. Kellogg Foundation and Clear Lake Camp. A new camp was then being built in Tyler. It was designed as a school camp and has served the entire community, providing facilities for schools during the school year and for agencies during the summer. When the new program was ready to begin in June 1949, Dr. Donaldson was called to become the director at Camp Tyler. Leslie Clark became Director at Clear Lake Camp.

In 1950 Dean George Makechnie, Jean Young, his assistant, and other staff members from Sargent College, Boston University, visited Michigan to get information about outdoor education in camps. Shortly thereafter it was decided to make the Sargent College Camp available to schools of the area. Dean Makechnie and Miss Young, who later gave leadership to outdoor education, Pontiac Public Schools, Michigan, established the new program in 1950. The schools of Newton, Massachusetts were the first to participate. In a few months a director was sought; Leslie Clark was called from Clear Lake to accept this position and the late Don Randall replaced him as Director at Clear Lake; later followed by Jack Wykoff. Northern Illinois University employed Don Hammerman of the Clear Lake staff as program director at the Lorado Taft Field Campus, which was one of the first extensive programs to combine teacher education with a resident program; he later became head of the Department of Outdoor Teacher Education of Northern Illinois University. Other staff members of Clear Lake Camp have taken positions throughout the country.

During the decade beginning in 1947 at Clear Lake Camp, many leaders from colleges and universities throughout the nation visited the camp. They were assisted whenever possible by the Clear Lake staff in acquiring information, and in some instances were given consultation service in developing outdoor education programs.

During the same decade other states began to give leadership through state departments of education. The W. K. Kellogg Foundation provided grants of funds for statewide workshops in New York, California, and Washington. A number of significant programs developed through these efforts. During the same period, a number of interested education leaders, including some members of the Clear Lake staff, attended summer workshops conducted by L. B. Sharp at National Camp in New Jersey.

Many other illustrations could be given of how one good program influences the initiation of others and how the cooperative efforts of a group of enthusiastic leaders are instrumental in effecting innovations in education. Each state where the outdoor classroom idea has developed has an interesting and significant story of growth. It is not possible to identify all of the many school districts involved in the various states, but a few brief descriptions will indicate the wide spread of this type of education in over half of the states.

Alabama. One of the earlier interesting developments in outdoor education occurred in Alabama. When sites on the TVA lakes were made available to school districts several schools acquired land in the late 1940s for future use. Recognizing the need for outdoor teacher education, the Florence State Teachers College (now Florence State University), through the interest of its President, E. B. Norton, was one of the first to create a staff position in outdoor education. George Gibbens assumed this position and his services have been made available as a consultant to the counties of northern Alabama served by the University.

California. Following the lead of the earlier programs in San Diego, Los Angeles, Long Beach, and others, over 200 school districts now have programs. Statewide interest in outdoor education was stimulated by the State Department of Education under the leadership of the late Verne Landreth, who was then Chief of the Bureau of Health Education, Physical Education and Recreation. A grant from the W. K. Kellogg Foundation, which resulted in a statewide workshop and an excellent publication, was helpful in the early stages of development in California. Later, the Association of Outdoor Education was formed in California. It has sponsored in-service training activities and preparation of materials, and has created much enthusiasm among school and college leaders. Legislation was enacted when the legality of schools operating programs outside of school boundaries was questioned. The law enables school districts to conduct outdoor science and conservation education programs in camps. School laws in California now make it possible to administer programs on a county basis through the county superintendent of schools. Several counties have provided staff leadership to assist local school districts.

New York. A number of school districts in New York became interested in using camps for outdoor education experiences and initiated programs during the 1940s. Caswell Miles of the Bureau of Physical Education, Department of Education, gave leadership to this new development as did the late Jay B. Nash, Head of the Department of Health, Physical Education and Recreation, New York University, and the late L. B. Sharp, then Director of Life Camps, Inc. More rapid progress in the use of camps by schools was impeded when an opinion was rendered by the legal counsel in the Department of Education that schools could not collect state aid for education during the time that children were in camp facilities outside the school district. This block was later removed by the enactment of legislation enabling schools to use facilities outside district boundaries. A considerable number of schools now are conducting outdoor schools in publicly owned facilities and agency camps.

Washington. Through the leadership of Harley Robertson, then Supervisor of Health, Physical Education and Recreation in the State Office of Public Instruction, Washington was one of the first states in which a number of schools initiated programs in camps. Much impetus was given to developments in the state of Washington by a pilot program conducted at Camp Waskowitz, a former CCC camp, by the

State Office of Public Instruction, the State Parks and Conservation Agencies and the Highline Public Schools. This pilot effort and a film entitled "Classroom in the Cascades" were made possible by a grant from the W. K. Kellogg Foundation. Later the Highline Schools purchased Camp Waskowitz and now operate an extensive program. Among the other early programs in the state were Snohomish County, Auburn, and Omak.

STATE AND NATIONAL DEVELOPMENTS

While the program was developing in the Battle Creek area, a statewide program was being carried on by the Michigan Department of Public Instruction. Eugene B. Elliott was the first chief state school officer to recognize outdoor education in a state by providing leadership in the Michigan Department of Public Instruction. In 1947 he was appointed President of Eastern Michigan University and was replaced by the late Lee M. Thurston, who continued to extend the State Department's efforts in outdoor education. Michigan's leadership had far-reaching results throughout the United States. Hugh B. Masters was then Educational Director of the W. K. Kellogg Foundation and had much to do with the development of school camping and with making it possible to initiate the experimental program in the state. The late P. J. Hoffmaster, then Director of the Michigan Department of Conservation and a leader of great social vision, was responsible for committing the vast resources of his Department in the development of the program. It was the privilege of one of the writers, Julian W. Smith, to direct this experiment. Over a period of seven years, more than 100 school districts in Michigan developed programs in camps. Many of these schools now provide outdoor classroom experiences for periods of several weeks and months.

The program in Michigan has had public endorsement in the form of an act passed by the Legislature in 1945 which enables school districts to acquire camps and operate them as a part of the regular educational and recreational program of the schools. The act reads in part:

355.35. SEC. 35. The board or boards may acquire, equip and maintain the necessary facilities and employ the necessary persons for the operation of the camp program which may be conducted on property located either within or outside the territorial limits of the school district.

Until 1948, no secondary schools had developed programs comparable to those in the elementary schools. In the fall of 1948, however, through the efforts of the Michigan Department of Public Instruction, the Department of Conservation, and the W. K. Kellogg Foundation, a pilot program for secondary school youth was initiated. Sixty high school youths from three schools and interested teachers from thirteen schools, along with state educational leaders, conducted a week's experimental program at the Chief Noonday Outdoor Center in the Yankee Springs Recreation Area near Hastings, Michigan. This program featured conservation-centered work experiences and was visited by many educational leaders throughout the state. The venture was so successful that in the following spring, nine of the thirteen schools represented in the Yankee Springs experiment conducted high school camping programs. Among these new developments were Dearborn, Bay City, Allegan, Lakeview of Battle Creek, and Ann Arbor. Barbra Holland directed the Dearborn program for many years.

In 1949 the Legislature set aside funds in the State School Aid Bill to encourage secondary and elementary schools to initiate outdoor classroom programs. This plan of financial aid designed to stimulate new programs extended over a period of several years.

National Camp took quite a different approach to stimulating interest. Working through the Teachers Colleges in New Jersey and New York, it began a series of "institutes" and conferences to which were invited selected faculty members and students. One such visit by faculty members from the Trenton, New Jersey, State Teachers College resulted in one of the early education-in-camp projects. Four faculty members and 32 youngsters from Trenton's Lanning Demonstration School were "camping guests" at National Camp for a ten-day encampment. Then they returned and established a college-sponsored day camp in a wooded area on campus.

National Camp also carried on graduate level summer sessions which were attended by educators and youth workers from all over the nation. Credit was offered by New York University.

Following the lead of the program operated by the Battle Creek public schools and others, the City-County Camp Commission of San Diego was established. The Commission has provided extensive education opportunities in camps for children in the city and county schools throughout the school year. Other California schools operate camps on a year-round basis. Tyler, Texas was the next school system to initiate a year-round program. A new camp was built in 1949 by the Smith County Youth Foundation, designed for school use for nine months and community youth-serving agencies during the summer.

The Smith County Youth Foundation is a nonprofit corporation whose only project has been that of providing the camp facilities. There are many other programs in various stages of development in most of the states.

The school camping idea has had much attention by national leaders in education. In the early 1940s, the W. K. Kellogg Foundation of Battle Creek, Michigan sponsored conferences at Clear Lake Camp, which set forth many of the educational values of camping experiences for school children. This resulted in one well-known publication, *Marks of Good Camping*,[1] prepared by the American Camping Association. In 1949 a National Conference on Community School Camping [2] was held at the Haven Hill Lodge, Highland Recreation Area near Milford, Michigan, during which approximately 100 leaders from various parts of the nation observed the Michigan program and carefully studied this rapidly unfolding venture in education. This group referred to community school camping as a partial answer to the problems of youth, the vitalizing of educational content and method of the school curriculum, the utilization of human and natural resources, and the cooperation of the many agencies concerned with youth and natural resources. In recent years, many books and periodicals have devoted attention to resident outdoor education, and the topic has been considered at numerous state and national conventions, conferences, and workshops.

ORGANIZATION AND ADMINISTRATION OF
PROGRAMS IN CAMP SETTINGS

The resident outdoor education experience, as an integral part of the curriculum, would employ the same administrative and organizational policies used in other phases of the educational program. The only variations would be those necessitated by the responsibilities the school incurs in taking pupils from their homes for several days, and by the use of a camp facility separated by some distance from the school building.

staff

The staff for an outdoor classroom consists of the teachers who go to camp with their groups and any others who may be employed to

[1] *Marks of Good Camping*, report of the workshop on Camp Standards conducted by the American Camping Association (New York: Association Press, 1941).

[2] *A Report of the National Conference on Community School Camping*, Lee M. Thurston, Superintendent, Department of Public Instruction (Lansing, Mich., 1950).

coordinate the program or who may be needed to supplement the classroom teachings. The latter should be appropriately educated and have the competencies necessary in the camp setting. In recent years, paraprofessionals have been used successfully to augment services of the regular staff in many schools. The coordinator should have administrative ability in addition to being well versed in curriculum practices and child development principles. Outdoor skills and a general knowledge of camp administration are desirable. The position requires versatility, for the coordinator usually becomes a combination of administrator, teacher, and handyman. Ideally, the staff should consist of a team of teachers whose interests, skills, and training are varied enough so they become resource leaders to each other. Special backgrounds in science, social studies, homemaking, arts and crafts, music, physical education, and recreation are among those readily applicable to school camping. The first and last requirement is to be a *good teacher*, with competencies for teaching *in* and *out* of the classroom. With adequate background in child growth, the learning process, skills in direct experience teaching, and some acquaintance with the outdoor laboratory, teachers should be able to provide profitable learning experiences for children. The education of such teachers will be discussed in more detail in a later chapter.

In general, specialists should be used in outdoor schools in the same way as in any phase of the school program. Unless the camp is in an isolated area far from the school, it is not considered necessary for physicians or registered nurses to spend full time at camp. Most schools have a physician on call from the nearest town, with arrangements for emergencies. The city, county, or school nurse should also be on call and make inspection visits if necessary. At all times, a staff member trained in first aid should be present.

instructional materials, tools, and equipment

The school should provide instructional materials and tools necessary for the maximum use of the camp and outdoor environment. First aid kits, small tools, art materials, and reference books on outdoor activities are commonly used. Special interests in photography, science collections, music, archery, angling, shooting, boating, and camping should be anticipated. In continuous year-round programs, all such material and equipment are provided as a part of the facility; schools that rent or lease camps for shorter periods will need to give much thought to matters of supplies and equipment. Personal equipment, including proper clothing and bedding, should be given consideration long before the camping period.

operational patterns

Resident outdoor education programs in camps are operated under a variety of patterns for a number of reasons:

1. Initial programs are often established on an experimental basis and upon a rather small scale.
2. Existing facilities are used and programs developed without creating additional administrative machinery.
3. Until resident outdoor education becomes more extensive, several school districts can join together to pool and share resources.

To date, several administrative plans have been used to facilitate a program that meets existing needs. They include:

1. Individual school district operation, with facilities owned or leased.
2. The resident outdoor education program administered by one school, but shared with others, according to a mutually acceptable plan or on a contract basis.
3. The formation of a nonprofit corporation with a controlling and cooperative board.
4. A multi-district plan whereby several school districts operate a resident outdoor education program cooperatively.
5. Administration by a county through an educational authority such as a superintendent of schools or county school board.

As more schools become involved, and as programs become more extensive, administrative patterns develop with legal sanction and authority to hold property, spend funds, and employ staff. The fact that there is no one best way to administer resident outdoor education experiences should encourage schools to be more imaginative in developing procedures to meet the needs of individual communities.

An examination of the more common trends in operational patterns indicates four general classes. They are described below, with examples.

1. A year-round operation of one or more school districts that (a) have access to a camp facility for continuous use, (b) select specific grades or groups for the outdoor classroom experience, and (c) often employ a central staff to assist the classroom teachers involved in the program.

Examples:

San Diego (California) City and County Schools. The program is operated by a legally constituted governing authority, known as the San Diego City-County Camp Commission.[3] The Camp Commission was created by a joint ordinance adopted by the City Council and the County Board of Supervisors. This constitutes a separate governmental agency, whose members represent the City Council, the County Board of Supervisors, the city schools, the county schools, and the Parent-Teacher Association. It has authority to plan and develop summer camps and resident outdoor education programs, receive and expend funds, and enter into contractual agreements for facilities and staff. The Commission now operates several resident outdoor education programs for fifth and sixth grade children of the city and county schools. A permanent, professional staff is employed.

Tyler (Texas) Public Schools. A year-round program of the Public Schools of Tyler for fifth and sixth grade children is provided. The camp is owned by the Smith County Youth Foundation and built specifically for school camping and for summer use by youth agencies. Children are at the camp each week throughout the school year. There is a full-time director and permanent staff.

Jefferson County (Colorado) Resident Outdoor Education Program. The Phelps-Dodge Ranch near Evergreen, Colorado, purchased by the Jefferson County Public Schools in 1962, is the scene of an extensive resident outdoor education program in which 5,500 sixth grade students and their teachers spend one week during the school year. The Jefferson County Outdoor Education Laboratory School is well equipped for the interdisciplinary program which extends and enriches the sixth grade curriculum. The Laboratory School Principal and a program specialist, with the assistance of resource leaders and selected high school students, constitute the staff for the resident outdoor education program.

Battle Creek (Michigan) Public Schools. The Battle Creek Schools now own Clear Lake Camp, which was deeded to them by the W. K. Kellogg Foundation. The Outdoor Education Center, which combines the camp property with a one-hundred-acre farm, operates during the entire year. The schools use the camp for fifteen to twenty weeks of the school year and contract it to eight or ten other school districts for the remaining weeks. The other school districts pay their proportionate share of cost and maintenance. A permanent staff of direc-

---

[3] Wilbur Schram, *Classroom Out-of-Doors* (Kalamazoo, Mich.: Sequoia Press, 1969).

tor and teacher-counselors is employed by the Battle Creek Public Schools. Fifth and sixth grade children spend a week at camp. Student teachers from Michigan State University, Western Michigan University, and several other colleges participate for varying periods of time.

2. A part-time operation by a school district that (a) rents or leases a camp facility as needed, (b) selects certain classes or groups for the outdoor classroom experience, and (c) uses the regular classroom teachers and resource personnel to give leadership to the program. This is the pattern most frequently found at present and usually seems to be the logical way to initiate a program. Existing camp facilities are acquired when needed, and a program designed to meet the needs of the participating group is planned. The extent of the outdoor classroom experiences in the school varies from one week to the entire school year. The usual period for each group is one week. In most instances, a director or coordinator is designated, and spends full time at camp, returning to school duties when the program is not in operation.

3. The use of an outdoor center or camp facility that is under the management of another agency such as a college or public agency (a) for selected classrooms and groups, (b) using classroom teachers as staff members, and (c) contracting for certain managerial and camp services. This type of program, when under the direction of a college, combines teacher education and outdoor classrooms rather effectively. It is helpful in initiating outdoor programs since the facility, and often food services, are made available and some leadership is provided by the college. It is equally helpful to the college in teacher education and provides opportunities for student teachers to work with regular school groups in camp. Some examples follow.

Southern Illinois University. With a long history of involvement in outdoor education, the University has an outdoor laboratory of 6,000 acres at Little Grassy Lake and has entered into a cooperative program with the Crab Orchard Wildlife Refuge of the U. S. Bureau of Sport Fisheries and Wildlife for conservation education. The outdoor education programs at the Little Grassy Outdoor Laboratory vary widely and include an Outward Bound type program, conservation workshops for high school students, and day use and resident camp programs for area school children; facilities include a nature center, a wild animal enclosure, and a host of camping and recreational facilities. The camp also sponsors a number of experimental programs for mentally and physically handicapped children. University classes in botany, zoology, orienteering, and outdoor education are held there. The Department of Conservation and Outdoor Education, created in 1969, is responsible for basic courses in conservation education, environmental education, nature interpretation, and outdoor education within the College of Education, and also for a master's degree program in Conservation and Outdoor Education.

Northern Illinois University. The Department of Outdoor Teacher Education is housed at the 140-acre Lorado Taft Field Campus near Oregon, Illinois. Each year approximately 5,000 University students majoring in elementary education, biological science, physical education for women, and industry and technology engage in a series of resident practicums at the Field Campus. The professional laboratory experience for seniors involves a week of student teaching at the outdoor school. The Department offers an extensive program of graduate study leading to the degree M.S. in Education. Extension courses are offered over a 23-county area. The Department also sponsors a series of foreign study tours on outdoor education. NIU's program of outdoor teacher education was initiated in 1954 and is one of the leading programs in the United States.

Bradford Woods—Indiana University Outdoor Education, Camping and Recreation Leadership Training Center. Indiana University, in cooperation with the James Whitcomb Riley Memorial Association, began in 1952 to develop the 2,300-acre university-owned Bradford Estate into a center for outdoor education, camping, and recreation leadership training. The educational program is under the direction of the University's Department of Recreation in the School of Health, Physical Education, and Recreation. The property makes available land and facilities for the training of teachers and other youth leaders. It also contains camping areas for school groups, handicapped children's groups, and youth agencies. Private funds have financed most of the physical developments, including roads, trails, camp buildings, a workshop center, and a lake. The University provides funds for the direction and administration of the program and some of the maintenance.

The purposes of Bradford Woods are two-fold: (1) to provide a center where leaders may be educated in an outdoor situation with direct relations to the setting, with opportunities for both actual leadership and observation of school and youth agency programs; and (2) to provide areas and facilities for outdoor programs for school groups, handicapped children, and youth agencies.

The property is approximately four miles long. A creek runs through the total length. A 110-acre lake with four waterfront areas has been created artificially. Two resident camps have been established with funds from both the original will and gifts. Camp James Whitcomb Riley is a winterized facility; Camp Pioneer, while primarily a summer facility, serving Boys' Clubs and other groups, also serves some school groups during the spring and fall. A day camp has been developed for summer school groups and other agencies. These camps provide opportunities for leadership training and observation. A workshop center, operating on a year-round basis, accommodates up to fifty persons and is used by various educational organizations during the year. Throughout the summer, workshops and summer session courses for University graduate and undergraduate students are given. With the American Camping Association national headquarters and library also at Bradford Woods, additional educational resources are available to students.

During the summer Camp Riley is used entirely by handicapped children's groups, including physically handicapped and mentally retarded children. The programs are financed and operated by either the Riley Memorial Association or associations for the handicapped. The Riley Hospital of Indianapolis assists with medical supervision. During the spring and fall Camp Riley is used by school groups. Camp Pioneer serves Boys' Clubs for six weeks during the summer and is available to other groups at other times. It has been used by school groups for day and overnight stays. Various school groups use Bradford Woods to study natural science. Boy Scouts, Girl Scouts, and Camp Fire Girls have leased property on which they have built their own camps.

4. Outdoor classroom programs operated during the summer months. It is not unusual to find educational programs in camp settings operated by schools during the summer months. This may occur for a number of reasons: (a) the community's desire to have the school provide educational and recreational opportunities during the summer months, as is often done with community recreation programs, music, and agriculture; (b) the lack of other camping opportunities for children in the area; and (c) in the north, the difficulty of using camps during the fall, winter, and spring months. It would appear that this pattern for outdoor education will not be extensive, since it is more difficult to relate it to the regular school organization and curriculum. In many communities agency-operated camps offer some opportunities for summer camping. However, the trend toward an extended school year may encourage day and resident camping in some sections of the country. Some of these summer programs are operated by schools and recreation departments. Some examples of outdoor classrooms during summer months are to be found in Michigan and Florida. Examples:

Iron County, Michigan.   For many years the school districts of Iron County, through the County Board of Education, have operated an extensive outdoor education program at the Youth Camp on Indian Lake. Elementary children have the opportunity to spend a week or more at the camp; the Boards of Education pay stipulated amounts covering the cost of instruction, and the parents assume the food costs. The camp is owned and maintained by the county. A fraction of a mill tax is earmarked for use of the County Board of Education in operating the camp. A director and competent staff of teachers are employed, and an excellent educational program is operated for seven or eight weeks.

Cadillac, Michigan. The Cadillac Board of Education was the first school in Michigan to acquire camp property and construct facilities. A program is operated during the summer months and for some periods during the school year for children in elementary schools in the community. A member of the school staff is employed as director. Community organizations and civic groups have assisted the Board of Education in improving the property.

It should be emphasized that although the patterns described reflect different operational procedures, every outdoor classroom program is somewhat different. This is as it should be, since the program grows out of needs and conditions of the local school. The most important principle of organization is that it be consistent with good practices in school administration and be operated according to the same principles as other units of the school program.

finance

The problem of finance is common to all aspects of the school program, and, since outdoor classrooms are integral parts of the curriculum, the same principles of finance apply. The only aspect that is different is the fact that the school takes on certain responsibilities of the home while children are at camp. This may require expenditures over and above classroom costs. More staff is needed, which may necessitate a budget item for substitute teachers or for additional staff. Other personnel are usually required for kitchen staff and maintenance. In relation to the total educational budget, the amount of money for these items is relatively small. Rental of the camp, heat, light, transportation, and supplies are usual costs for any out-of-classroom programs and are relatively minor items. If a school builds a camp, these expenses should be considered a part of the program of capital outlay and might partially reduce the costs of some of the central buildings if the school operates an extensive camping program. Little additional instructional equipment and tools are required, since many of those things can be taken to camp as needed.

The following general principles have been followed in the financial operation of outdoor classrooms:

1. The family should assume the cost of food for students while at camp. The home should keep its right to assume the responsibility for maintenance of its members.
2. The board of education should assume the cost of instruction, as always has been done in public education. In outdoor education, as in other aspects of the school program, the board of education should maintain its function to provide instruction for youth.
3. For children whose families are unable financially to assume the cost of food, the regularly constituted social agency or service club which normally provides for them at home should assume this responsibility at camp. Frequently, local service clubs and organizations that believe in the camping program provide funds so that no boy or girl will be denied a camping experience because of the lack of financial resources.

It is difficult to cite accurate figures on costs of school programs in camp settings because of the many different situations and types of programs. In most states schools are using existing facilities, making it unnecessary as yet to spend funds for capital outlay.

The cost of resident outdoor education programs will be proportionate to the quality and quantity of instructional services provided and the arrangement for rental, lease, or ownership of camp property. To date, experiences indicate that significant educational experiences can be provided for relatively little cost, as compared to other special aspects of the school program such as athletics, music, or shop.

facilities and resources

The general problems of facilities are treated at length in a separate section, so a brief review of those new ones which are being used for schools will suffice here.

To date, most of the schools in the United States providing educational experiences in camp settings have made use of available existing facilities. In Michigan, more than one-half of the nearly one hundred school districts have used state-owned outdoor centers which were rarely used except during the summer months. In several instances, former CCC camps throughout the country have been converted by the state or local government and made available to schools and other groups. Some youth-serving agencies have leased their camps after the summer season to schools, and, in some cases, private camps have been utilized during off seasons. As publicly owned camps receive full use, an increasing number of conveniently located agency and private camps will be sought by schools. A recent study indicates, for example, that there are enough camp facilities near New York City to serve the children of that metropolis. There is evidence now that schools in some areas will develop facilities on their own lands, such as forests. One trend is certain—when state departments (such as parks and conservation) construct group camps they will be designed for use by agencies during the summer and by schools for the rest of the year. In northern climates this will mean that facilities will be winterized when they are constructed. The trend is already noticeable in many areas, where new agency and state camps are being built especially for school use. In several instances, school leaders were called in when plans were being developed for such facilities.

When needs warrant the construction of camps by schools, those charged with the planning will be urged to select sites adjoining or near publicly owned lands, so it will be necessary to purchase only small land parcels for building purposes. Such developments should be preceded by community planning so that facilities will serve the greatest number of people and organizations. The camp at Tyler, Texas, built by the Smith County Youth Foundation, is a good example of community planning. The camp is used by community agencies during the summer and by the schools for the remainder of the year. In some communities consideration should be given to a facility owned by one school, but contracted to others for available periods. Such is the plan used by the Battle Creek Public Schools in making the camp property available to several other schools in the area.

Many resources, including leadership, are available to schools for outdoor education; they are discussed in more detail in another chapter.

teacher preparation for outdoor classrooms

The matter of teacher preparation for outdoor education, included in another chapter, applies generally to school programs in camp settings. There are unique opportunities in teacher training in camping situations not present in some of the other types of outdoor education activities. Camping, by its nature, provides living situations with children and teachers. In addition to demonstrating good teaching methods outdoors, the resident camp offers a great variety of other types of training, such as guidance, observation of child development and behavior, social living attitudes and skills, and a combination of approaches to classroom situations. The continuity of the experience in camp makes it possible in a week, for example, to plan, initiate, execute, complete, and evaluate teacher-pupil activities that might not be possible in weeks or months in the classroom. Some school staffs have noted the conclusion of several complete processes in a week. Consequently, resident outdoor education, offering many situations for pre-service and in-service training, has implications for better ways of preparing teachers. There are indications that an increased number of field experiences in pre-service education will soon be required, some of which may be in camp settings.

In some areas several teacher education institutions have arrangements with schools having resident outdoor education programs whereby student teachers or observers spend a week at camp. Some colleges have used camps for summer courses, whereby teachers and leaders spend the summer in the camp while taking outdoor education and counselor training courses.

The increasing number of colleges and universities that are acquiring camps for leadership training, or cooperating with existing camps, indicates a decided trend in the preparation of teachers and leaders in outdoor education. The combination of actual experience in camp with courses in educational foundations and methods is an interesting approach in teacher education for out-of-classroom activities. It is conceivable that most of the college offerings in outdoor education should be in camps and other outdoor laboratories or closely associated with them.

PROGRAM ACTIVITIES IN CAMP SETTINGS

objectives

It would be impossible to describe all of the possible activities in the various outdoor education programs in camp settings. They include those experiences that cannot be achieved as well, or at all, in the classroom. In addition, the outdoor classroom experiences should supplement and enrich many of the in-school learning opportunities. There are instances where programs in camp settings are developed for special purposes—science, conservation, music, athletics, and others. Such programs also have many general educational values, inherent in all good camping situations. School programs in camps, for the most part, however, are broad and the experiences would be considered among the common learnings of general education. It would be beyond the scope of this book to list all of the learning situations that are unique in camp settings. Many of them could be categorized under the following general objectives:

1. Experiencing democratic and social living.
2. Learning to live happily and healthfully out-of-doors.
3. Understanding the physical environment and man's relationship to it.
4. Learning to appreciate natural resources and how to use them wisely.
5. Providing direct learning situations, including purposeful work experiences, where many of the skills and attitudes developed in the classroom may be applied.
6. Initiating and completing effective teaching processes in pupil-teacher planned experiences.

The educational objectives of outdoor classroom programs may also be classified as social living, healthful living, work experience, recreational living, and outdoor education activities related to classroom subject matter.

The listing of program activities is to help identify the many potential learning situations inherent in the outdoor classroom; it should not give the impression that the program is fragmentized or divided according to subject matter areas.

program planning

An outdoor classroom program is developed in much the same way as good classroom activities. The freedom from tradition and classroom pressures makes it easier to follow the best procedures in the learning process. The following general principles are important in securing the greatest value from experiences in camp settings.

1. The entire experience should be planned jointly by students, teachers, parent groups, and resource leaders.
2. The facility and surrounding area should be carefully studied so maximum use can be made of its unique teaching and learning resources.
3. The planning should begin with the interests and purposes of the students, in terms of what can be learned best during the period at camp.
4. The structure for achieving the purposes should provide for maximum participation of students and teachers.
5. The program should, whenever possible, grow out of classroom planning, and in the post-camp period, be utilized to the greatest extent.

6. There should be careful evaluation, by students, teachers, and parents, of the camp-related experiences.

To date, one of the most impressive characteristics of unfolding resident outdoor education programs has been the pupil-teacher planning and the assumption of responsibility for the activities by students. The new relationship established between students and teachers, plus the genuineness of the experiences, is conducive to cooperative planning. It is common practice for student committees to explore the camp in advance, consider items of food and clothing, to establish committees with specific responsibilities, and participate in evaluation activities. Often the group is completely organized and ready to start exploring or preparing the camp meal when the bus unloads.

program activities

The program consists of a series of complete activities centered around (1) the natural living situations that occur, and (2) the best use of the camp environment for learning activities that grow out of the children's interests and the on-going school curriculum. Some schools carefully plan class-related activities: operating a camp bank and store, for example, involves arithmetic; running a weather station relates to the study of natural and physical sciences. Others build the activities around problems of food, clothing, shelter, and the physical environment. Still others combine these two effectively in a series of living activities, explorations, and adventures.

A helpful device in planning outdoor experiences is to conceive of the camp setting as another school laboratory. Pupils and teachers go to the outdoors to have certain experiences just as they go to the library or the science room, the bank or the post office. The emphasis is consistently on direct as opposed to vicarious experience.

In the elementary school program, students may participate in exploratory trips throughout the camp area, cookouts, shelter construction, trail building, development of simple nature trails, use of the compass, developing weather stations, arts and crafts activities with native materials, and many comparable activities that have interest and meaning for children. In secondary school programs, the outdoor activities are more intensive and involve a maximum of *doing.* Specific projects to improve the camp community become problem-solving experiences in the improvement of the physical environment—building shelters, tree planting, timber management, improving the park, game and fish management, and correction of soil erosion. There are many social activities, including special interests in music, arts and crafts, use of tools, and outdoor recreational activities. Interspersed in the program for all age groups will be explorations to points of interest, such as marshes, quaking bogs, seashore, glacial lakes, sand dunes, high cliffs, desert areas, tropical swamps, historic landmarks, farms, sawmills, mines, and others unique to the camp environment. There are seasonal interests, such as gathering and preparing wild fruits, maple sugaring, and taking canoe trips. Some of the most important experiences are those associated with meals, evening campfires, and other living activities. The opportunities for leisurely family-style meals, with hosts and hostesses, servers, and kitchen helpers are unique to a camp setting. The introduction to new outdoor skills and interests is particularly significant in giving balance to the traditional school program of mass games and athletics. Many of these have lead-on values into adult living, such as hiking, skating, skiing, swimming, archery, orienteering, casting, shooting and gun safety, boating, outdoor photography, woodcraft, cookouts, use of hand tools, or building shelters.

The following outline represents a composite of program activities from several outdoor classroom programs. Its purpose is to stimulate others in exploring the potential learning situations in their own settings. Most of the situations mentioned are not isolated experiences, but are interwoven with others.

Social living. The camp setting is rich in common living experiences. For example, eating together affords many situations for learning. Opportunity is presented for practicing proper table etiquette and for engaging in social conversation. Staff members and guests are usually invited by student hosts and hostesses to sit at the various tables during each meal. Grace at meals is arranged each day by the responsible program unit. A small but significant experience presents itself here when grace at the meals is said, or sung, sometimes by the group, and sometimes by individuals representing various faiths. There are additional learning activities at mealtime, such as decoration of the room and tables, after-dinner speeches, and so forth. Meals should not be announced by gongs—campers should enter the dining room leisurely and visit in social groups until the meal is served. Such experiences are basic in developing a sensitivity to gracious living.

Other types of social living activities include:

1. Children and teachers living together 24 hours a day.
2. Cooperative learning person to person, group to group, and teacher to teacher.

3. Opportunities for growth in social amenities, religious tolerance, intercultural understandings, race relations, and socioeconomic problems.
4. Social growth through planning activities, cooperative endeavors, evaluations, camp citizenship, and group activities for camp living.
5. Children living together with their peers in social patterns that are different from those usually found in the home and school.
6. Additional opportunities for youth to be inducted into society through participation in service activities such as conservation and camp improvement projects.

Healthful living. Health becomes a program of action, rather than a set of abstract facts. The camp, being a complete community, presents community health problems for the camper citizen to solve.

The preparation and serving of food at camp can provide a wider variety of learning situations than exist in school or in the modern home. Even though the general planning and preparation are done by a professional staff, camper participation in these activities can have many implications for health. Each program group may have the responsiblity for one day of assisting in preparation and serving of food, together with clearing of tables and caring for dishes. In some instances county health inspectors and sanitarians work with the groups in developing skills for sanitation in food handling. A variety of activities are included here, such as peeling potatoes, preparation of fruit, serving the food, clearing tables, cleaning the dining room and kitchen, and caring for utensils. These experiences apply to social living, since social living is a cooperative venture and involves many relationships. Some groups may even devise a sanitation checklist and elect health inspectors to make daily checkups on practices throughout the camp.

Some of the other implications for health include:

1. Engaging in a proper balance of outdoor activity, work, and recreation.
2. Practicing good habits of eating, sleeping, and care of the body; having opportunities to observe the benefits of an orderly plan of living.
3. Being in a good environment for mental health, with fewer tensions from the rapid tempo of adult society.
4. Working with problems of food, clothing, and shelter—having direct experiences in personal health such as planning menus, preparing foods, and wearing proper clothing.

5. Considering camp health problems, such as water supply, sanitation, cleanliness, garbage disposal, and general health conditions.

Like the other types of activities, the health aspect is a part of the whole camp venture, with many of the suggested experiences having significance in various phases of the curriculum.

Purposeful work activities.   Since outdoor education programs are based on the principle that children and youth learn best by doing, purposeful work activities are significant. Answer giving is kept at a minimum and exploration at a maximum. Work activities in camp are, of two types:

1. Those necessitated when a group lives together in camp, such as the routine activities relating to food, shelter, and comfort;
2. Projects for the improvement of the camp and the physical environment.

In the first group, campers learn by doing—planning, preparation, and serving of meals, washing dishes, building fires, and general camp housekeeping. The second group is particularly significant in developing good citizenship and desirable attitudes toward natural resources and the improvement of the natural environment. In well-planned programs, children and youth have an opportunity to give service to the community and state, and to exercise some of their prerogatives as citizens, functions which are generally not fully exploited in the regular curriculum.

Work experiences on the land are an important contribution of the camp setting to education, particularly for secondary school youth. Some of these activities include:

1. Improvement of the camp.
   a. Building shelters, footbridges, and boat docks
   b. Cleaning and redecorating buildings
   c. Installing and repairing plumbing
   d. Constructing roads and parking areas
   e. Improving beaches
   f. Building trails and labeling interesting phenomena
   g. Solving pollution problems
   h. Landscaping building area
2. Forest management.
   a. Planting seedlings
   b. Selective cutting and studying of timber growth
   c. Cleaning and brushing

  d. Controlling disease, insects, and fires
  e. Sealing of lumber
  f. Comparing grazed and ungrazed woodlots
3. Wildlife management.
  a. Making animal population studies—census, trapping, banding
  b. Engaging in environmental improvement, such as building brush shelters, planting game cover, and constructing bird houses and winter feeding stations
4. Fish management.
  a. Improving lakes and streams
  b. Studying food in lakes
  c. Studying fish population
  d. Preventing lake and stream pollution
5. Soil conservation.
  a. Building check-dams
  b. Maintaining or restoring fertility
  c. Planting shrubs, trees, and grass to prevent erosion
  d. Soil testing
6. Fire prevention and fire fighting.
  a. Learning use of power machinery
  b. Participating in actual fire control
  c. Studying fire fighting methods, fire towers, ground and air equipment, lanes and backfires
7. Gathering of data.
  a. Maintaining weather records
  b. Keeping stream flow and ecological records

Recreation and outdoor living. A new field of experience in recreational activities and outdoor living presents itself in outdoor education programs in camp settings. There are opportunities for children and youth to participate in leisure-time activities that have leading-on qualities. New skills connected with some of the basic activities of man, such as fishing, hunting, trapping, canoeing, swimming, skating, nature photography, and hiking, are possible in the new outdoor curriculum. Many of the primitive skills involving food, clothing, and shelter become interesting recreational activities for a generation that has removed itself from the land. Creative recreation is more often possible when children and youth are away from an environment of "manufactured" entertainment. Folk dancing, singing together, storytelling, square dancing, campfire programs, and simple dramatics supplement the school's list of competitive games and activities.

All types of outdoor education are viewed by many educators and by parks and recreation officials as a unique way to teach

American people to enjoy the out-of-doors and come into possession of the abundant natural resources. Contact with nature and the adjustments necessary to live under many conditions of weather and climate are appealing to modern adventurous youth and may constitute a partial answer to some of the youth problems of our day. Learning and living outdoors are and always have been fun, and outdoor classroom experiences are not exceptions. Fun and learning go well together. The following list of activities will illustrate only a few of the opportunities for recreational living:

1. Social activities in camp
   a. Games and play activities
   b. Singing and storytelling
   c. Dramatics
   d. Ceremonials
   e. Dancing
   f. Campfire programs
2. Outdoor activities
   a. Hiking and excursions
   b. Cookouts and campouts
   c. Swimming and boating
   d. Skating, skiing, snowshoeing
   e. Archery and riflery
   f. Photography
   g. Fly tying and bait casting
   h. Hunting and fishing
   i. Orienteering
   j. Woodcrafts
   k. Whittling
   l. Use of camping tools
   m. Care of tools and equipment
   n. Arts and crafts

Outdoor education activities. There are many opportunities relating classroom experiences and subject matter to reality out-of-doors. Some of these activities are specifically planned in conjunction with the curriculum, whereas others are concomitants of explorations of the environment. Following are some activities which may be identified with subject areas:

1. Science—experiences with soil, water, weather, plants, animals, and birds; collections of leaves, seeds, fruits, nuts, and bark
   a. Game and fish management
   b. Developing a library and simple museum

   c. Understanding forests, soil, and water through visits to points
       of special interest
   d. Activities in geology through visits to stone quarries or gravel
       pits
   e. Weather station activities
   f. Making maple sugar
   g. Photography
   h. Study of stars
   i. Use of simple keys for identification in botany and zoology
   j. Museum preparation, such as elementary taxidermy, foliage
       impression, and making casts of animal tracks
   k. Use of compass
   l. Activities involving land use and types of soil
   m. Sanitation and water testing
   n. Study of poisonous plants and methods of protection
   o. Use of fire fighting equipment
   p. Use of plants for food
   q. Development of nature trails
   r. Mapping and aerial photo interpretation
   s. Soil testing
2. Social science
   a. Land-use problems and reasons for shifting population; charts
       and maps
   b. Study of deserted farms
   c. Indian lore and stories of lumber camps
   d. History of the camp area
   e. Improvement of the camp community, such as landscaping
   f. Study of local industries, such as commercial fishing, saw-
       mills, mining, agriculture, and forestry
   g. Study of dams and electric power, watershed concept and re-
       lation to other resources
   h. Care of public property
   i. Problems of stream pollution
   j. Visiting nearby rural schools
   k. Participation in government of the camp community
   l. Recreation patterns as determined by the land and people
3. Communication
   a. Daily logs and journals
   b. Trip reports
   c. Evaluation reports
   d. Storytelling with use of visual aids
   e. Written reports

    f. Reading of camp stories and legends

    g. Pre- and post-camp planning in English classes

    h. Writing letters to family and friends, land owners, and participating agencies

    i. Appearance before clubs and organizations to report camp experiences

    j. Labeling nature trails

    k. Use of literature involving the out-of-doors

    l. Writing poetry at camp

    m. Preparation of mimeographed take-home material

    n. Preparation of radio and television programs

    o. Preparation of assembly programs

4. Mathematics

    a. Computing costs of food and purchasing supplies

    b. Use of compass

    c. Surveying and mapping

    d. Operation of camp store and bank

    e. Developing financial report of camp—obvious and hidden costs

    f. Drawing plans for camp buildings, birdhouses, and other structures

    g. Making requisitions for supplies

    h. Mathematical computations involved in logging, determining board feet

    i. Angles in determining heights of trees and buildings

    j. Studying depth and surface of lake

    k. Use of laws of leverage

    l. Determination of land values

    m. Aerial photography interpretation

    n. Meteorology

    o. Inventories of camp materials and supplies

5. Shop

    a. Construction of bridges, cabins, deflectors

    b. Construction o fneeded equipment, such as birdhouse, feeding stations, line traps

    c. Care and use of tools

    d. Reading blueprints

    e. Making or maintaining waterfront equipment

    f. Repairing boats

    g. Making simple boat equipment

    h. Making simple weather instruments and housing them

    i. Constructing exhibits

    j. Making and keeping bulletin boards

    k. Constructing outdoor museum

6. Homemaking
    a. Planning menus
    b. Preparing and serving foods
    c. Being responsible for personal sanitation
    d. Decorating
    e. Using proper clothing
    f. Making beds
    g. Providing for cabin sanitation
    h. Practicing social graces at meals
    i. Greeting guests and making introductions
7. Music, art, dramatics
    a. Singing camp songs
    b. Using native materials
    c. Creative drawing and sketching
    d. Taking part in ceremonials, pageantry, storytelling
    e. Playing recreational charades
    f. Preparation of visual materials to tell stories of things seen while at camp—posters, charts, exhibits, museums, layouts, and nature trail signs
    g. Preparation of take-home materials, printed or mimeographed

Exploration activities. Previous mention has been made of explorations both in the camp area and to places of interest. Although the richness and variety in these extensive adventures cannot be described adequately in the limited space available, a few types of such activities are briefly reviewed:

1. *Blazing a trail.* It is natural for a group of young outdoorsmen to choose this project. There is a lack of foot trails in many areas. The groups, with maps and a compass, may start on back country courses that lead over a creek, skirt a thicket, cross a clearing to the edge of a lake, and possibly proceed over gently rolling ground to the foot of one of the prominent hills in the area. The campers could blaze this trail with markers, or decide that it is unnecessary because future park visitors can easily follow the natural terrain of the country. School campers might climb the hill and consider the purposes of a trail—to prevent park visitors from becoming lost, to invite them into the most scenic parts of the area where wildlife and flowers can be observed, and to give hikers a safe footpath free of poisonous plants and obstacles.

At one camp a river trail can be begun; at another, the development of a trail to the beach from the camp is of major importance. Trees might have to be felled so that footbridges may be constructed at marshy places. At all of these camp locations, trail location and construction work are done in a spirit of community contribution. Campers are justifiably proud of their work.

2. *Cookouts and hikes.*   Every group takes some kind of hike. The purpose is to see as much of the back country as possible, to enjoy the scenery, or to visit one of the geographical oddities. Hikes and excursions often are taken to neighboring communities so that local economy may be discussed. The hikes are not aimless rambles, but are always carefully planned with definite objectives. Usually they include planning and preparing an outdoor meal, using the area maps and a compass, and making systematic observations.

On cookouts, the use of an open fire is a skill each individual learns and will probably never forget. Student campers learn, too, that campfires must be put out because they have seen in fire-scarred trees the results of careless campers. They learn to work together by sharing the work involved in menu planning, fire building, cooking, and cleaning up the cookout area. Students discuss hills, planting of evergreens and other trees to prevent erosion, and the beauty they find in the outdoor scenery. They usually recommend that every camper have the experience of a hike and cookout.

3. *Historical explorations.*   Most children and youth have an instinctive desire to explore, and the program should incorporate it in a learning situation. Children are very interested in investigating the historical background of land areas. An exploring opportunity at one camp is an oddly shaped hill visible from the lodge. The mystery surrounding the peculiar mound on top of an otherwise regularly shaped hill is quite sufficient to arouse the exploring instinct of children in the outdoors.

A hike to the hill produces interesting evidence along the way. A gravel pit at one side of the hill, now completly grown over, shows where the soil came from for building up the mound on top. Tree stumps on the man-made mound suggest its probable age. Finally, at the top, a brick- and stone-lined hole, with a pipe running out one side and the absence of branches on the side of the surrounding trees, prove the presence at one time of a water tower. A little research in the local library by a camp counselor has already disclosed the fact that the tower was originally intended to be one of a series to furnish drinking water for a city. How the original idea failed and how the tower was subsequently used to supply water for a large horse stable, to provide steam baths for a private sanitarium, and finally as a station in the underground railroad for smuggling southern slaves into Canada, make an interesting story involving much local and national history. On such an exploratory trip, students learn that the methods of science apply to history as well as to biology. Acting as an amateur archeologist can be exciting.

Other explorations will give an appreciation of land use. One or more groups may set out on a trip. The leaders employ different techniques for stimulating the campers into finding out for themselves, as well as they can, the history of this locale. They visit old dooryards and examine them quite thoroughly. By deduction and discussion, they determine many interesting facts from the evidence they find in the scraps of old building materials, concrete building foundations, old berry patches, and old orchards. Firsthand knowledge, combined with material in books in the camp library, gives many of the campers their first live history lesson.

The same story repeats itself in other areas, where the remnants of flower gardens and flowering shrubs present an image of life among pioneer women. The limited leisure-time enjoyments of our forebears were directed toward making their lands and homes more beautiful. There is keen appreciation of this among the students. Historical hikes impart in a few hours a volume of knowledge. The picture of hardship, struggle, and accomplishment of earlier years becomes an absorbing and vivid lesson in little more than a class hour.

Fire-scarred trees at the edges of clearings suggest danger from forest fires that can destroy in a few moments the unharvested crops, stock, and personal possessions of a family. A nest of great-horned owl fledglings at the top of a hollow stub arouses interest in the relative harm or good that birds of prey can do.

Campers may wonder why once-productive fields are nearly barren. Examination shows meager topsoil and starving vegetation. Thoughts of soil treatment and pollution control, use, and adaptation enter the minds of the campers. They pause from time to time to discuss it. Later, in their cabins, the history, biology, agriculture, social customs—and the land—are further discussed.

4. *The quaking bog.* A worthwhile trip from camp is a visit to a quaking bog. One such spot has been visited over and over again by groups from a school camp. Each exploration of the area results in new discoveries for both the children and the teachers. As the seasons change, the swamp and surrounding woodlands take on a new and interesting appearance when explanations are sought and reasoned out by observation and group discussion.

The bog consists of a large swamp having three small ponds extending its length. The whole area is surrounded by hogbacks, making it possible to explore either by the water route or by the dry-land trail.

Having planned and prepared for the trip, and finally having arrived at the spot, children are anxious to begin exploring. First, it is necessary to talk things over. Poison sumac is present and, until all come to know its red twigs and white berries, it is necessary to stay together, and wise that the leader go first and point out the offending shrub. Every child will have new experiences on this trip—most of them have never been on an expedition of this type. In the late summer and early fall, fringed gentians are in bloom. Carnivorous pitcher plants are always in evidence. Also new to many are larch trees, some prematurely yellow and already dropping their once-green needles. It is a new experience to walk out over the water on a closely-woven carpet of spagnum moss and swamp grasses. The fact that shrubs, trees, and other plants are living over the water is proved by performing the "bogtrot"—all jumping in unison and watching trees and bushes shake fifty feet away. On occasions, woodcocks have been flushed from their natural habitat. When the group returns to the starting point, two-thirds of the area is still unexplored.

By now it is time to put on dry stockings, gather wood, start the fire, and prepare the meal planned two days ago. The frying pans are put over the fire and the onions sliced and put on to brown. Next, ground meat is added to the pans containing the onions. When the meat is completely done, it is transferred from the frying pans to No. 10 tin cans, already provided with wire bails by the children at camp. Tomatoes, beans, and chili sauce are added and stirred together, put over the fire, and allowed to simmer until hot enough to serve. Served on bread toasted by individual campers, with raw carrots and celery on the side and apples or oranges for dessert, it makes a balanced one-dish meal, easy to carry and prepare. It also provides plenty of energy for the afternoon exploration.

After cleaning up, putting out the fire, and resting a short time, the campers are anxious to discover what the high ground has to offer. The hogbacks provide a new terrain, with entirely different plant and animal life. Hardwoods predominate; oak, hickory, elm, and maple are in the majority. Occasionally an old scaly-barked black cherry tree is found, different from the smooth-barked roadside cherry. There are found evidences of a ground forest fire leaving triangular scars at the bases of the larger trees, all on the windward side, from which the fire must have come. One scar, upon investigation, proves to have been made by a farmer attaching barbed wire to the tree as a fence post. A lightning scar is evident, starting at the top and twisting down the trunk. There is also a man-made or, more probably, a boy-made scar—a hatchet cut in an otherwise perfect tree. Squirrel tracks and freshly disturbed earth in the trail give evidence of a recently buried nut.

Such a trip can mean for children a day full of real and lasting experiences in the out-of-doors, vital to an appreciation of living things and to promoting the idea of conservation, often difficult to attain in later life.

Tree planting.   Learning to love and appreciate the land on which we live is only part of the picture. Preventing its loss and waste, by knowing and understanding the tremendous importance of topsoil to all living things, is another part. Youth should gain the knowledge and be stimulated to do something constructive about it.

Soil conservation is accomplished in various ways. Certainly campers cannot become expert farmers overnight. But they can learn the purpose of contour plowing, and can come to understand the importance of planting trees and shrubs on areas not suitable for ordinary farm crops in order to utilize fully all of the land. They may plant trees and grasses on hillsides threatened by erosion; and they may pile brush to halt the gaping gullies in order to benefit the wildlife.

Many trees are planted by students, but more important they realize they are doing something of lasting value. On returning to camp they will speak about the prevention of erosion, improving the wildlife habitat of the area, the relationship of all wild things to their environment, and soil conservation and watersheds. They learn that only certain kinds of trees and plants will grow on certain types of soil, only certain kinds of animals and birds will be helped. They know they can return in years to come and see the fruits of their efforts— the growing forest. They perform an important task for the benefit of others.

A visit to a nearby sawmill, followed by actual timber cruising, can be one of the most interesting features of the whole program. Watching logs sawed into boards and learning from the sawyer which lumber is good for various purposes, and how it is graded, impresses the groups. Cruising timber, estimating the number of board feet, the age of the trees, determining the grades, and then with all this knowledge, computing the amount of material necessary and the cost involved to construct a house or some other building, is a practical lesson in appreciation of resources.

program organization

Organizing the outdoor school program for the week is an important learning process for children. Much of the planning is done prior to the camping period, but final details are sometimes completed after arrival at camp. In order to use the camp resources most effectively, the classroom group needs to be oriented to the resources of the camp, by advance exploratory visits and/or discussions with resource leaders or school staff members. After listing things that the group would do at camp, a tentative schedule can be made. The usual plan of organization is to divide the group into program units, with ten to fifteen students in each. In most instances, these program groups, with assigned teachers, stay intact throughout the entire camp period. Often, a group name is chosen and loyalties are developed. Planning sessions of the program units are held, and activities are considered. Days when special resource leaders, such as foresters, arts and crafts leaders are available, are indicated. Each group then makes choices of activities for every day spent in camp. Time blocks are normally set up on a half-day basis. Usually, representatives are elected from each of the program units to become members of the camp council to indicate their group's choices; then a composite schedule is made for the week. The staff program coordinator works with the council in assembling the activities and ironing out conflicts in the use of facilities and resource leaders. Procedure will vary, but the method of organization should insure maximum student participation in planning.

Student-teacher program planning is one of the most significant contributions of outdoor living to education. Perhaps no single aspect of the program has made such an impression on pupils as the opportunity to plan their own learning activities for camp. This should be constantly kept in mind lest there be temptation to dictate a rigid schedule, and rob the program of one of its greatest values.

pre-camp planning by staff

It is possible that the most important kind of planning is done by teachers, counselors, and resource people. In a camp with a permanent staff, this planning process ideally goes on all year with peaks of emphasis before the arrival of each new group of campers.

In situations where there is no regular staff or where pre-camp planning is usually done in an intensive manner, the usual procedure is for the staff to assemble at the camp one or two days before pupils are due. This session often begins on a Friday evening or Saturday morning, with the pupils arriving Sunday afternoon or Monday morning. The pre-camp session is important, particularly where several classrooms or even schools are involved, because this may be the first opportunity for the staff to become thoroughly acquainted with the area, to agree on general principles, and to search out new learning activities.

At this session, members of the staff usually commit themselves to be learners and counselors who forswear formal and prescribed courses of study, rules of the classroom, and the traditional role of the pedagogue.

In camp, where no schedule of classes and no set of rules are enforced, the director or chairman of the group engages in democratic planning seldom found in the classroom. The difference in enthusiasm and spontaneous reaction is evident. The result in creative action should give a clue to how local staffs might participate in the entire community school program. When one school is involved, much of this planning is done prior to arrival at camp and extended over a longer period of time.

examples of resident outdoor education programs

Similarities and points of difference in outdoor classroom programs are illustrated by the following examples from actual programs:

EXAMPLE 1—SUGGESTED ACTIVITIES FOR ELEMENTARY
CLASSROOM GROUPS AT CAMP

Hikes (with approximate time required)

Paul Bunyan's Woods—half-day or half-day with cookout
Around the lake—all-day, including a cookout meal
Half way around the lake (pick up by boat)—half-day, with or without cookout
Mystery Swamp—half-day or less
Hidden Valley—1½ hours to half-day
Abandoned Farm—half-day with or without cookout
Indian Village area—half-day with or without cookout
Dairy Farm—1½ hours to half day
Sawmill or Grist Mill (small groups to hike one way, pick up by station wagon)—half-day with or without cookout
Rural village—half-day to visit blacksmith shop, library, gravel pit, and general store

Things to do on hikes.

Study of wildlife; conversation; map and compass work; scavenger hunt; making collections; playing games; conservation projects; cookout preparations

Other activities at camp.

Crafts: whittling, carving, clay modeling, tin can crafts, sketching, primitive crafts, birdhouses, using and caring for tools

Lumbering; boating; cookouts; fishing; making ice cream, popcorn, punch; archery; night hikes; folk, square and social dancing; star study; treasure hunts; camp improvement; campfires; digging clay; parties; building check dams and retaining walls; conservation activities; singing, story telling, games; tree planting

The following schedule is generally followed at camp. It is suggested that the teacher plan with her students to fill in most of the activity periods before coming to camp.

8:00 a.m.	Breakfast
9:00—12:00	Morning activity period
12:00 noon	Lunch
until 2:00 p.m.	Lazy period
2:00—5:30 p.m.	Afternoon activity period
5:30 p.m.	Dinner
until 8:00 p.m.	Evening activity period
8:30 p.m.	Lights out

EXAMPLE 2—AN ELEMENTARY SCHOOL

Classroom work was done in each subject in preparation for the resident outdoor education experience.

Arithmetic—Opening and keeping of bank accounts—knowledge and interest in various areas of banking obtained in classroom and from a resource person (Assistant Manager of a branch bank); experiences in reading and using weather instruments; planning and estimating the cost of food; practical application of the fundamentals in daily activities.

Language and spelling—Practical application of paragraph writing, punctuation rules and outlining by means of reports, letter writing, and evaluating activities; acquiring new vocabulary and spelling in all areas.

Reading—Reference and research reading in the various units, pointing up the value and use of a library.

Science—Preparatory study of units relative to outdoor living via conservation, weather, health, and safety, through identification and workshop experiences in these subjects.

Social studies—Due to modern inventions, the goal in social studies is to become neighbor-minded, human-minded, world-minded. We must be able to appreciate and understand all people. To accomplish this the need is first, to understand oneself; secondly, to appreciate oneself in the classroom organization; and thirdly, to participate in a community living situation at camp. In the follow-up, these experiences aided in the understanding and appreciation of "our neighbors across the sea."

In the outdoor classroom at the Outdoor Education Center during a week in mid-winter each child was given a set of suggestions including problems and projects for water, soil, wildlife, plants, astronomy, and weather. They were to solve the problems and select one project in each unit. These were checked by the group leader as they were completed. The children answered the questions by observation, by questioning camp staff, teachers, and resource leaders, and by library research. Examples of each of the units include the following (there were from ten to twenty questions in each unit, and about seven projects):

Water

Problems:
1. How wide and how long is the river? Where does it begin and end? In which direction does it flow?
2. Find a place where water is cutting away a tree. What will happen to the tree? Will anything happen later as a further result?
3. How thick must ice be before it is safe to walk on?

Projects:
1. Map out trips and mark points of interest.
2. Observe under a microscope drops of water from various places. Identify microscopic organisms.
3. Write a story or poem about our trip.
4. Make a chart or report on different forms of water that you have observed. Give reasons for each form.

Soil

Problems:
1. Why does the ground freeze? How deep is it frozen? Where did you test it, and what was the temperature of the air?
2. What do the words "percolation" and "capillary" mean when re-referring to different soils?
3. How can you tell precious and semiprecious stones?

Projects:
1. Collect several kinds of soil. Put them in a jar of water, then shake and observe settling. Consult a resource person to find out what this means.
2. Collect rocks turning to soil—moss covered, lichen covered, rust colored, rock being split by roots, rock being crumbled by weathering.
3. Test for acidity (samples taken from various locations).

Wildlife
Problems:
1. What are some necessary game laws? Why?
2. Why do teeth and eye placement differ in animals? What is comparable in fish? How do bird beaks differ? Why?
3. Which animals hibernate? Semi-hibernate?

Projects:
1. Build game refuges and shelters.
2. Build and supply a bird feeding station.
3. Make casts of tracks.
4. Observe and explain how the chickadee, downy woodpecker, tufted titmouse, white-breasted nuthatch, and brown creeper work as a team to protect the trees in the winter.
5. Observe—then sketch your observations.

Plants (trees, mosses, lichens, plants)
Problems:
1. Study some lumbering operations. What does it mean to thin a forest?
2. How can you tell the age of a cut tree? An uncut tree?
3. What are different uses of plants? (as for soap, tea, rope)

Projects:
1. Collect leaves, twigs, weeds, fruits, fungi, galls, insect eggs, cocoons, etc., for identification and display.
2. Make some winter bouquets.
3. Demonstrate how plants turn toward light. Explain.
4. Do trees hibernate?
5. Set out some trees (plan with conservation officer).
6. What trees, plants, birds, and animals are listed in the Bible?

Astronomy
Problems:
1. How many miles is a light year? Why is it so measured?
2. What is a comet? A meteor? A meteorite? Of what are they composed? What are some evidences found in the United States and Canada? What is a meteorite crater? Where are some located?

3. How many have seen a man-made satellite? What causes it to stay in orbit? How can it be controlled from earth? What will it tell us about outer space?

Projects:
1. Chart layers of space and explain to the group.
2. Draw charts of constellations you have observed.
3. Tell the group about early legends (Indian and Greek mythology).
4. How is a telescope made?
5. Make a star finder out of materials at hand.

Weather
Problems:
1. Read weather instruments in our weather station.
2. Discuss and observe cloud formations.
3. What does the IGY research hope to tell us about weather?
4. How have certain people adapted to their particular climate—artificially and genetically?

Projects:
1. Keep a record of weather for the week, using the barometer, hygrometer, anemometer, weather vane, rain gauge, and thermometer. Observe cloud formations. Forecast.
2. Tell how the pioneers observed and predicted weather.

The schedule included resource people for forestry, science, crafts, music, and language arts. Groups were scheduled for certain activities, and had choices for some activities. The weekly schedule included a hike to a lake, ice tobogganing, local history, science (samples, observations, microscopic study, building terraria), communication skills (sketching, painting, writing, dramatizing, discussing, singing), group recreation (planned by children, by adults, or together), snow sculpturing, bird study, animal study, and related areas.

SUGGESTIONS FOR FURTHER STUDY AND RESEARCH

1. Develop a plan for the use of a camp setting for a school system which you know or in which you are interested.
2. Outline a plan for a community camp which could be used on a twelve-month basis by schools, recreation departments, and agencies.
3. What research has been done that identifies some learning experiences that are more effective in a camp sitting?
4. Prepare a sample agreement or contract between a school district

EXAMPLE 3—AN ELEMENTARY SCHOOL RESIDENT OUTDOOR EDUCATION PROGRAM

	MONDAY	TUESDAY	WEDNESDAY	THURSDAY	FRIDAY
		B	COOK-OUT-A E	COOK-OUT-C F	COOK-OUT-D F
8:00 BREAKFAST		GRADE 6	GRADE 5	GRADE 4	ALL GROUPS PACK AND CLEAN UP
MORNING ACTIVITIES 9:00-10:30	LEAVE FOR PROUD LAKE OUTDOOR CENTER	A FORESTER B FISHING C HIKE D INTEREST HIKE E WEATHER STATION; HIKE F HIKE	A&F TRAPPER B PLAN AND EVALUATE C ICE FISHING D PLAN AND EVALUATE E CONSERVATION RESOURCE	A COMPASS B CRAFTS C BIRD HIKE D PACK FOR COOK-OUT: NOTES E HIKE F FORESTER	ALL GROUPS PACK AND CLEAN UP
10:30-12:00	SETTLE DORMS	A FORESTER B ICE FISHING C CRAFTS D&E HANDCRAFTS; F WEATHER STATION; NOTEBOOKS	A HIKE B&E TRAPPER C ICE FISHING D CONSERVATION RESOURCE F CRAFTS	A ICE FISHING B WEATHER-COMPASS HIKE C CRAFTS D PACK FOR COOK-OUT E HIKE F FORESTER	ALL GROUPS - TOBOGGANING TRACKING GAMES
12:00 LUNCH	SACK LUNCH	C	COOK-OUTS-A, E, F. D	COOK-OUTS B&D, E&F C	A
QUIET TIME		ALL GROUPS	ALL GROUPS	ALL GROUPS	ALL GROUPS
AFTERNOON ACTIVITIES 2:00-3:30	MEETING WITH CAMP STAFF	A B C } FIREARMS DEMONSTRATION D } AND RIFLERY E F CRAFTS	A CONSERVATION RESOURCE C&D TRAPPER B CRAFTS F STORY-TIME	A B, E, F FORESTER C CRAFTS D ICE FISHING	LEAVE FOR WILL ROGERS SCHOOL
3:30-5:00	ORIENTATION HIKES PLANNING SESSION CRAFTS KNIGHTS OF THE PANTRY I.D. BADGES LETTER HOME	A NOTEBOOKS B NOTEBOOKS C&D FORESTER E OUTDOOR SKILLS F HIKE 6th. GRADE - RIFLERY	A STORY-TIME & LIBRARY B NOTEBOOKS & LIBRARY C CRAFTS D HIKE F CONSERVATION RESOURCE	A FORESTER B RIFLERY C ICE FISHING D FORESTER F HIKE 6th. GRADE - RIFLERY	
5:30 DINNER	A	D	B	E - BIRTHDAY DINNER	
EVALUATION	ALL GROUPS	ALL GROUPS	ALL GROUPS	ALL GROUPS	
EVENING ACTIVITIES 7:00-8:30	GENERAL EVALUATION BY PRINCIPAL RECREATION - COUNCIL FILM	CAMPFIRE TALENT SHOW ASTRONOMY	ASTRONOMY DORM PROGRAMS POPCORN PARTY STORY-TIME	STATE TROOPER CAMPFIRE SQUARE DANCE	
	DORM DEVOTIONS	DORM DEVOTIONS	DORM DEVOTIONS	DORM DEVOTIONS	
	ALL GROUPS EVALUATION	ALL GROUPS EVALUATION	ALL GROUPS EVALUATION	ALL GROUPS EVALUATION	
9:00 LIGHTS OUT					

EXAMPLE 4—A SECONDARY SCHOOL RESIDENT OUTDOOR EDUCATION PROGRAM

DAY	LOGGERS	TEAMSTERS	CRUISERS	LUMBERJACKS	SAWYERS
MONDAY	Weather station Historical hike Sunset vespers	Find the history of the area Weather station Hike to old homestead Sunset vespers	Felling trees and cutting wood Sunset vespers	Building a dam Completion of dam building Sunset vespers	Bird hunt Blazing a trail and woodcutting Sunset vespers
TUES.	Fish conservation Evening cook-out	Trip to Devil's Soup Bowl Noon cook-out and hike	Planning session Building game shelters	Building animal shelters Fish conservation (scaling)	Trip to Devil's Soup Bowl Cook-out
WED.	Build brush piles for game Deer census	Find depth of lake Fish conservation Deer census	Tree planting Deer census	Tree planting Deer census	Fish conservation Bird trip Deer census
THURS.	Axe demonstration Gun demonstration Scaling and lumber mill trip	Axe demonstration Gun demonstration Clearing underbrush Build brush piles animal shelter Felling trees	Axe demonstration Gun demonstration Trip to Devil's Soup Bowl Noon cook-out Historical hike to Yankee Springs	Trip to Devil's Soup Bowl Noon cook-out	Axe demonstration Gun demonstration Sawmill visit and cruising
FRIDAY	Evaluation	Evaluation	Evaluation	Evaluation	Evaluation

EVENING

DAY	LOGGERS	TEAMSTERS	CRUISERS	LUMBERJACKS	SAWYERS	
SUNDAY	Planning by group		Camp council	Games		Snacks
MONDAY	Planning session and daily evaluation by groups		Singing	Games	Square dancing	Snacks
TUES.	Planning session and daily evaluation by groups		Guest speakers	Singing	Story telling	Snacks
WED.	Planning session and daily evaluation by goroups		Guest speakers	Games	Square dancing	Snacks
THURS.	Planning session and daily evaluation by groups		Story telling		Dancing	Snacks in cabin

Note: One group was responsible each evening for planning the evening's activities.

and an agency for using a camp facility for an outdoor education program.

5. Prepare a directory of camp facilities in your state that might be available for schools in conducting an outdoor education program.

REFERENCES

books

Gabrielsen, M. Alexander, and Holtzer, Charles. *The Role of Outdoor Education*. New York: The Center for Applied Research in Education, 1965.

Garrison, Cecil. *Outdoor Education: Principles and Practice*. Springfield, Ill.: Charles C Thomas, 1966.

Mand, Charles L. *Outdoor Education*. New York: J. Lowell Pratt, 1967.

Michigan Department of Education. *Outdoor Education in Michigan Schools*. Lansing: Michigan Department of Education, 1970.

Schramm, Wilbur. *Classroom Out-of-Doors*. Kalamazoo, Mich.: Sequoia Press, 1969.

Smith, Julian W., *Outdoor Education*. Rev. ed. Washington, D. C.: AAHPER, 1970.

films

Beyond the Chalkboard (16 mm., sound, color). Northern Illinois University, De Kalb, Ill. 60115.

Nature's Classroom (16 mm., sound, color). Division of Conservation, Department of Natural Resources, Box 450, Madison, Wisc. 53701.

Outdoor Education (16 mm., sound, color, 28½ min.). NEA Sound Studios, 1201 Sixteenth Street, N. W., Washington, D. C. 20036.

6

education for the outdoors

The universality of interest in the outdoors is exemplified by the multitude of outdoor pursuits which attract increasing millions of people. The activities range from the appreciation arts to manipulative skills, all of which have the potential for the enrichment of human living. Many outdoor sports, such as fishing, hunting, boating, and archery, are as old as man. In earlier cultures, they served primarily as a way of acquiring food and of surviving, but they also had the elements of sport and adventure.

For the most part, the outdoor sports mentioned now serve the latter purpose and are becoming significant outlets for fitness and for the constructive use of time in an age of mechanization and automation. Shooting and hunting, casting and angling, boating and water activities, archery, and others, in addition to their potential for adventure, fun, and relaxation, are related to natural resources and are important for a better understanding and use of the outdoors. They are wholesome and desirable activities for children, youth, and adults.

In past decades, such activities were a normal phase of the growing-up process of children, and an essential part of the off working hours of many men. Skills were learned from parents or neighbors, and it was assumed that outdoorsmen would know their way in the forests and in the lakes and streams. The change in living has now removed many of the opportunities to learn these skills in the home. As in music, art, and athletics, it becomes necessary for the community's educational program to broaden its offerings to include outdoor skills, particularly those which have life-long interests and values.

Some people feel that interest should be diverted from outdoor sports that involve the use of natural resources such as fish, wildlife, and land areas. However, with good conservation management, many of these resources can be provided indefinitely, if future citizens are educated to use them wisely. Much has been accomplished in recent years to emphasize sport and adventure outdoors with less concern for bag limits. The satisfactions of skills in shooting, casting, or boating and the pleasure of outdoor living outweigh the importance of game for food; good game management requires the taking of game as a crop. There are also those who decry sport that involves the killing of game or fish and want to substitute only the appreciation arts. Both kinds of interests in the outdoors are necessary and important, and with education there will be the necessary balance in all activities. It is important to interest people in a wide variety of activities that will teach care and protection of natural resources and bring man and his physical environment into harmony.

The outdoor sports, therefore, are not only compatible with the appreciation arts related to the outdoors, they are complementary and interrelated. It is the purpose of this chapter to describe a variety of activities that provide education for the outdoors.

CASTING AND ANGLING

Angling is an old and ever popular activity. Its origin dates back to the time when early man fished to obtain food; but for ages it has also been considered fun. There has been an increasing emphasis on angling as a sporting activity rather than as a source of food. Of all sports, its claim to universality is best founded, for over thirty million people are involved in fishing each year.

The techniques of taking fish from lakes and streams have changed from primitive methods to a great variety of highly skilled operations through the use of well-designed equipment and lures. Thus, casting, one form of angling, has in itself become a specialized but satisfying skill. Much of the modern fisherman's pleasure is in the selection, use, and care of equipment. While no one would deny that the simpler forms of angling with the cane pole are fun, especially for boys and girls, increasing numbers of people desire specialized equipment for many types of fishing on streams, lakes, and oceans. Since much of the fun in sport fishing is related to matching skill and proper equipment with hard-to-get fish, skills in casting and angling become more important in providing satisfying recreational experiences. While most people find enjoyment in acquiring angling skills in anticipation of fishing, many find equal pleasure in learning accuracy through practice and in competitive distance and accuracy casting. The making of equipment and lures, fly tying, and construction of fishing coops and boats are examples of constructive and worthwhile use of leisure time for more and more people.

Casting, angling, and allied activities are becoming important experiences in educational and recreational programs and are finding their place in schools, colleges, recreation departments, and other agencies. They are carry-over activities which have life-long values and in which people of all ages can participate. Many, who do not take part in more strenuous sports, find casting and angling challenging and satisfying. For example, they are suitable for the handicapped and may have therapeutic value.

In schools and colleges, casting and angling are appropriate offerings in physical education and recreation courses and activities. They are relatively easy to teach and administer; they fit logically into later elementary grades and secondary schools and into service and professional courses in colleges and universities. The diverse interest in angling makes it desirable to teach all types of casting —bait, fly, spincast, and surf casting. Many schools and colleges provide additional opportunities for casting and angling through clubs, outing organizations, intramural sports, and after-school programs. Likewise a large number of school and community recreation departments and agencies offer casting and angling activities throughout the year or during the summer.

Competitive games such as skish (a casting game) and tournament casting offer opportunities to create more interest and competence. Postal and telegraphic tournaments are often conducted for casting teams in high schools and colleges. The American Casting Association is the official organization for sport casting. It sets the rules, administers the official tournaments, gives awards, qualifies instructors, and provides services to those interested in competitive casting. The Association is made up of hundreds of local casting clubs in communities throughout the country. These clubs and their enthusiastic members are helpful to schools, colleges, and other groups who wish to initiate casting activities. Information and materials concerning tournament casting may be obtained from the American Casting Association office in Nashville, Tennessee.[1]

The Outdoor Education Project of the American Association for Health, Physical Education, and Recreation (AAHPER) has stimulated much interest in angling and casting in the physical education and recreation programs of schools and colleges throughout the nation. Regional and state Outdoor Education Workshops, which included casting clinics, have been held in nearly every state and section of the United States, and as a result many schools and colleges represented in the workshops include casting and angling in physical education classes, clubs, and recreational activities. A manual published by the AAHPER gives much helpful information about the teaching of these activities and offers suggestions on equipment specifications.[2] The American Casting Association has cooperated with the AAHPER in supplying instructors and materials to workshops, clinics, and local school and college programs. The American Fishing Tackle Manufacturers Association,[3] Chicago, one of the sponsoring agencies of the Outdoor Education Project, through its member companies has made the services of casting experts available to schools and organizations to help initiate programs.

casting and angling instructional activities

The inclusion of casting and angling in a physical education class, in a school club, or as a recreation activity is relatively simple. Casting should be taught first as a skill, beginning with the fundamentals of each type of equipment. In physical education it can be one of the several activities taught over a period of weeks, and fits well into a rotation plan through teaching stations. This plan requires a minimum amount of equipment. Casting is easy to administer since it can be done on a gymnasium floor, in multi-purpose rooms and corridors with high ceilings, on a lawn or playground, or in the water. Indoor or outdoor swimming pools are excellent for casting instruction and practice. In the club or recreation program, casting and angling can be conducted in much the same way, beginning with simple skills, followed by drill, competitive events, and fishing trips. The study of habitat, baits, and lures will add to the value of the instruction, and opportunities for fly tying, and construction of accessories

[1] American Casting Association, P. O. Box 51, Nashville, Tennessee 37202.
[2] Casting and Angling (Washington, D.C.: AAHPER, 1958).
[3] American Fishing Tackle Manufacturers Association, 20 North Wacker Drive, Chicago, Illinois 60606.

will add to the interest. Shop teachers often find interest in angling reflected in the construction of boats, fishing shanties, and related accessories.

Casting and angling have importance in a variety of curriculum activities. Teaching the skills in physical education, for example, can and should be related to science when angling and casting techniques are associated with fish management, bait, and habitat. The propagation of minnows and raising earthworms add interest. There are many other subject matter correlations in the physical and social sciences.[4] Conservation leaders have long recognized the value of teaching attitudes and concepts through school and college outdoor education programs, camping agencies, and recreation departments.

THE SHOOTING SPORTS

Shooting and hunting began with primitive methods of hurling projectiles and have developed into the use of modern sporting arms. Shooting is a recreational sport in itself, as evidenced by the millions that engage in target shooting, skeet, and trap shooting. Sporting arms are employed in various types of hunting, which has been a popular activity from pioneer days until the present when over twenty million hunting licenses are issued each year. Hand guns are used for recreational activities by many adults, but rifles and shotguns are more appropriate for instructional activities for children and youth. In the United States 25 million homes have guns for the shooting sports or as collector's items.

Shooting and hunting activities are included in many instructional and recreational programs in schools, colleges, and youth agencies. The natural interest in shooting and hunting is usually associated with childhood, beginning with toy wooden guns and cap pistols, and progressing to spring-type air rifles and gas guns. It is estimated that there are eight to ten million such guns in the hands of boys and girls in the United States. Many of these young Americans will some day use rifles and shotguns. Shooting and hunting provide adventuresome and wholesome fun, and lead into related activities in outdoor living, such as camping, boating, and hiking. They offer unusual opportunities for teaching conservation, safety, outdoor manners, and citizenship. Schools, colleges, and community agencies should provide basic instruction in shooting and hunting to help make

[4] A six-part filmstrip, *Beginning Fishing* (The Athletic Institute, 805 Merchandise Mart, Chicago, Illinois 60654) includes some of the subject matter correlations.

these sports safe and satisfying for the increasing numbers of people who seek participation in outdoor activities.

Ideally, the home should provide early instruction in the care and use of sporting arms. Otherwise, instruction should be available elsewhere to those interested.

The first instruction is recommended during elementary school age, with the air gun. Marksmanship, safety, and good citizenship can be taught in later elementary physical education classes, clubs, after-school programs, and in recreation departments and organized camping programs. Many youth-serving agencies also have shooting programs for later elementary and junior high school age groups using air rifles, pellet guns, and .22 rifles. A publication of the AAHPER on shooting, designed for recreation departments and agencies and elementary schools, is available.[5]

instruction in the shooting sports

Shooting instruction and hunter safety are appropriate to physical education and recreation curricula. They may be included with other activities in the regular class period or be a part of clubs, intramural sports, after-school programs, or special activity periods. Rifle shooting, especially, has often been administered as a club activity, but the physical education class can provide basic instruction for all those who need it. Clubs are excellent for field experiences and competitive events. Many schools offer concentrated instruction in hunting and correct gun handling during activity periods and after-school hours prior to the hunting season. In colleges and universities, shooting and hunting may be offered as service courses or as part of the professional classes in physical education.

There are many resources and materials available for instruction. The Outdoor Education Project of the AAHPER, through in-service training activities, has stimulated many schools, colleges, and agencies to broaden their offerings in physical education and recreation to include shooting sports and hunting workshops and clinics which are helpful in alerting teachers and administrators to the need for giving more emphasis to these sports. Excellent publications for teachers and leaders are now available. The National Rifle Association (NRA), an old and established membership organization, has championed safe and satisfying shooting activities since its inception in 1871. The NRA, in cooperation with the National Education Association, developed a hunter safety course, and millions of young shooters and hunters have

---

[5] *Marksmanship for Young Shooters* (Washington, D.C.: AAHPER, 1960).

received training from qualified NRA instructors. The Association cooperates with the AAHPER in the Outdoor Education Project in conducting shooting sports clinics in state and regional workshops and in providing instruction and materials.[6]

The National Shooting Sports Foundation and the Sporting Arms and Ammunition Manufacturers' Institute (SAAMI) have done much to stimulate instruction and participation in the shooting sports. These organizations have contributed funds, personnel, and materials in the leadership training efforts of the Outdoor Education Project. The National Shooting Sports Foundation[7] has excellent publications and visual aids—some especially appropriate reference materials for teaching—and is an invaluable service agency in making shooting sports available to all. Member companies of the Foundation also have excellent materials available. One of the most complete teaching aids is a shooting and hunting manual available from the AAHPER.[8] A significant study in shooting and firearms safety which includes much helpful information on instructional programs was made by Dr. Jack George.[9] The Daisy Manufacturing Company was one of the sponsors of the Outdoor Education Project and has contributed much to making the spring-type air rifle an instructional tool in marksmanship and safety.

Hundreds of Sportsmen's Clubs in the United States offer resources through facilities and leadership in shooting and hunting. While many new school and recreation buildings now have shooting ranges, many communities will find the local sportsmen's club the best facility for shooting activities.

Conservation agencies offer many services in interpreting conservation through shooting and hunting. In most states consultants are available to work with schools and other local agencies in initiating and developing effective shooting sports and hunting safety programs. In fifteen states, legislation makes hunter safety training a prerequisite to securing the first hunting license. The National Rifle Association, working with state education and conservation departments, administers shooting and hunting activities and has provided basic instruction to hundreds of thousands of youth. Most of the teaching is done by volunteer leaders, but an increasing number of schools and colleges are taking on this function. The opening of the small and large game

[6] Hunter Safety Packet (National Rifle Association, 1600 Rhode Island Avenue, N.W., Washington, D. C. 20036).

[7] National Shooting Sports Foundation, 1075 Post Road, Riverside, Connecticut 06878.

[8] Shooting and Hunting. (Washington, D. C.: AAHPER, 1960).

[9] Jack F. George, "The Construction and Evaluation of a Course of Study in Firearms Education" (doctoral dissertation, Boston University School of Education, 1955).

hunting seasons are colorful events in many states, when thousands of hunters, many of them school youth—and most of them ill-prepared —swarm into the fields and woods and onto the lakes. Instruction and practice in shooting and hunting is a necessary prerequisite to the mass exodus into the outdoors and should receive attention comparable to that given to athletics, or music and dramatics.

School and community recreation departments and agencies have a great opportunity to include shooting sports in their offerings. This would extend opportunities for wider participation in recreational pursuits, and would add interest and vitality for many in the whole educational program.

ARCHERY

Archery as an outdoor sport is becoming increasingly popular in many sections of the country. Historically, the bow was used for protection, for securing food, and as a weapon. But since the days of the American Indian archery has become a sport activity. Its appeal to all ages makes it a significant skill activity which should be taught in schools, colleges, and other community educational and recreational programs.

Archery is a versatile sport with a number of games and activities, in addition to target and field archery, which use the bow and arrow. They include:

Target archery rounds, with distances from shooting lines to targets ranging from 5 to 100 yards.

Clout shooting with large targets on the ground at distances of 120 to 180 yards.

Wand shooting with a two-inch diameter wand at a distance of 100 yards.

Flight shooting for distance.

Archery golf, set up in units of nine targets, each at varying distances with the bull's-eye four and one-half inches in diameter.

Field archery courses, set up in units of ten or fourteen targets with shots and shooting positions simulating hunting situations.

Roving, shooting one arrow at various inanimate objects at unknown distances.

Hunting with bow and arrow.

Fishing with bow and arrow.

instruction

The teaching of archery skills can begin with elementary age children, and should progress and extend into secondary schools and colleges. In schools and colleges, archery is logically a part of a good physical education program and is often included in clubs. Archery clinics are effective in stimulating interest in improving skills. Opportunities for participation in archery activities are often found in recreation agencies, youth organizations, and summer camps. The sport is an excellent coed activity, and mixed competition can be arranged in groups of two or more. Safety is an important phase of instruction and participation, and good teaching will include safe use. Much helpful information on archery instruction and competition may be found in *Archery*, an instructor's guide published by the American Association for Health, Physical Education, and Recreation.[10]

Archery is relatively simple to administer in a school, college, or agency program. A school gymnasium, all-purpose rooms, and protected areas of the playground may be used. In many communities, indoor and/or outdoor archery ranges are available through archery and sportsmen's clubs, youth centers, and public and commercial recreation facilities.

Archery as an all-season sport is becoming popular for family recreation and adult groups. There are organized clubs in many communities. In addition to the many directed and informal activities in archery, there are opportunities for local, state, and national competition.

Hunting with bow and arrow has had sensational growth in recent years. In many states, the opening of the season for bow hunting comes early in October, when fall colors are at their best, adding to the pleasure of being in the outdoors. It is estimated that approximately a million people hunt with the bow and arrow annually.

Bow and arrow fishing is a thrilling sport. In some instances this method is used to eradicate carp and similar types of rough fish. Many ardent archers respond to this opportunity.

equipment

Archery equipment today ranges from simple wood products to fiber glass and laminates. Specifications are important for adapting equipment to age and diversity of activities. Beginners tend to use equipment that is too heavy. Many archery instructors feel that elementary age children should use 15- to 20-pound bows. In the second-

---

[10] AAHPER, *Archery* (Washington, D.C.: AAHPER, 1972).

ary schools and colleges, it is well to start with 20- to 25-pound bows. Gradually the more experienced archers may find heavier equipment more appropriate for their particular interests and needs.

The increasing popularity of archery as an outdoor receational activity prompted the AAHPER to initiate a special effort to improve the quality of instruction and broaden the scope of archery in schools, colleges, recreation departments, and camping agencies. Originally known as Operation Archery, the program became a segment of the Outdoor Education Project of the AAHPER and is a cooperative venture with the archery industry as represented by the American Archery Council. Through selected pilot centers, research was conducted on methods of instruction and equipment. Archery instructors workshops are held in several sections of the country, and instructional materials have been developed.

BOATING AND WATER ACTIVITIES

While various forms of boating, such as canoeing, rowing, and sailing, have been favorite pastimes for generations, the increased availability of leisure time and the advent of the outboard motor have been largely responsible for the phenomenal increase in the number of people who participate in boating and water activities. Part of this increase has accompanied the growth of fishing, camping, and outing activities, but vacation use and the desire for adventure have made boating one of the leading outdoor sports. Today over 40 million people participate each year in all types of small craft activities.

Boating, like the other skills for the outdoors, requires training and experience to insure maximum satisfactions and safety. The growth in the number of people involved in boating is far ahead of the means of basic instruction, thus creating problems, accidents, and difficulties. In attempting to deal with the situation, legislation, ordinances, and regulations have come into being, but little has been done as yet to provide the education and training needed before boating and related activities can make maximum contributions to American living. National, state, and local agencies are increasing their efforts by providing a variety of training activities, among which are the American Red Cross, the Power Squadron, the Coast Guard Auxiliary, the Outboard Boating Club of America, the National Association of Engine and Boat Manufacturers, and many other trade and professional organizations, community agencies, schools, and colleges. Fortunately, the teaching of swimming has been extensive and well done in many schools and communities, but there are still many accidents due to the inability of people to care for themselves in and about the water.

Schools, colleges, and community agencies will eventually have to provide the basic instruction necessary for boating and water activities. Swimming and water safety skills must find their place in health, physical education, and recreation activities. Many feel that learning to swim should be a requirement for all school age children and youth. This can be achieved only by teamwork on the part of all community agencies, with the schools having a major role in basic instruction, supplemented with opportunities for extensive practice and application by many other recreation and youth agencies. The construction of thousands of public and private pools, and the development and improvement of beaches, have made it possible for great numbers of children and youth to learn to swim. Adequate instruction for boating and other water activities go beyond swimming skills. There need to be more educational experiences in canoeing, rowing, sailing, operation of outboard and inboard motors, transportation and launching of boats, safe equipment, first aid, and other related activities.

In schools and colleges, boating and water activities may be included in the offerings of health education, physical education, recreation, outing clubs, after-school and summer recreation programs, boating clubs, activity periods, swimming classes, and camping. Other curriculum areas such as health education and safety, general shop, and mechanics courses offer opportunities for instruction in small craft and motors. While canoeing, sailing, and rowing have long been a part of the curricula of some colleges, universities, and private schools, basic instruction is needed for larger numbers of students in all small craft operations. Much can be done without a large amount of equipment and extensive water facilities. Swimming pools can be utilized for some elementary instruction in boating skills and safety, while some of the preliminary activities can be done without water. In all instances, school and college instruction in boating must be supplemented by other community activities. Instructor training is being done through the efforts of the American Red Cross, Power Squadron, the Coast Guard Auxiliary, yacht and boating clubs, the Outboard Boating Club of America, and other trade and professional organizations. The AAHPER, through the Outdoor Education Project, has done much to stimulate boating and water activities by providing in-service training in workshops and clinics. Some states are now conducting boating and water safety clinics through the cooperation of departments of public instruction and conservation, safety committees, Red Cross, and other organizations concerned with water safety.

Water skiing and skin diving need much more systematic instruction than is now being offered in most communities. Good swimming skills are important prerequisites. More specialized, they require careful instruction and safety precautions.

Inasmuch as boating and water activities involve large numbers of people and provide excellent opportunities for fun, relaxation, and fitness, basic instruction should be part of a sound educational program. Many communities already have facilities and leadership necessary to initiate a more intensive program of training. Through cooperative action and in-service training at the local level, instruction in boating and water activities could be provided for all who want it.

SKIN AND SCUBA DIVING

There has been an interest in the underwater world for centuries, but not until recent years, with the advent of adequate equipment, have underwater recreational activities become extensive. Diving is the art of going below the surface of the water for a considerable length of time. Types of diving are roughly classified as military, open sea, commercial, and sport. Our concern here is with diving as sport—usually skin and scuba diving. The former requires no special equipment except mask and flippers, whereas scuba involves a self-contained underwater breathing apparatus, lightweight diving equipment, and in some instances helmet equipment.

Underwater diving is adventuresome and thus attracts the interest of all. Underwater constitutes a different physical environment for the human body, and precautions are necessary to eliminate danger. Equipment must be good, and instruction for its proper use competent.

Skin diving and scuba are becoming popular sports: they offer opportunities to fish, explore aquatic life, and satisfy the natural curiosity about the underwater environment. To date, diving is provided largely through diving clubs and private instruction. More recently schools, colleges, and agencies are beginning to offer opportunities to learn the necessary skills. In some states, clinics are conducted by teams of experts representing the American Red Cross, State Police, conservation officials, diving club members, and interested individuals. Some of the manufacturers of diving equipment are helpful in providing instructors and materials that will make underwater sports safe and satisfying.

OUTDOOR WINTER SPORTS

Winter sports are rapidly growing in interest and participation in many sections of the United States. Possessing excitement, they are suitable for various age groups and lend themselves to individual and family pleasure. Winter sports are of two types—snow and ice—and include downhill and cross-country skiing, ski jumping, bobsledding, tobogganing, snowshoeing, snowmobiling, skating, ice hockey, and a variety of games. Vacations and population mobility have made winter sports available to large numbers who do not live where there is snow and ice. Indoor ice rinks, and mechanical devices for manufacturing ice and snow have expanded the possibilities for many winter sports.

Vigorous winter sports make a distinct contribution to fitness and leisure. The skills are relatively easy to acquire, and facilities are becoming more available.

Many schools, colleges, and community agencies now offer instruction and opportunities for participation. Physical education and recreation classes, clubs, and sports clinics often include winter sports. Competition in several winter sports is popular in some sections of the country.

There has been a substantial development in publicly managed and commercially owned winter sports centers and facilities. In many instances, such facilities have been made available for school and college use, as has been done with bowling. Many school-community recreation programs find that winter sports are among their most popular activities, having the potential to satisfy the recreational needs and interests of a wide range of age groups.

MOUNTAIN ACTIVITIES

Among the more specialized outdoor living interests are those found in the mountain areas of the United States. Mountain climbing, pack trips, and hiking expeditions are included in a variety of popular activities, particularly in the western regions. Mountain climbing, particularly, requires much skill, and several colleges and private associations now include these activities in club and outing programs. Olympic Junior College, Bremerton, Washington, has an extensive program in mountain climbing and related activities, as does the University of Colorado at Boulder through its active Rocky Mountain Club. There are many public and private organizations and camps, such as the Sierra Club and Outward Bound, that feature outdoor activities in mountain areas.

ORIENTEERING

An outdoor sport which is gaining in interest and popularity in camps, youth agencies, and outdoor education programs is known as orienteering. This game, involving map and compass study, was first introduced in Sweden in 1917. It soon spread to other parts of Europe, is now a part of the educational program in Sweden and Norway, and is a popular national competitive activity in Denmark, Finland, and Switzerland. In recent years it has spread to Canada and the United States, being used primarily in Scouting and other youth organizations.

Orienteering is an appropriate activity for outdoor education programs in schools and colleges. It affords good experiences for those who engage in hiking, camping, hunting, fishing, and activities involving the use of larger land areas. Orienteering is a skill game involving the use of a compass and maps. It consists of a variety of activities including: reading and traveling by maps; exploring new territories; constructing maps of areas; judging and pacing distances; using a compass and landmarks to travel designated directional courses; and participating in contests using a compass.

OUTDOOR PHOTOGRAPHY

Outdoor photography has become one of the most popular interests for an increasing number of those who wish to capture the beauties and wonders of the outdoors. Good equipment—simple and sophisticated—for slides, prints, and movies has done much to add to the pleasure of outdoor pursuits and hobbies, and to motivate learning and facilitate instruction in many fields that lend themselves to outdoor learning.

Photography stimulates interest in outdoor education, and helps interpret outdoor learning experiences by supplementing instruction in visual terms. Outdoor photography helps the amateur or skilled photographer develop an awareness of and appreciation for the outdoors. Photographic instruction in classes and clubs of schools, colleges, and agencies, is helping to improve picture-taking quality. Much can be done in outdoor photography to supplement and reinforce outdoor learning experiences. Photography is also effective in informing the public about the need for and means of improving the outdoor environment.

FAMILY CAMPING

A phenomenal development in outdoor living is family camping. It is estimated that one of every six Americans participates annually in camping, usually as a member of a family group. The term *family camping* is used to describe the experience of a family living in an outdoor setting away from the usual routine, usually for a period of several days. The type of camping will vary from the more primitive experience in tent living to the use of elaborate mobile trailers. The goal may be to share an experience in outdoor living through camping, or to engage in sightseeing, fishing, boating, hunting, outdoor photography, or other interests and hobbies. Whatever its purposes, family camping makes it possible for millions of people to have satisfying outdoor recreation experiences within the limits of the family budget.

The objectives of family camping have been stated in unpublished materials by Thomas C. Slaughter and the late Ernest V. Blohm, well-known leaders in outdoor education in Michigan:

1. Provides a rich experience in family living on a 24-hour-per-day basis, different from the usual daily routine where a variety of obligations and interests tend to separate the family. Change from the normal daily routine is a relief from commonly known tensions.

2. Provides a cooperative family experience. Both work and play are shared. Is an opportunity for family togetherness.

3. Provides for healthful and wholesome living experiences.

4. Provides for wholesome relationships with other campers, often develops friendliness and neighborliness that breaks down the callousness of human relationships existing in other living situations.

5. Provides an opportunity for a comparatively inexpensive and economical vacation not otherwise possible. (Due consideration is given to the sizable initial investment for equipment, but this is absorbed in succeeding years as costs are averaged.)

6. Provides for learning experiences of all kinds: the out-of-doors, historical, social, and economic facts. Family camping—the skills involved and daily camp living—is a learning experience by itself.

7. Develops a variety of appreciations: for the land, the State, the beauty of nature, other humans, natural resources, such as trees and plants, animals, and creatures.

8. Develops spiritual and religious values. Helps develop a sense of judgment and concern required of adults in conservation matters and similar issues which are influenced by public decision and understanding.

9. Provides the opportunity to enrich life by the potential development of hobbies and interests.

10. Provides progressive experiences in romantic adventure and dis-

covery not as available in any other setting. The experiences of American pioneers can be recaptured and relived—a vital part of the American heritage.

11. Recalls the past economies of industries—lumbering, mining, quarrying—the culture of the people comprising those earlier societies, and the original Indian tribes. Historical interest and value may be of continuing personal interest.

12. Provides numerous occasions for creativity in improvisations often necessary; frequently provides freedom-of-choice situations.

Some noteworthy family camping programs are described later in the chapter in connection with adult education.

OUTDOOR EDUCATION FOR ADVENTURE

Outdoor education has many frontiers, including the more vigorous and adventuresome programs for high school and older youth. Some new developments in outdoor education challenge youth who, unlike their forebears, are being deprived of exciting encounters in outdoor areas that remain partially wild. Some of these programs have characteristics of the Civilian Conservation Corps of the 1930s which combined outdoor learning with work experiences on the land; others stress physical fitness and survival skills and are characterized by terms such as "risk," "plunge," and "quest for zest" (a phrase coined by Kirk A. W. Wipper, Professor, University of Toronto). Others feature outpost camping, pack and canoe trips, mountain climbing, and other outdoor adventures. Many feel that these aspects of outdoor education supply the needed emotional outlets for youths who might otherwise pursue less desirable activities, some of which border on crime and delinquency.

Much more thought and planning need to be done on this end of the outdoor education continuum if there is to be a greater impact on the education of secondary school and older youth. Some of the types of programs mentioned above are briefly described.

work-learn experiences

A Title III Elementary and Secondary Education Act program conducted by the Traverse City (Michigan) Public Schools, which continued after the termination of federal funding, will illustrate one kind of outdoor program for high school youth. A Michigan Department of Education publication explains the program as follows:

In the initial stage of the program, 70 high school boys from Traverse City schools who were low achievers, troublemakers, and potential dropouts were identified by teachers and counselors to participate in a work-learn program. During the entire school year, a half day is spent in the school and a half day on a 210-acre farm made available to the school district by Northwestern Michigan College. On this farm the boys engage in various outdoor projects through which there are practical learning opportunities in many areas of the curriculum, including outdoor and vocational skills. Some of the work-learn activities include building roads, restoration and use of an old saw mill for lumbering, well digging, shelter construction, stream improvement, tree planting, gardening, and other endeavors which help restore both human and natural resources. The group participates in outdoor skills such as angling, archery, shooting, skiing, and hiking.

As the project developed, the program has been expanded to include a comparable experience for junior high school boys on a day basis, a resident outdoor school program for elementary grades, and field trips for elementary, junior and senior high school classes.

The boys in the work-learn program experience success and enjoy activities that have interest and meaning to them. Changes in attitude and behavior are reflected in improved classroom achievement. Many of the boys remain in school who otherwise would have been dropouts. Much of the success of the entire program can be attributed to the leadership of high quality staff who understand the students and know how to work with them. An unusually effective resource leader is a pioneer lumberman, who adds much to the success of the lumbering and construction activities as well as to the welfare of the boys.

Programs of this type offer unique opportunities for the prevention of "human erosion" as well as soil erosion and present a pattern of outdoor education that can be designed for older youth—both boys and girls.[11]

outward bound

Outward Bound, a private program designed primarily for youth of secondary school age, presents a more rigorous approach to outdoor experiences with its emphasis on survival, adventure, and fitness. The movement originated during World War II as a crash program to

[11] Michigan Department of Education, *Outdoor Education in Michigan Schools* (Lansing, Mich.: Michigan Department of Education, 1970), pp. 25–27.

prepare young men for the harder challenges of life with a strong emphasis on saving lives. Starting with the first school in Wales in 1942, Outward Bound has expanded in a number of countries throughout the free world. The first school in the United States was held in Colorado in 1962. There are now several programs in various areas of the country. Each school has a special program feature, such as experiences in the mountains, in the wilderness, or on the water. All the programs include physical fitness and endurance activities, rescue and life saving, solo trips, and service projects.

The intensive and rugged 26-day experience is designed bearing in mind urban youth, who have few opportunities to participate in vigorous physical activities and to develop individual emotional resources. College-sponsored training courses and workshops are now available for those who are interested in becoming leaders and instructors in the Outward Bound movement.

While Outward Bound is a private venture and limited to a relatively small number of youth, many aspects of the program are applicable to outdoor education in schools and colleges, particularly older youth activities.

survival

Survival would be comparatively easy if skills providing for food, shelter, and clothing were all that were necessary to guarantee life. But survival calls for the individual to make rational choices, to have emotional maturity for living under extraordinary or adverse conditions, and to possess a degree of physical fitness adequate to perform difficult or unusual feats.

The major values necessary for survival are (1) the ability to face emergencies which change, even temporarily, the routines of life, and (2) a quality of independence and self-assurance which gives the individual mental, physical, and spiritual security to face life with vigor. The term "fitness," as conceived by some, would include survival.

relationship to outdoor education

The skills for living outdoors, in man's original habitat, are basic to survival. The best safeguards against panic and confusion arising during emergencies are broad educational experiences resulting in emotional and physical maturity, and a practical knowledge of the skills of everyday living. Ideally, an "educated person" would be able to survive in most situations, but changes in our society have removed many of the natural ingredients necessary for resourceful living. Man's dependence on machines and gadgets can be a handicap: little is required of adaptability and resourcefulness until daily routines are interrupted by unusual circumstances.

Survival, as conceived here, is the ability to live in the modern world, with the capability to perform during the unusual and unforeseen. Heredity and environment account for differences which must always be considered in educational experiences of any kind. Many phases of a good educational program contribute to survival other than those related to outdoor education. Most of the illustrations pertain to necessary skills, but they must be accompanied by proper attitudes. Survival and sanity in our society may well be one of the major objectives and results of outdoor education.

The following are examples of life situations and emergencies in which the ability to survive is paramount:

1. Sudden events due to accidents: fire; automobile, plane and train accidents; home and industrial accidents; failure of power in public utilities; getting lost in outdoor areas.
2. Emergencies and catastrophes occasioned by the elements: floods, cyclones, tornadoes, lightning, earthquakes, snow and ice.
3. Conditions due to war: nuclear warfare, bombing, poison gases; devastation of cities; destruction on and under the water.

In regard to the above situations, certain fundamental skills are necessary in most emergencies. Some of them include:

1. The ability to think and act quickly and wisely without panic.
2. Physical stamina and courage to perform tasks necessary for survival.
3. Knowledge of the outdoors and the ability to provide food, clothing, and shelter.
4. Ability to improvise.
5. Training in first aid and safety.
6. The skill to use simple tools.
7. General knowledge about utilities, such as gas, electricity, and water, and the ability to cope with disruption of service.
8. Simple skills in mechanics involving motors and machines.
9. Skills in outdoor sports such as boating, casting, shooting, archery, camping, nature crafts, mountain climbing, and others.

10. Strength and agility necessary for running, climbing, and jumping.
11. Spiritual qualities that might be described as moral courage, faith, or a belief in a Supreme Being.

Most of the above characteristics require a physical ability. Survival in another sense applies to the power of the mind to cope with life and its complexities. The ability to survive physically is interwoven with mental fitness. Security which comes from the knowledge that one can survive is as important as the process itself.

There is a tendency to compare people of today with the early pioneers. While it is true that individuals lack some of the important skills common in colonial days, it must be remembered that previous eras were fraught with disease, and lacked the advantages that are taken for granted today. However, some of the qualities and characteristics of the pioneers are needed as much today as in the past. The at-homeness in the woods, for example, of some of the frontiersmen and hunters would add to the pleasure and appreciation of outdoor living as we now know it. While impractical from a conservation standpoint, the belief that an American family could survive on an acre or two of forest land, knowing the skills required for such a feat, would be reassuring to those who panic when lights go out for several hours.

present-day needs for survival

Outdoor education can provide some of the elements lacking in today's educational abstractions. Simple skills pertaining to food and shelter, such as may be taught in camp settings and through outing activities, could give self-assurance during snowstorms in suburban communities. The experiences of stranded motorists and local residents reported without food, heat, or shelter during storms indicate what might be provided in an educational program.

incidents where survival skills and knowledge would be useful

Every year accidents are reported in which the knowledge of survival techniques would have saved lives. Lost hunters and hikers are among the most frequent victims. Knowledge of the woods, skill to determine direction with or without a compass, and the ability to keep comfortable and secure food would, in many instances, have prevented undue hardship or death. The possession of these skills combined with previous experience under instruction would usually prevent panic.

Accidents in activities such as mountain climbing, skiing, excavating, and exploring require a knowledge of first aid and skills necessary to perform under stress.

Emergencies such as occur in auto, train, and plane accidents require quick thinking and action in order to prevent loss of life or serious injury. Courage and emotional maturity are important in all accidents and catastrophes. The development of these qualities is a complicated process and depends much on the natural endowments of the individual. It is certain, however, that instruction and experiences under the direction of competent teachers are helpful. One needs only to observe the excellent training and service of the American Red Cross to understand the importance of education for survival and rescue.

Although little has been said about outdoor education as a basic factor in civil defense, a strong case could be made in this regard. When man-made homes and devices are destroyed or impaired, the human being must depend on his original habitat for survival. Much of the basic preparation for civil defense could and should be a part of the educational experiences of every person. The following brief outline will indicate some of the outdoor education activities which would be important in survival and pertinent to civil defense.

1. Classroom instruction
   a. study of science—plants and animals, geography
   b. learning to use maps and compass, weather instruments, and other scientific devices
   c. social studies—function and operation of government, public utilities, citizenship
   d. applied arts—food, clothing, use of tools
   e. outdoor classroom experiences
2. Health, physical education, and recreation courses and activities
   a. functional experiences in health education
   b. physical development—fitness
   c. first aid and safety
   d. special activities and clubs—outing clubs, survival trips, camping experiences, school recreation programs
   e. teaching of outdoor skills and sports—shooting and hunting, casting and angling, boating and water activities, camping skills, archery, winter sports, use of compass, hiking, hosteling, and others

3. Adult education—family camping courses and clubs, outdoor sports clinics, and the learning of outdoor living skills

CONCOMITANTS OF OUTDOOR PURSUITS

The *leading-on* qualities in many outdoor pursuits are as important as the events themselves. The preparation, anticipation, and afterthoughts of camping trips, fishing and hunting expeditions, boating and water activities, and numerous other outdoor ventures, constitute rich and interesting experiences.

The "leading-on" experiences involve planning, purchase and care of equipment, construction of needed items, perfecting skills, exchanging ideas, and photographing and developing pictures.

ADULT EDUCATION FOR OUTDOOR LIVING

Some communities, through adult education, provide opportunities for individuals and families to prepare for their leisure-time pursuits and share their experiences with others. Most outdoor activities and interests have the potential for originality and creativity.

Adult education is administered by school districts and is financed by regular school funds, course fees, and, in some instances, state aid. Usually offered in the evenings for the convenience of employed citizens, the programs include a wide range of activities, ranging from fundamental subjects and vocational courses to classes in recreational activities. More recently there has been an increased interest in activities which will provide skills and knowledge for the use of free time, including those related to outdoor recreation. Some of the offerings in adult education which have a direct relationship to outdoor education are family camping, construction of outing equipment, boat and trailer building, making fishing shanties, casting and angling, shooting and gun safety, fly tying, production of bait, game preserve management, instruction in small crafts, lapidary activities, nature crafts, flower arranging, and gardening.

A number of school districts administer combined programs of adult education and recreation. There are nationally known programs in Milwaukee, Wisconsin; Pasadena, California; and Kalamazoo, Michigan. Brief examples will illustrate.

Milwaukee Outdoor Education Program. Milwaukee, Wisconsin has the largest Family Camping Association in the United States. It is under the supervision of the Department of Municipal Recreation and Adult Education of the public schools. Starting with six families in 1955, the Association now has over 2,000 family memberships and assists hundreds of other families who are interested in family camping and outdoor living.

The basic purpose of the Association is to provide an exchange of ideas and information about family camping and outdoor living. For a small fee a family receives all the benefits of membership, including five bulletins which offer information on camping techniques, equipment, campsites, and outdoor areas. A series of family camping programs is conducted through the winter season. The attendance at each of these sessions varies from 1000 to 1500 people. One of the major services of the Association is to respond to the many requests for speakers, materials, films, and information about how and where to go camping. Television programs, clinics, displays of equipment, equipment trading center, and the conducting of institutes are important phases of the program.

The effect of this Association is far-reaching. Hundreds of families camp in Wisconsin and neighboring states during the spring, summer, and fall months, and the quality of outdoor living improves each year as the Family Camping Association serves the Milwaukee community. Milwaukee also has a large and active hiking club and several city 4-H clubs which offer outdoor education opportunities for hundreds of youths and adults each year. A farm program for all age groups has been added to the extensive education-recreation program.

Pasadena Outdoor Recreation Program. The Pasadena, California, Department of Recreation conducts an extensive outdoor recreation program. The Department is set up as a coordinated plan for operation with the schools, the city, and the county, with its activities designed for all age groups. One activity for adults is the family camping course, with an attendance of several hundred each year. An important part of the course is a weekend practice camping trip. Other outdoor activities of the Department include: Elementary School Nature Science Program; the Children's Museum; nature study; ski instruction; a fly tying class; angling instruction; gun safety; hiking and camping. Thousands of children and adults have learning and participating experiences each year through the school Recreation Department.

South Western Michigan Family Camping Association. Through the leadership of Western Michigan University, a large and growing family camping association has been established in the Kalamazoo area. The Association was formed to provide an opportunity for those interested in family camping to learn more about outdoor living, and for the exchange of ideas on skills, activities, equipment, and camping sites. Western Michigan University conducts a non-credit course during the winter months through the Extension Service. It is not unusual for three to four hundred people to participate in the series of meetings. The year's activities for the Association are climaxed by a Family Camping Day, featuring exhibits, displays, and clinics. Universitiy staff members give leadership to family camping activities.

The impact of such courses on education for the outdoors is immediate and extensive. Family camping courses conducted during the fall and winter months are followed by camping trips and outings in the spring and summer. Outdoor skill courses and clubs result in immediate participation in activities in the mountains, woods, lakes, and streams. Many community recreation departments now assist local residents in planning and organizing their camping, boating, and caravan travel trips. School and municipal recreation programs, which in the past were entirely devoted to organized and mass activities, are now increasing their coverage of individual and family interests. This trend of meeting the needs and individual interests of people is gaining momentum.

A VIEW OF TODAY'S OUTDOORSMAN

While the outdoorsman of today lives in an outdoor world far different from that of his forebears, he nonetheless faces a "frontier" that may be as challenging as any in our history. While the pioneers of other days cut their way through wilderness in search of a better life, today's outdoorsman may well be the savior of our way of life, if not our survival. Not only must he have the characteristics of a good citizen and be sufficiently educated to enjoy and survive in the outdoors if necessary, but he also must bear the awesome responsibility of maintaining an environment that has helped to make this nation great. Who, other than the outdoorsman who loves the outdoors, finds recreation and adventure in it, and thus has a stake in the natural resources that have bettered his life, will fight to restore our outdoor heritage?

This book contends that the outdoors not only offers unlimited opportunities for learning, but also effects behavioral changes that will be reflected in an appreciation and understanding of man's relationship to his physical environment and his responsibility for improving it. Outdoor education, making its greatest contribution to education in the affective and psychomotor domains supported by the cognitive, is a powerful agent for improving the quality of man's life and, consequently, the environment. Children and youth who learn to love and appreciate natural beauty and who are fully able to pursue and enjoy outdoor interests, will become citizens conscious of the forces that destroy the outdoors and determined to exercise the rights and responsibilities of a citizen to protect and maintain the land that has supported a life that is the American heritage. Crash programs and political promises will not solve the problems of an impending environmental crisis. A sustained program of sound education, of which outdoor education is a part, is required. Today's children and youth—tomorrow's adult outdoorsmen—need to find adventure in learning and involvement in the solution of human and environmental problems that are relevant to their own interests and needs. Education in and for the outdoors will determine the quality of millions of future outdoorsmen, providing the educational system considers this aspect of education.

SUGGESTIONS FOR FURTHER STUDY AND RESEARCH

1. Survey and analyze the growth of interest in outdoor sports during your lifetime in your own neighborhood.
2. What is the economic significance of outdoor recreation sports in your own state? Consult publications from the state conservation department, tourist council, and other agencies.
3. What are the outdoor recreation needs in your state? Design a plan that would help provide outdoor recreation opportunities to meet these needs.
4. Identify the places in the curriculum where outdoor skills and sports can be taught.
5. Evaluate the effectiveness of legislation in coping with outdoor recreation problems such as those concerned with boating, water skiing, misuse of outdoor areas, vandalism, and others.
6. What facilities are already available in your community for teaching outdoor sports?
7. What are some of the significant implications for education in the Outdoor Recreation Resources Review Commission report, "Outdoor Recreation for America," pertaining to people's outdoor recreation interests?

REFERENCES

archery

AAHPER. *Archery.* Washington, D.C.: AAHPER, 1972.

————. *Physical Education for High School Students,* 2nd ed. Washington, D. C.: AAHPER, 1970.

ABC's of Archery. American Archery Council, 618 Chalmers, Flint, Mich. 48503.

Division for Girls' and Women's Sports. *Archery-Riding Guide,* current ed. Washington, D. C.: AAHPER.

How to Improve Your Archery. Chicago, Ill.: The Athletic Institute, n.d.

Keaggy, Dave, Sr. *Power Archery.* Rev. ed. Drayton Plains, Mich.: Power Archery Products, n.d.

Klann, Margaret. *Target Archery.* Reading, Mass.: Addison-Wesley, 1970.

Miller, Myrtle K. Archery pamphlets. "Unique Acres," 67 Old Stone Church Road, Upper Saddle River, N. J. 07458.

National Archery Association. Instructions and rules for archery tournaments. Box 48, Ronks, Pa. 17572.

Niemeyer, Roy K. *Beginning Archery.* Belmont, Calif.: Wadsworth Publishing, 1962.

boating

American Red Cross. *Canoeing.* New York: Doubleday, 1956.

Carter, Samuel, III. *How to Sail.* New York: Sentinel, 1957.

"Outboard Seamanship Course." Outboard Boating Club of America, 333 North Michigan Avenue, Chicago, Illinois 60601.

camping

Jaeger, Ellsworth. *Wildwood Wisdom.* New York: The Macmillan Company, 1957.

Miracle, Leonard, with Decker, Maurice H. *Complete Book of Camping.* New York: Outdoor Life: Harper & Row, 1961.

casting and angling

AAHPER. *Casting and Angling.* Washington, D. C.: AAHPER, 1958.
_____. *Physical Education for High School Students.*

Gabrielson, Ira N., and LaMonte, Francesca. *The Fisherman's Encyclopedia.* Harrisburg, Pa.: Stackpole and Heck, 1950.

family camping

Better Homes and Gardens. *Family Camping.* Des Moines, Iowa: Meredith Publishing, 1961.

Sunset Books and Sunset Magazine. *Family Camping.* Menlo Park, Calif.: Lane Publishing Company, 1959.

orienteering

Kjellstrom, Bjorn. *Be Expert with Map and Compass.* New York: American Orienteering Service, 1955.

the shooting sports

Amber, John T. *Gun Digest.* Chicago, Ill.: The Gun Digest Co., annual.

AAHPER. *Physical Education for High School Students,* 1970.
_____. *Shooting and Hunting.* Washington, D. C.: AAHPER, 1960.
_____. *Marksmanship for Young Shooters.* Washington, D. C.: AAHPER, 1960.

Camp, Raymond R. *The Hunter's Encyclopedia.* Harrisburg, Pa.: The Stackpole Company, 1957.

Smith, W. H. B. *Gas, Air and Spring Guns of the World.* Harrisburg, Pa.: Military Service Publishing, 1957.

survival

Angier, Bradford. *Living Off the Country.* Harrisburg, Pa.: Stackpole, 1956.

Colby, C. B., and Angier, Bradford. *The Art and Science of Taking to the Woods.* Harrisburg, Pa.: Stackpole, 1970.

Nesbitt, Paul H. et al. *The Survival Book.* Princeton, N. J.: Van Nostrand, 1959.

Olsen, Larry Dean. *Outdoor Survival Skills.* Provo, Utah: Brigham Young University Press, 1967.

Whelen, Townsend, and Angier, Bradford. *On Your Own in the Wilderness.* Harrisburg, Pa.: Stackpole, 1958.

winter sports

Peterson, Gunnar A., and Edgren, Harry D. *The Book of Outdoor Winter Activities.* New York: Association Press, 1962.

_____. *Fun in Winter Camping.* New York: Association Press, 1967.

Proceedings, Third National Institute on Girls' Sports (ice skating, skiing). Sponsored by the Women's Board of the United States Olympic Development Committee and the Division of Girls' and Women's Sports of the AAHPER, 1966.

films

Archery (4 Super-8 film-loops). Ealing Films, 2225 Massachusetts Avenue, Cambridge, Mass. 02140.

Outdoor Education (16 mm, sound, color, 28½ min.). Prepared by AAHPER. NEA Sound Studios, 1201 Sixteenth Street, N. W., Washington, D. C. 20036.

III

outdoor education through public, professional, and private agencies

7

outdoor education
through park and
recreation agencies

While the school is society's basic educational agency, education is a continuing process. It takes place through the home, church, mass media, and various public and private organizations. Much of the application and continued use of the knowledge, skills, and appreciations acquired in school is furthered by local community agencies. Public agencies, such as park and recreation departments, have a special responsibility to assist the schools in providing the essential facilities and leadership for outdoor recreation.

PARK AND RECREATION AGENCIES IN THE
AMERICAN COMMUNITY

Open spaces for recreation and inspiration have been set aside by man ever since he first began to live in cities. The Greeks and the Romans had their park areas. As western European cities grew, parks of various types were established. While these were primarily for the benefit of the nobility or royalty, in some cases they were open to the general public. By order of the King of Spain, every new city in Spanish America was to have its "plaza."

The first park lands in our country were secured in colonial days. In Boston, the common pasture, when no longer needed as pasture, became a public park, purchased in 1660 by the Board of Selectmen for that purpose. William Penn set aside five parks when Philadelphia was established in 1682; and the Dutch had a bowling green in the lower end of Manhattan, when it was known as New Amsterdam. There was, however, very little in the nature of town planning in colonial days. An exception was the city of Savannah, in which General James Oglethorpe attempted to create an ideal colony. He laid out public gardens and 24 open squares as part of his plan. The District of Columbia was designed as a city of beauty, with "stately parks and pleasure gardens." Major Pierre L'Enfant drew up the plan for the city in 1791, and the formal French influence is still evident in Washington.

Most influential in present park development was the establishment of Central Park in New York City around 1853. As the city grew, there was fear that the country areas would soon disappear unless land was reserved for park purposes. The park was intended to offer relief from urban conditions by providing a rural setting. The 843 acres of land have been held inviolate since that time and today form one of the best-known city parks in the United States. Other large cities followed the lead of New York, and similar parks were established in most of the major metropolitan areas.

Early park planners were concerned with aesthetic values primarily and sought as their goal the peaceful enjoyment of beautiful surroundings. However, some provisions were made for active recreation. For example, the parade ground and three small playgrounds (three to ten acres each) were included in the original Central Park plan. Frederick Law Olmsted, who is generally credited with the planning and development of Central Park, became an important figure in municipal planning throughout the United States. Charles Eliot, the first metropolitan park commissioner for Boston, was another influential figure in the early park movement.

In the 1890s and early 1900s, the concept of community responsibility for recreation began to change, partly because of the growth of the large cities and the resultant lack of play space for children. The earliest playgrounds had been established under private auspices; but pressures to include active recreation and athletic facilities, such as swimming pools and golf courses, soon came from the general public.

Special agencies and organizations, public and private, began to develop to provide recreation, particularly for children. Recreation divisions were created within park departments or as separate divisions of government. By 1900 some 14 cities had made provisions for supervised play. In 1906, following a White House Conference called by Theodore Roosevelt, the Playground and Recreation Association of America (now the National Recreation and Park Association) was organized. This organization began the active promotion of community recreation facilities and programs. Through the early years of the twentieth century, public-supported recreation programs increased in number, and professional recreation leadership came to be regarded as an essential.

Although the original recreation movement was concerned for the most part with children, organized public recreation today embraces all ages and segments of society. The concept of recreation has expanded to include all worthy pursuits engaged in during leisure—arts and crafts, sports and games, music, dramatics, social recreation, dancing, mental and linguistic activities, and outdoor recreation—activities which may be distinctly educational as well as recreational. The field of outdoor recreation includes nature interests, camping, gardening, fishing, water sports, and winter sports.

Outdoor recreational pursuits are dependent upon land, particularly parks and forests. Many parks have made special provision for outdoor recreation, and today one of the principal functions of parks is to offer opportunities in the outdoor education-recreation field.

There are commonly three types of administrative organization for recreation: organization as a separate division of government, as part of the park department, or as part of the school system. In recent years, the public recreational functions of many communities have been combined under one jurisdiction, usually called Recreation and Park Departments.

Park departments are generally the major public land-holding agencies of the communities. Under standards developed by authorities, at least one acre of park land should be reserved for every one hundred persons. Much of this land should be set aside for outdoor education, while some is designated specifically for sports and other recreational pursuits.

The types of areas and facilities held and operated by local public park and recreation agencies will be discussed more fully in another chapter. However, because of their program connotations, several kinds of areas are noted here. *Playgrounds* and *playfields* are areas in which the primary interest is on sports and games. *Park* generally refers to an area in which the aesthetic values of the landscape predominate. It may contain some active recreation areas. Parks range in size from small city squares to hundreds of acres of land on the periphery of cities or in outlying areas and may include both natural and horticultural lands. Local parks may be under the jurisdiction of municipal, metropolitan, or county park departments. Large areas in which natural features predominate are often called *reservations* or, as in the case of Cook County, Illinois, *forest preserves*. While neighborhood recreation areas are devoted largely to sports and games, the emphasis upon activities dependent upon the natural environment increases materially in parks and reservations more distant from the hearts of cities. It is these areas that have the greatest significance for outdoor education.

Public property may provide city children with their only access to natural lands. Through their program services, the parks serve both the general public and the organized groups in a community. Park officials are both custodians of land and administrators of active programs in outdoor education for youth and adults.

PURPOSES OF PARK AND RECREATION SERVICES

From the time of the first parks, one of their main purposes—and sometimes their sole purpose—has been to provide aesthetic satisfactions through the maintenance of areas of beauty—natural or horticultural. To attain the highest values these areas can offer, certain knowledge and understanding of nature is necessary. The interpretive programs of parks are designed to help visitors gain this knowledge and to develop appreciation.

The park and recreation movement of today is concerned also with helping people make the best use of their increased leisure time. Outdoor-related pursuits rate high as a satisfying interest for many.

Physical and mental well-being is an additional goal of park and recreation services. Parks have often been considered the "breathing spaces" of crowded cities—places where people can get into the open air and engage in pursuits conducive to physical and mental fitness.

Local public park and recreation agencies have a particular contribution to make to the outdoor education of children: (1) they provide areas and facilities; (2) they cooperate with the schools and give direct service to the schools; (3) they provide special programs for those who visit the areas; (4) they provide materials in the form of pamphlets, booklets, radio and television programs.

PARK AND RECREATION AREAS AND FACILITIES
RELATED TO OUTDOOR EDUCATION

In most communities the best and in some cases the only areas available for outdoor education are those managed by local park and recreation departments, which are planning more and more for such purposes. The joint use of facilities by schools and other agencies is not only good economics but is also an improvement over the services offered by any single agency. Land made available by public agencies for outdoor education should be located within an hour's travel of the homes of the users, except where overnight accommodations are provided.

The use of park and recreation areas falls into four groups:

1. *General public use.* Users may come as family groups or as individuals. General public use must be permitted on most public property.

2. *Programs under leadership of the park and recreation agency.* Most communities carry on recreation programs under trained leadership for children and older youth, although there are some programs, such as the interpretive services in parks, that cater largely to adults.

3. *Use of park areas by school groups.* School groups at all levels use park and recreation lands and facilities, including trails, museums, zoos, picnic areas, meeting sites, camps, and special facilities such as aquariums and planetariums.

4. *Use by organized community groups.* Many of the organized groups in the community, such as the voluntary youth serving agencies, church groups, and service clubs, conduct extensive parts of their programs on public lands.

Areas valuable in outdoor education programs range from the highly developed to those consisting of natural woods, fields, and waters. Some types of areas are: landscaped parks; playgrounds and playfields with some landscaped areas; forests and reservations—largely natural; swamps and bogs; wildlife refuges, sanctuaries, and preserves; wildflower preserves; lakes, ponds, and streams; and horticultural gardens.

Special facilities may include trailside museums, special museums, general museums, zoos or other wildlife exhibits, botanic gardens, greenhouses, planetariums, aquariums, day camps, resident camps, overnight camps, hiking trails, nature trails, council rings, amphitheaters, and weather stations.

PROGRAM SERVICES OF LOCAL PUBLIC AGENCIES
RELATED TO OUTDOOR EDUCATION

The extent of services related to outdoor education differs widely from community to community, according to local resources, the vision of local administrators, and the kind and extent of leadership. It is difficult to draw any line between recreation and education in outdoor activities, where the acquisition of knowledge and the learning of skills accompany participation in the program.

interpretive services

Interpretive services may be thought of as educational services. The term *interpretive* implies more than the acquisition of factual knowledge. Such programs give significance to what we see and hear in the out-of-doors through the development of enjoyment, perception, understandings, and appreciations.

Programs in this field have also been referred to as *naturalist* programs. This term is inadequate because the field is broader than the natural sciences, including relationships between the outdoor areas and history, art, literature, and human needs and uses.

Interpretive programs have existed for countless years, though not so labeled. Some of the best teaching in natural science has been in this category. Interpretive programs of public park agencies received their initial impetus through developments in the national parks; most of the national parks and monuments today have special interpretive staffs. State parks were the next to establish this type of program. Many municipal and metropolitan parks have followed suit. The interpretive services usually include a trained staff with special competence working out of a trailside museum or nature center, although such centers are not essential. The programs described in the following pages are typical of interpretive services.

FIELD TRIPS

Taking groups afield for direct experiences with the environment is at the heart of interpretive services. Such trips may be general in nature, intended to acquaint participants with anything of interest along the way. Trips may be taken to particular locales, such as a special rock formation, a swamp, a lake shore, a historical site, or a reforestation project. Or, the trips may be intended to acquaint groups with some particular area of interest, such as trees, birds, rocks, or local history. Special trips are often conducted for school groups, camp groups, or teachers.

Field trips are usually quite informal. The leader endeavors to capitalize on interests manifested within his group. He is more concerned with making the participants aware of their surroundings and with making the ordinary significant than with the mere transfer of information.

SPECIAL SERVICES TO SCHOOLS AND OTHER GROUPS

Many school groups and youth agencies take advantage of the interpretive services offered by park and recreation departments. Day or half-day visits by school classes may be used for field trips with naturalists, viewing museum exhibits, participating in observations, hearing illustrated talks, or watching slides or movies related to the local area. In some communities the interpretive staff prepares materials for school use, including question sheets to follow up museum visits, pamphlets on local natural science or history for use in classroom instruction, and even display materials for loan to classrooms. In some cases the interpretive staff visits school classrooms to conduct discussion sessions, give talks, and show pictures or exhibits. In Cook County a summer staff is provided to help day camps and resident camps with field trips, talks, and demonstrations for campers.

Services of a small interpretive staff have the most far-reaching effect if they are devoted to assisting teachers and youth leaders rather than to conducting programs directly for children. Field training courses for teachers are conducted on Saturdays and during vacations and are sometimes combined with indoor evening classes which provide a background for the field experiences. Some interpretive centers find themselves unable to meet the numerous demands from school and youth groups and must schedule their activities for many weeks or months in advance.

PUBLICATIONS AND AUDIO-VISUAL MATERIALS

One of the responsibilities of the interpretive staff is the preparation of written materials. Among the materials often prepared are news releases for local newspapers; magazine articles on topics of outdoor interest; pamphlets covering such topics as what to do and see in a particular area, guides to nature trails or auto tours, and guides to local birds, trees, geology, history, and animals; and booklets on crafts of various kinds and on outdoor living skills or outdoor good manners. Slides, movies, and exhibit materials are sometimes prepared for the use of community groups.

INTERPRETIVE CENTERS

The types of interpretive centers and their facilities are discussed more fully in Chapters 4 and 10. They usually include a museum with meeting rooms and display cases; outdoor displays, including small wildlife displays; radiating trails; outdoor activity centers; and outdoor meeting places.

Displays in interpretive centers generally explain the locale in which they are placed and are intended to help users understand what they see outdoors. Visitors are often casual, therefore labels must be short and catchy, and displays must tell a story and stimulate interest. When groups of children or teachers come to the centers, the displays are explained more fully by a member of the staff as part of a lecture and demonstration program. The centers, also called "nature centers," are often located in parks and operated as part of a park interpretive program.

Talks and demonstrations are an important part of the center's activity. In Washington, D. C., where the interpretive program in the local parks is under the jurisdiction of the National Park Service, evening campfire programs with illustrated lectures are presented to the general public throughout the summer. The response has been very enthusiastic. Special services are offered to day camps and youth agencies through a trailside museum. During the summer children participate in regularly scheduled programs at the center.

In addition to centers maintained by public park and recreation departments, there are centers operated by schools. However, most are privately financed and managed, sometimes as part of a museum. There may be various combinations of ownership and management; for example, development by a school or private organization may take place on public park or forest land.

LEADERSHIP INTERPRETATION

A leader in the interpretive program must be a person with a broad background in science and history. He must have an attractive and friendly personality, be able to speak well and meet people easily. Such leaders are hard to find, and training programs in colleges and universities are few. Most leaders now in the field have had college backgrounds but have acquired much of their training elsewhere, sometimes through apprenticeship in museums, sometimes in camping or in other work with youth agencies. Summer workers are often teachers with a particular interest in the out-of-doors.

ZOOS

Interest in living animals ranks extremely high with both children and adults. Most large cities and many small cities maintain zoos or wildlife displays. Although educationally and recreationally important, only a few communities have recognized and developed their possibilities to the fullest.

The modern zoo endeavors to provide attractive and natural-looking habitats which appeal to the visiting public and show the animals off to advantage. Good labeling adds much to zoo exhibits.

Some zoos sponsor interesting and educational lectures and demonstrations with information relative to the life histories and habits of the animals. Demonstrations may include trained animal acts. Publications available in many zoos provide information on their animals and on animal life throughout the world. Moving pictures, slides, and photographs are also often provided.

In some zoos, club programs for both children and adults have been organized. Zoology clubs, or specialized groups such as those with a special interest in birds or snakes, are included.

A useful development in some cities is the traveling zoo or barnyard. Small wild or domestic animals are taken during the summer to playgrounds, and programs are developed around the animals. Such exhibits are of particular interest and value in large cities where children may have little chance to become acquainted with animals.

clubs

Clubs with outdoor interests are often set up through local public agencies in connection with playgrounds, community centers, neighborhood parks, day camps, nature centers, zoos, and botanic gardens. The leaders may be paid or volunteer. Adults with special interest in outdoor fields usually assume the major responsibility. A club organized by a public agency may affiliate with a voluntary or private organization, such as the Audubon Society. There are outdoor-related clubs for all age groups. Adult groups are usually centered around such interests as gardening, birds, or one of the special craft fields such as rock polishing.

Sometimes a public agency provides only the initial impetus in organizing outdoor interest clubs. Adult groups usually become self-sufficient once established and ask only occasional leadership from the public agency, though the meeting place, equipment, and natural areas of the agency may continue to be used.

Some types of clubs which may be affiliated with public park and recreation agencies are those concerned with gardening, birds, snakes, forestry, conservation, hiking, outings, boating, fishing (including casting and fly tying), zoology, geology, paleontology, and Indian lore.

For many years, Omaha has had a very successful city-wide Junior Foresters' program. Forestry clubs have been organized in the schools under the auspices of the local park department. The relationship illustrates the possibilities inherent in cooperation between public park and recreation agencies and the schools.

outdoor-related classes

Classes may be organized in connection with nature centers, interpretive centers, community centers, zoos, museums, and sometimes parks and playgrounds. Some of these classes are intended for teachers and leaders; others, for the general public, either adults or children. Some classes are conducted weekly, some in the daytime, some in the evening. Others are set up on a seasonal basis to study topics of seasonal interest, such as spring migration or spring flowers. Whereas some classes are organized to study nature, others are concerned with outdoor skills, including camping and outings.

outdoor-related crafts

Like clubs and classes, craft centers are often included in museums, interpretive centers, community centers, and sometimes playgrounds. Adults and children may come to work in their own free time and at their own pace, with the craft center providing tools, equipment, and technical help when needed; or instruction may be scheduled on an individual or class basis. The crafts may be outdoor-related only in part or according to the emphasis given. For example, one ceramics group might study the source, composition, and method of formation of clay and might collect and prepare their own clay from local clay banks. Another might use commercial clays about which they learn little. The photography and art classes likewise may or may not have outdoor relationships, according to their emphasis.

Some of the outdoor-related crafts provided by local agencies include lapidary, ceramics, photography, sketching, painting, modeling, and crafts with native materials such as carving, weaving, and basketry.

playground nature corners

Where the leaders have skills and interest and where there are areas that are suitable, playground nature corners and activity centers have been successful. Here children may work on insect and leaf collections, terraria, live insect displays, and other local natural materials. Short field trips and games may be conducted in conjunction with the program.

One city has a staff of nature leaders who move from park to park, spending one day at a time at each. They conduct various nature activities and use resource materials which they may bring with them, as well as materials found in the areas themselves. Such programs are most popular with children from nine to twelve years of age.

fishing, casting, and the shooting sports

In some communities small lakes in public parks are open for fishing to children under a given age, usually twelve years. Special instruction may be given in fishing techniques. Casting classes and fishing derbies may be organized. Skills such as fly tying, plug construction and the making of rods may also be taught, although such instruction usually appeals to adults.

Public agencies in many places have constructed shooting ranges and offer instruction; or they may merely provide the facilities and permit other groups to conduct the programs.

trips and excursions

Many kinds of trips and excursions are conducted by public agencies. These may include hiking trips, camping trips, visits to points of interest, boat trips, auto caravan trips, and various types of cookouts. Such programs may be a part of the interpretive services or some other community program.

evening programs

Evening programs, particularly campfires, are conducted by some local park and recreation agencies. They usually include community singing and other entertainment, followed by illustrated talks pertaining to some outdoor subject. Evening lecture programs under the auspices of local recreation agencies have also been successful.

camping

Various camping programs have been conducted under the auspices of local recreation and park departments. Family camping programs operated by local public agencies are particularly popular in western cities, where areas are leased or purchased away from the city and developed for family use. Family-sized cabins, dining halls, lodges, and various types of recreation facilities are usually included. The use of the camp is limited to residents of the sponsoring city who pay membership fees equal to the cost of camp maintenance. Program services are sometimes made available to children's groups as well as participating families.

A number of cities have established children's resident camps under the auspices of recreation agencies. These camps often serve the underprivileged, although there is an attempt to serve all children to whom camping would not otherwise be available. Factors limiting the growth of public-sponsored resident camping include high costs, the relatively small number of people who can be served, and the fact that voluntary agencies often serve the same groups in the community. Need should determine whether a public agency should establish a camp. In some cases public agencies merely develop the facilities, then make them available to voluntary agencies in the summer and to schools for outdoor education during the rest of the year.

Day camping under public auspices is more widespread than resident camping, but some of the same considerations apply. Many communities feel that public agencies, even when they do not administer the program, should supply facilities and offer certain program services, such as those related to the use, understanding, and appreciation of the environment.

Day camps are operated by hundreds of recreation departments in the United States, usually in public parks or outlying reservations. Picnic facilities are often adapted to day camp use, although some park departments set aside and specifically develop areas for this purpose.

Overnight camping is provided in special areas by some public agencies. Elsewhere, extended camping trips are taken by groups under the leadership of public agencies. One large county recreation department conducts travel camping trips, sometimes covering several hundred miles.

Whatever the type of camping, the purposes are similar to those of camping programs conducted by voluntary, religious, and private agencies: the development of outdoor interests and skills and the building of a sense of social responsibility, individual initiative, resourcefulness, health, and moral fitness.

gardens

Various types of children's gardens are discussed in Chapters 4 and 10. Many public agencies operate children's gardens either independently or in cooperation with public schools. Gardens for adult apartment dwellers may be available in the form of small plots of land, rented by the season. Some cities maintain garden centers which provide printed information and technical help to amateur gardeners. Garden shows and festivals are often held as a part of the services of local public agencies.

special events

Many kinds of special events significant in outdoor education are sponsored by public agencies, sometimes on a city-wide basis and sometimes on a neighborhood basis. Among them are:

Science fairs. Natural science or all aspects of science may be included.

Hobby shows. Some hobby shows are outdoor oriented, with natural materials such as living animals and plants, collections, crafts with native materials, and models of living things.

Garden and flower shows. Local garden projects sponsored by local agencies usually include exhibits or fairs. The municipality may cooperate with community groups or may merely provide the facility.

Pet shows. Pet shows are popular activities of many public agencies.

Festivals. Special festivals, such as those centering around harvests, fall colors, and spring wildflowers, are often sponsored by public agencies.

Camping demonstrations. The popular interest in family camping has resulted in a number of successful camping shows and demonstrations designed to help families camp easily and happily. Sometimes commercial exhibits of camping equipment and demonstrations of camping skills are included.

There have been, in recent years, many more outdoor-related activities provided by local public agencies who make a definite effort to find the trained leadership needed. The expanded recreational use of the out-of-doors, resulting in problems of vandalism and litter, makes increasingly important the need for educating every person in outdoor skills and conservation.

Park and recreation departments should coordinate their programs with the outdoor education programs of schools. Schools can benefit greatly from the leadership services of park personnel and from the use of park lands and facilities. There has been an increased concern for community planning to meet future needs for outdoor areas and facilities. Schools and other public agencies have an important responsibility in meeting these needs.

SUGGESTIONS FOR FURTHER STUDY AND RESEARCH

1. Make an analysis of the park-school concept. Analyze its advantages and problems.
2. Examine the purposes of park and recreation programs. Compare these with the purposes of outdoor education.
3. Develop a plan for the integration of school, park, and recreation services for a particular community.
4. Analyze the park and recreation resources of a particular community. Determine their value and how they might be used as part of a school outdoor education program.

REFERENCES

American Association of School Administrators. *Conservation—in the People's Hands.* Washington, D. C.: AASA, 1964.

Butler, George D. *Introduction to Community Recreation.* 3d ed. New York: McGraw-Hill, 1959.

Carlson, Reynold E.; Deppe, Theodore R.; and MacLean, Janet R. *Recreation in American Life.* 2d ed. Belmont, Calif.: Wadsworth, 1971.

Jensen, Clayne R. *Outdoor Recreation in America.* Minneapolis, Minn.: Burgess Publishing Company, 1970.

Meyer, Harold D., and Brightbill, Charles K. *Community Recreation.* 4th ed. Englewood Cliffs, N.J.: Prentice-Hall, 1969.

The Recreation Program. Chicago, Ill.: The Athletic Institute, 1953.

van der Smissen, Betty, and Goering, Oswald H. *A Leader's Guide to Nature-Oriented Activities.* 2d ed. Ames: Iowa State University Press, 1968.

8

state and federal
relationships to outdoor
education

With the 1970s comes the recognition of governmental responsibility at all levels to protect and restore the quality of the environment. Air and water pollution, overcrowding, misused land and mineral resources, endangered plant and animal life, noise, and population growth gather greater support as problems that can be solved only by strong governmental action.

State and federal governments play an important part in outdoor education by providing lands and facilities for outdoor education programs and in supplying leadership and services for such programs. A growing interest on the part of state and federal agencies encourages the use of public lands for educational purposes more closely related to school programs.

Until recently, conservation education and outdoor education dealt largely with the nonurban environment. Government itself was concerned primarily with the rural scene—the protection of soil, forests, plants, animals, lakes, rivers, and outstanding examples of scenic beauty. The importance of these has not lessened; the government still bears responsibliity for land reclamation for recreation, soil conservation, construction of dams and reservoirs, lake and stream improvement, parks and forests, wilderness, and scenic areas. However, the government now recognizes that more attention should be paid to serious environmental problems caused by crowding in metropolitan areas.

Outdoor educators have a responsiblity to the urban as well as the nonurban environment. The knowledge of governmental responsibility for air and water quality, open space, and city planning is essential.

STATE AND FEDERAL SERVICES

The federal government has begun to assume a major role in environmental improvement in the following ways:

1. the setting of standards
2. the securing of state cooperation in adherence to the standards
3. research upon which action may be based
4. enforcement of federal laws related to the environment
5. the examination of its own activities to determine whether they are in harmony with good practices
6. alerting the people to the seriousness of the situation
7. allocation of federal funds, particularly for the abatement of air and water pollution.

To administer its accelerated program, the federal government established in 1970 the President's Council on Environmental Quality and the Environmental Protection Agency. The first Conference of Natural Beauty was called in 1966. The government has increased funds for abating air and water pollution, and has strengthened measures against the dumping of wastes. Federal grants to communities for environmental improvement has spurred local planning and the setting of standards to meet requirements for such grants. Growing public sentiment supports strong governmental action in controlling deterioration of the environment. Federal agencies related to outdoor education lie in various departments which, in a country as large and complex as the United States, often overlap in functions and relationships. In some cases, there is competition.

Some of the federal agencies with a particular relationship to outdoor education are:

In the Department of Agriculture
Federal Extension Service
Forest Service
Soil Conservation Service

In the Department of Defense
Corps of Engineers

In the Department of Health, Education and Welfare
Public Health Service
Office of Education

In the Department of the Interior
Bureau of Indian Affairs
Bureau of Land Management
Bureau of Outdoor Recreation
Bureau of Reclamation
Fish and Wildlife Service
National Park Service

The states' adoption of standards for water and air quality was an important step in environmental improvement. In most states there are counterparts of federal agencies which on the whole render more direct services to local communities than does the federal government. The states also assume more responsibility for schools than the federal government. Yet, in spite of these differences, there is a great deal of similarity in their functions and their provisions for outdoor education. As an illustration, state parks, like national parks, may have museums, naturalist programs, and other educational features. State park areas are, however, generally smaller and of less widespread interest than the national parks.

Under various names, state agencies concerned with outdoor education include departments, divisions, commissions, or boards concerned with the following functions:

Air and water pollution

Education

Planning

Conservation (This includes forests, parks, recreation, fish, and game. In some states these are administered by one agency; in other states they may be divided among two or more agencies.)

Agriculture

Interagency cooperation (usually secured through interagency committees)

Youth welfare

Some of the state and federal services relating to outdoor education will be briefly described.

land management

Because of pressures on the land due to increased population and competition by various elements in society, it is important to use wisely the resources of all levels of government and to coordinate more effectively than in the past. Planning must be on a scale wider than the local community; regional planning for outdoor education and recreation is a growing necessity.

State and federal agencies control about 38 per cent of the land of the United States, including our most prized historical, scientific, and scenic areas, encompassing forests, mountain ranges, wildlife refuges, deserts, historical sites, and lakes. State and federal lands also have within them most of the last true wilderness left in our country with much of our remaining wildlife, some of which would otherwise perish.

These lands belong to the people and are open to everyone for study, inspiration, relaxation, and recreation. Through them we may become acquainted with America's outdoor heritage. In many parts of America no other natural lands are available for public use.

Certain lands are managed for economic reasons, such as to insure the continuation of forests, water resources, and soil. Other areas are set aside primarily for aesthetic, educational, and recreational purposes. Still other areas are designated for multiple use, with recreation, timber production, and wildlife conservation all taking place. Parks as a general rule fall into the second of these three categories.

development of facilities for public use

Developments on government lands are generally planned to make possible public access and use while still protecting the resources for future generations. Various kinds of facilities have been developed on public lands for the convenience of the public. Some of these are owned, developed, and operated by the government, such as roads, trails, camping facilities, and educational exhibits. Other facilities may be constructed and owned by the government, but operated by concessionaires, or private commercial groups may both develop and operate them. Generally hotels, lodges, stores, restaurants, and riding stables are privately operated. In a few cases governmental agencies themselves operate all facilities with their own personnel.

The following types of facilities are often government built and operated. They are discussed in greater detail in Chapter 10.

Means of access: roads, trails, beaches, boat ramps

Structures for comfort and shelter: lodges, campgrounds, organized camp facilities, shelter houses, winter sports warming houses, toilets

Developments related to outdoor education: museums, nature centers, historical reconstructions, trailside displays and markers, nature trails, observation centers, wildlife exhibits, amphitheaters

Special facilities which can be used for outdoor education: agricultural experiment stations, game farms, weather stations, forest fire lookouts, fish hatcheries, research stations

protection of natural resources

State and federal governments are the custodians of large segments of the nation's natural resources. Wildlife belongs to the state. The federal government is concerned, however, with migratory wildlife and enters into international agreements for its protection. The federal government is also active in the protection of off-shore fisheries.

The states assume responsibility for wildlife within their borders and establish and enforce fish and game laws. They may give complete legal protection to certain species. The federal government cooperates in determining desirable regulations.

propagation of plants and animals

Government fish hatcheries and game farms provide for the distribution of wildlife for stocking. There is cooperation between the states and the federal government in the propagation of plants and animals and the restoration of natural habitats, with costs shared. Federal funds secured through application of the Pittman-Robertson Act of 1937 and the Dingell-Johnson Act of 1950 (which provide for taxes on fishing and hunting equipment, including ammunition) are distributed to the states for the improvement of wildlife. State and federal governments also cooperate in the propagation of forest tree seedlings for distribution to private land owners.

education in resource use

Educational services related to resource use are rendered by both state and federal agencies. They include radio and television presentations; magazine and newspaper articles; leaflets, brochures, and books; the use of consultants and specialists in work with individuals, schools, voluntary agencies, and private groups; and interpretive services such as those of state and national parks.

The conservation education programs in public schools are, in part, state services. State departments of education in many states have conservation and outdoor education specialists on their staffs, and state committees have often been constituted to improve services on a local level. The federal government also, through the Office of Education, serves the outdoor education interests of local and state school groups.

consultant services

Consultant help is available from both federal and state sources to political subdivisions and to private individuals and agencies. The federal government usually offers direct services to the state counterparts of federal agencies. Thus the United States Fish and Wildlife Service works closely with state fish and game agencies, and the United States Forest Service with state forestry agencies.

The Extension Service of the Department of Agriculture is an excellent illustration of how the federal and state governments cooperate with local governments. The cost of the services of the county agent are borne by the local, state, and federal governments. Publications from state and federal sources are channeled through the county agent.

research

Some of the types of research relative to resource use and outdoor education carried on at state and federal levels are land use, recreation needs and services, wildlife, educational methods, and all aspects of conservation.

FEDERAL AGENCIES RELATED TO OUTDOOR EDUCATION

A multiplicity of federal agencies administer public lands and are engaged in providing services related to outdoor education. The pages that follow describe those with the most direct relationship. They may be considered as educational, recreational, or conservation agencies. While their functions are in many cases primarily economic, in other cases they are educational and recreational.

The federal agencies have potentialities for outdoor education far beyond their present utilization.

national park service (department of interior)

The concept of reserving the superlative scenic, scientific, and historic areas for the benefit of all the people is something new in the history of government. Parks, forests, and hunting grounds have been reserved by governments in other parts of the world, but the United States was probably the first to develop a nationwide system of acquisition and preservation in the public interest and the first to make these areas meaningful to visitors through planned programs.

In 1832 Hot Springs in Arkansas was reserved for protection as a health resort; but it is not generally regarded as the first national park, even though it was incorporated in 1921 into the national park system.

The *national park* idea is generally accredited to a small group of men, members of the Doane-Washburn-Langford Expedition, who entered the Yellowstone region in 1870. They were deeply impressed by the scenery and the geyser phenomena. At a now famous camp-fire meeting, one member of the party, Cornelius Hedges, proposed that since the area had outstanding national significance, it should be protected forever in the public interest. Subsequently, these men began stirring up public sentiment for its protection. As a result, in 1872, Congress established Yellowstone National Park, first of a series of national parks. By 1900, Sequoia, Yosemite, and Mount Rainier National Parks had been established.

The national parks increased at a rapid pace through the early part of the twentieth century. In 1906 Congress passed what is generally known as the Antiquities Act, which made possible the setting aside as national monuments areas of historical, scientific, and archeological interest.

In the early years of the national parks there was no adequate system of development nor unified responsibility for administration. The agitation of leaders interested in the parks led to the establishment of the National Park Service in the Department of the Interior in 1916. Stephen T. Mather, an outspoken critic of previous park administration, was made the first Director, with jurisdiction over the 15 national parks and 21 national monuments then in existence. With his assumption of authority, Mather began enlisting the support of wealthy and prominent Americans in the expansion and development of the parks. Many of the policies under which the parks operated through the succeeding years were developed during Mather's administration. His vision and enthusiasm made possible the acquisition of many areas that might otherwise have been lost to the public.

Through Congressional acts of 1933 and 1935, the National Park Service became the custodian of the national monuments, national military parks, certain national cemeteries, historic sites, and other government-held areas of educational and recreational value.

Thus the National Park Service has come to be charged with the management in the public interest of about 288 pieces of property totaling 29.5 million acres of wide variety. Thirty-five of these are national parks.

Assistance to state parks.   During the depression of the 1930s, the National Park Service worked with state agencies in the development of state parks and recreation areas, using labor resources of the Works Progress Administration and the Civilian Conservation Corps. Among the depression projects were 52 recreation demonstration areas, intended to show how cheap land could be improved for outdoor recreation purposes. On most of these areas the National Park Service developed artificial lakes, picnic areas, roads, and trails, and constructed demonstration camps for the use of agencies that could not otherwise afford to conduct children's camp programs. At the end of the depression, the Recreation Demonstration Areas were, with a few exceptions, turned over to the states to become part of their park systems. Since then, time and management have greatly improved their beauty. They have proved that inferior land can be developed to serve outdoor needs.

Use of national parks.   That the national parks have captured the interest of the American people is shown by the growth in numbers of visitors through the years. In 1917 there were less than half a million visitors to areas administered by the National Park Service; in 1969 there were nearly 164 million. These multitudes create serious problems for the National Park Service.

The 1916 act creating the Service contained the following statement of purpose:

To conserve the scenery and the natural and historical objects and the wildlife herein and to provide for the enjoyment of the same in such manner and by such means as will leave them unimpaired for the enjoyment of future generations.

How can the parks be unimpaired while providing for the enjoyment of those who visit them? The expansion of roads, parking lots, camps, hotels, and service stations of necessity destroys certain natural features. Moreover, the mere presence of crowds detracts from the satisfactions which most individuals seek in the parks.

Already campground use is limited in some areas. If pressures continue, limitations on use may become more widespread to avoid serious depreciation of the parks.

Educational implications of national parks. The National Park Service has developed an approach to education somewhat different from the traditional one. The park visitor comes, not primarily to be educated, but eager to learn and to enjoy what the park has to offer.

The Service attempts to keep national park resources unspoiled. Forces of nature have free play as far as possible. Lands are managed from an ecological viewpoint, with complete protection for plants and animals, for the predator as well as the song bird. Dead trees are allowed to stand or fall, to provide homes and food for wildlife, and eventually to decay into the forest floor. In some areas it is possible to see land as it was when the first white man appeared. In historical sites efforts are made to reconstruct the area and events in such a way that the visitor captures the feeling of the time.

The educational and inspirational values of the parks were recognized early. Colleges and universities took classes into the areas, and efforts were made to develop the human and scientific histories of the parks. Interpretive services began in 1918 with the first conducted field trips for visitors. The program has expanded into a very important attraction for park visitors, by which they are told in scientifically accurate yet simple language the story of the parks. Extensive research in history, geology, archeology, or biology is usually carried on in each park to provide a background for the interpretive staff. Interpretation is regarded not merely as the transfer of information but also as an effort to develop appreciations and understanding.

Various facilities and devices are employed in interpretation— trailside museums, historical museums, exhibits, displays in place, nature trails, and low cost or free publications. It is through personal contacts with park visitors, however, that the most effective education takes place. These include guided field trips, auto caravans, informal talks, and individual contacts by well-trained staff members who can arouse interest and interpret clearly.

Although contacts with interpretive services may be brief and few, they make a deep impression on visitors and give them new perspectives. History comes alive at Jamestown, Kings Mountain, and Lincoln's birthplace. Ancient cliff dwellers walk again at Mesa Verde and Canyon de Chelly. The variety and interdependence of life become evident in the Great Smoky Mountains, the Everglades, and Olympic National Park. The great stories of earth movement, rock formation, and glacial action are told visibly at Yosemite, Glacier, Mount Rainier, and Grand Canyon.

A step forward in outdoor education would take place if all young people could visit national park areas where, under the guidance of outstanding teachers, they could experience a form of learning impossible inside the classroom.

In recent years the NPS has expanded its service into local outdoor education in an effort to make its vast natural and cultural resources more responsive to the educational community. The NPS has established experimental school programs, local trails, and park developments for outdoor education. With the cooperation of the American Association for Health, Physical Education, and Recreation (a national affiliate of the National Education Association) the NPS has initiated *Project Man's Environment*, under which a study of the present status and direction of environmental education in the United States has been undertaken.

forest service (department of agriculture)

With the depletion of timber resources of the eastern part of the United States, sentiment began to develop in the nineteenth century for government protection of western timber lands. A Division of Forestry, purely advisory in nature, was created in 1881. In 1891 Congress authorized the President to reserve, by proclamation, forest lands in the public domain; and President Harrison set aside 13 million acres of forest land before his term expired. This reserve, increased by succeeding presidents, was administered by the General Land Office of the Department of the Interior.

Gifford Pinchot become head of the Division of Forestry in 1898. Through his effort the United States Forest Service, in much its present form, was created in 1905. The forest reserves were transferred to its control, and Pinchot became its first chief. The primary purpose of the Forest Service was economic; it was to manage federal timber lands in the public interest. Under the administration of Theodore Roosevelt, Forest Service holdings were expanded to more than 160 million acres.

Educational or recreational uses of forest land received scant attention in the early days of the Forest Service. When the National Park Service was established in 1916, some of the outstanding scenic areas were transferred to its administration. There developed some conflict of interest between the two agencies, the National Forest Service being concerned with the long-term economic use of the land and the National Park Service with its complete preservation.

From their establishment, however, there was public demand for recreational use of the forests. The act of 1897, which outlined policies for forest management, recognized the recreational use of these lands. A few forestry leaders saw the values of forests for the inspiration and well-being of the people.

A system of land leases for cabin sites and for other services to the public began early. Some areas with particular values for recreation were set aside for public use. Pressure for recreational use continued to grow and led eventually to the establishment of a recreational division that placed the administration of recreation on a level with the administration of timber production, water protection, grazing, and wildlife conservation. The appointment of Robert Marshall as the first Director of Recreation for the Forest Service marked the full official recognition of the recreational use of forests. Marshall had been a strong proponent of the protection of wilderness areas. Through his efforts and those of others of like mind, the Wilderness Society was organized in 1935, and the Forest Service was encouraged to set aside wilderness areas for posterity.

The depression brought a great impetus to developments in federal forests. The Civilian Conservation Corps, in particular, developed many camping facilities, trails, and ski facilities.

By 1969 the United States Forest Service managed nearly 187 million acres of land. Much of this land was in the western states, although in recent years considerable land has been acquired in the east.

Use of national forests by visitors. The numbers of visitors to the national forests testify to the importance they have assumed in the lives of American people. In 1969 there were nearly 163 million visitors, as compared with 14.3 million in 1939. Several million use the family camping areas, the organized camps, and the wilderness areas. Others using the forests are sightseers, picnickers, occupants of family cabins, participants in winter sports, hunters, and fishermen.

Funds for the development of facilities and services, scarce since the days of the Civilian Conservation Corps, were allocated in 1957 to Operation Outdoors, a five-year plan which received about 85 million dollars for the improvement of public-use areas. In the 1960s an Accelerated Public Works program further stepped up facility developments.

Because of their variety and extent, the national forests are invaluable for outdoor education. They contain more than 80,000 miles of fishing streams and more than 40,000 lakes. There are about 4,900 developed campgrounds with a capacity of 294,000 people. About

14 million acres have been set aside to be preserved in a wild or wilderness condition. With their varied wildlife, outstanding geological features, and plant communities, they range from the high mountain tundras to the southern forests.

The national forests offer a superb laboratory for the study of land management. Under the *multiple-use* principle, land may be used for various but compatible purposes. In some areas recreation and education may be designated as the dominant uses. Such designated areas are less than 5,000 acres in size but may be located at spots of particular interest. In other areas, recreation is coordinated with timber production and watershed protection. In still other areas, recreational use may be subordinate. Each area is managed with what is believed to be its best use in the interests of the public.

Educational significance of national forests.   The national forests are assuming a greater and greater function in the field of education. Almost 600 organized camps operate on national forest land, the great majority owned and operated by nonprofit agencies. There is a trend toward year-round use of the camps, thereby expanding their usefulness.

The Multiple Use Bill passed by Congress in 1960 gave recognition to the varied functions of the Forest Service and opened the door for a great expansion in its educational functions through the use of foresters, historians, and naturalists in leadership capacities both with the general public and with organized groups from schools and other agencies. A Visitor Information Service was begun in the 1960s.

The Forest Service might provide worthy work experience to young people who would benefit by getting away from the city environment. The multiple-use concept of forest management makes possible the use of forests for educational programs related to land use. The national forests constitute one of the major resources for outdoor education in America.

Like the National Park Service, the Forest Service is now trying to make its services more relevant to the city dweller. Accordingly, the Forest Service makes its technical services more available than previously to community agencies and has begun an educational program in the forest areas accessible to community groups.

federal extension service (department of agriculture)

The federal government works through the extension services of the state agricultural colleges and county extension agents to provide a direct service at a local level. The extension program is designed to improve the rural economy and to assist the rural land holder, and a large segment of its work consists of the education of rural youth through the 4-H programs in which several million children participate. The 4-H program, which functions chiefly in small towns and rural areas, is a major outdoor education service, emphasizing not only farm and home skills, but natural sciences, camping, and outdoor recreation. Some of the 4-H publications are excellent basic material for outdoor education.

Possibilities for enriched outdoor education programs lie in closer working relationships between city schools and the Extension Service. The city programs would be enhanced through visits by city youth to rural areas to participate in programs organized through extension services.

fish and wildlife service (department of the interior)

In 1940 two existing services, the Bureau of Fisheries and the Bureau of Biological Survey, were consolidated to form the present Fish and Wildlife Service. Today this agency consists of two separate bureaus: the Bureau of Commercial Fisheries and the Bureau of Sport Fisheries and Wildlife.

The Fish and Wildlife Service is responsible for the protection and increase of wildlife, the dissemination of information about these resources, and the enforcement of federal game laws. It also conducts extensive research in wildlife problems and cooperates with states in their wildlife programs.

The Service administers about 26 million acres of land in its various refuges. These areas protect certain species in danger of extinction, offer nesting areas for migratory waterfowl, and serve as winter habitats and temporary refuges for birds in migration. The refuges are open to visitors interested in wildlife and in recreation activities consistent with the purposes of the refuges.

Inasmuch as hunting and fishing are among the major recreational pursuits of a growing American public, the Fish and Wildlife Service performs a significant function in assuring the continuance of a fish and game supply.

Although millions of Americans visit the refuges to observe wildlife in their natural habitat, the educational resources of the Fish and Wildlife Service have not as yet been fully realized. However, a new educational division has been created in the Service. Those planning outdoor education programs might well explore the opportunities herein. The published materials of the Service constitute a large reservoir of wildlife information. The refuges themselves are outstanding for field trips and study projects.

bureau of outdoor recreation (department of the interior)

In January 1962, after more than two years of study, the Outdoor Recreation Resources Review Commission issued the most comprehensive report on outdoor recreation interests and needs that had been made in the United States. Among its recommendations was the establishment of a Bureau of Outdoor Recreation, which in April 1962, was created in the Department of the Interior. Some of the more important functions of the Bureau are to:

coordinate related federal programs

stimulate and provide assistance in state planning

administer grants-in-aid

sponsor research

encourage interstate and regional cooperation

formulate a nationwide recreation plan

In 1965 the Land and Water Conservation Fund bill was passed. This bill was intended to provide funds for outdoor recreation and gave the Bureau, as administrator, leverage to influence planning and development. The act provided that money received from a tax on marine gasoline, the sale of surplus military lands, and admission fees to federal lands be divided between federal agencies concerned with outdoor recreation and the states, each receiving half. The states' portion was to be distributed on a matching basis, and the states in turn could grant the funds on a matching basis to local government divisions.

The act specified that, to receive funds, a state must develop an acceptable outdoor recreation plan. As a result all fifty states have produced master plans. Each state has designated a state department to serve as the clearinghouse for funds. In some states new divisions or departments of outdoor recreation have been created. In many of these states the new divisions have assumed the responsibility for coordinating the efforts of the many state agencies involved.

The Bureau has been at work on the development of the national master plan for outdoor recreation. It is assumed that this task will involve a continuing program of studying the needs of outdoor recreation.

In performing its function of coordinating related federal programs, the Bureau serves as a resource for the evaluation of new developments by other federal agencies and acts as a clearinghouse to prevent duplication.

Funds for research have been very limited. The Bureau has co-operated with the research efforts of colleges and universities, and some projects have been carried on by the Bureau's own staff.

The original sources of funding have produced less revenue than had been expected, and Congress has from time to time found it necessary to make direct appropriations to support the services of the Bureau.

united states army corps of engineers
(department of defense)

The Army Corps of Engineers, organized in 1775, is responsible for a federal program of management, improvement, and maintenance of rivers and harbors in the interests of navigation and flood control. In this capacity it has constructed reservoirs and managed land adjacent to them. The Corps holds approximately seven million acres, half of which is water. Generally the Corps endeavors to turn the management of its areas over to local, state, and national agencies, but in many cases it assumes management itself.

The tremendous growth of interest in water sports in recent years has resulted in heavy use of reservoirs. In 1960 about 109 million people visited Corps of Engineers reservoirs. Picnic grounds, access roads, observation points, boat ramps and landings, public campgrounds, and organized youth camps have been developed around these waters. Many wildlife refuges and parks are maintained.

Properties managed by the Corps of Engineers are valuable for outdoor education as well as for recreation. Schools and other community groups should not overlook opportunities to secure leases for the development of facilities for outdoor education.

united states office of education (department
of health, education and welfare)

The primary function of the Office of Education, established in 1867, is to influence schools to provide the best education. Its services are channeled in part through the state departments of education to the local schools. It publishes materials related to education, conducts workshops, promotes training, represents education within the federal government and to many voluntary and private organizations, and attempts to raise standards for both teachers and educational programs.

The Office of Education has prepared many pieces of literature useful in outdoor education, such as those dealing with conservation education, science education, and related subjects, as well as outdoor education itself.

educational resources information center (eric)

The Educational Resources Information Center (ERIC) is a national network for acquiring, abstracting, indexing, storing, retrieving, and disseminating significant and timely educational reports and program descriptions. ERIC consists of a coordinating staff located at the U. S. Office of Education, supportive technical subcontractors, and a number of decentralized clearinghouses, each focused on a separate area of education. The basic objective of ERIC is to provide acquired information promptly and inexpensively to a wide audience. *Research in Education (RIE),* a monthly journal, contains abstracts of documents from all ERIC clearinghouses; abstracts of on-going research projects; and indices by subject, institution, and author or principal investigator.

Outdoor education is one of several areas of education assigned to the ERIC clearinghouse originally known as ERIC/CRESS (Clearinghouse on Rural Education and Small Schools), located at New Mexico State University, Las Cruces. This clearinghouse provides a great service to outdoor education by acquiring, indexing, and abstracting information. Subscriptions to the quarterly newsletter are free upon request and various monographs are prepared and distributed. It has been a policy of ERIC/CRESS that anyone wishing to submit materials on outdoor education for inclusion in the ERIC system may send them to the clearinghouse at New Mexico State University. Types of materials desired include research reports, newsletters, conference papers, bibliographies, curriculum guides, speeches, journals, articles, and books. Several monographs on outdoor education prepared by the clearinghouse are included in the references of several chapters in this book.

bureau of reclamation (department of the interior)

Federal reservoirs built primarily for irrigation and power have been the responsibility of the Bureau of Reclamation. Hoover Dam and Grand Coulee are among the Bureau's large developments. Management of recreational aspects of reservoirs and adjoining lands has usually been turned over to other agencies. For example, Lake Mead, formed by Hoover Dam, and other large units are administered by the National Park Service, with which the Bureau of Reclamation works closely. Other areas are administered by the Forest Service, Fish and Wildlife Service, and state and local agencies.

In general, uses not inimical to the principal purposes of the reservoirs are permitted. Before a reservoir is constructed, a study of its recreational potentialities is made, frequently by the Bureau of Outdoor Recreation.

More than 7.5 million acres of land are held by the Bureau. Many of the areas are excellent centers for school visits to study water conservation and its relation to land use. Classroom study followed by field trips are of great help in clarifying problems of soil and water management.

tennessee valley authority

The Tennessee Valley Authority, created in 1933, was authorized to develop the Tennessee River for navigation, flood control, production of electric power, to aid regional development, conserve natural resources, and in other ways aid the general welfare. It has been a successful demonstration of the effect of comprehensive multiple-use planning on a region's social and economic life.

A significant resource for outdoor education is the TVA's demonstration area in Kentucky and Tennessee known as the Land Between the Lakes. Although primarily a recreation area, it contains noteworthy outdoor education developments and programs. A youth education center with housing for school groups and a museum have been built. Extensive plans to expand programs for schools and other youth groups are in the making.

Groups within visiting distance of the TVA dams can benefit from the tours led by specially trained personnel who explain the operation of the dams.

Lands adjacent to the reservoirs are usually developed by other agencies or private groups. Many of them have been and still are available to municipalities, schools, and youth agencies for camps and outdoor education.

other federal agencies

Space does not permit detailed discussion of the many other federal agencies related to outdoor education or involved in the management of land resources. The following agencies should, however, at least be mentioned.

Bureau of Land Management (Department of Interior).   This bureau manages over 470 million acres of federal unreserved lands and has the authority to sell, lease, or exchange lands to political subdivisions.

Bureau of Indian Affairs (Department of Interior). There are about 55 million acres of land in Indian reservations. These lands attract tourists and are of particular interest to school children.

Children's Bureau (Department of Health, Education and Welfare). This agency is concerned with strengthening families in their rearing of children and therefore encourages education, welfare, and recreation services for children.

Soil Conservation Service (Department of Agriculture). This service is concerned with the improvement and management of soil. Its educational division has been devoting attention to means of educating children in conservation.

Public Health Service (Department of Health, Education and Welfare). Sanitation and health in outdoor resources are matters on which the Public Health Service will give information and assistance. Prevention of water pollution and means of refuse disposal are among its concerns.

STATE SERVICES IN OUTDOOR EDUCATION

The responsibility of states to provide for education in cooperation with local communities places them in strategic positions in relation to outdoor education. Through legislation, the state determines the educational patterns of local communities. Since it works with and provides services to local school boards and other agencies, the state has a direct channel through which educational programs are instituted or made more effective.

Although many functions of the state have federal counterparts, other functions lie primarily with the states. Those related to outdoor education include:

Provision of conservation and outdoor education consultants particularly for work with schools

Provision of leadership education through colleges and universities or through workshops and institutes

Direct services to local communities, to local organizations, or to individuals

Protection and conservation of wildlife and other natural resources

Establishment of state committees to coordinate materials and services within the state

Maintenance of lands and waters for public use

Allocation and distribution of federal funds for fish and game and outdoor recreation

State government services vary greatly from state to state. There are, however, services which may be found in all states, even though the administrative structure and the names of the agencies may differ. These services are discussed in the pages that follow. In addition, special services found in only a few states are discussed because of the challenge they offer to other states.

state departments of education

All states have established state departments of education with professional staffs. These departments have a major responsibility in determining courses of study, standards for school operation, requirements for teacher certification, distribution of state funds, and the like. Their staffs may include specialists in various areas, among which may be individuals responsible for conservation education and outdoor education.

A number of state departments of education have set up statewide outdoor education committees, composed of interested individuals and leaders in outdoor education programs. Such groups, often working under the direction of state school officers, have accomplished such things as:

Conducting studies of the status of outdoor education in the state

Conducting leadership training courses

Developing booklets and outlines for the operation of local outdoor education leaders

Working with state agencies in securing sites and facilities for outdoor education

Encouraging the development of new programs

Publishing informative bulletins and other helpful materials for outdoor education leaders.

Encouraging cooperative programs with related groups

state departments of conservation and
natural resources

Special services related to outdoor education are carried on by most states in connection with their conservation functions. The state authorities responsible for these services include a variety of agencies with a multiplicity of names and are concerned with such conservation interests as outdoor recreation, forests, parks, fish, game, water, and history. In some states a Department of Natural Resources combines most of these concerns; in other states there are separate departments of parks, forests, fish and wildlife, and others. Whatever the state administrative structure, there is a similarity of functions performed.

The first state park, a forerunner of the national parks, was established when the federal government committed the Yosemite Valley and the nearby Mariposa Grove of Big Trees to the state of California in 1864—eight years before the first national park, Yellowstone, was established.

Yosemite Valley had been visited by a number of prominent individuals who, impressed by its majestic cliffs, waterfalls, and superlative glacier-cut valley, began advocating its protection for the public. The establishment of the state park began the development of extensive state and national park systems. In 1906 the park was receded to the federal government as part of the national park system.

Michigan, in 1885, created a park on Mackinac Island, and in the same year a small reservation was set aside by the state of New York at Niagara Falls. In 1895 the Palisades Interstate Park of New York and New Jersey was created, and development of the extensive area up the Hudson began. A few other states followed in the early 1900s, but progress was generally slow.

Meanwhile, the National Park Service, established in 1916, was assuming the responsibility of holding areas with national significance. There was, however, a definite need for state areas of a character intermediate between the municipal parks and the national parks. Stephen T. Mather, director of the National Park Service, in cooperation with other prominent park leaders, called a meeting in 1921 to discuss the place of state parks and means of expanding and strengthening the state park movement. As a result of this meeting, the National Conference on State Parks, dedicated to the expansion and improvement of state parks, was organized.

The depression brought further development in the state parks. The National Park Service was made responsible for improvements made with the use of emergency funds provided by the federal government. The Civilian Conservation Corps, in existence from 1933 to 1940, provided the labor. Many states that had made little progress in the development of parks were assisted in acquiring areas and developing facilities such as roads, hotels, lodges, shelter houses, picnic areas, trails, and camping grounds.

There were in 1967 over 7.3 million acres in approximately 3,200 state parks. There is tremendous diversity in size. Some historical parks are less than an acre in extent, while there are eight parks containing more than 50,000 acres each. There is equal variety in the types of parks. There are large wild areas that contain scenic and wilderness values, such as Baxter State Park in Maine, Porcupine Mountains in Michigan, and Anza Desert in California. There are areas set aside primarily for their outstanding scenic, scientific, or historic values, such as Spring Mill State Park in Indiana and Valley Forge in Pennsylvania. There are also parks reserved primarily for their value in active recreation. These parks provide for such activities as swimming, boating, fishing, and archery.

State parks have purposes somewhat similar to those of national parks, but because of their accessibility to large centers of population in many instances, their use has tended to differ. Among the functions served by state parks are:

1. The protection of significant scenic, historic, and scientific areas. There is usually an attempt to preserve qualities that are characteristic of the state in its natural condition or in its early history.
2. The provision, where appropriate, of outdoor recreation activities. What constitutes appropriate types of recreation differs from state to state and from area to area. Where natural features predominate, the provisions for recreation should not detract from nor depreciate the natural resources.
3. The development of facilities to serve the general public in a manner consistent with the purposes of the particular park.

In some states, particularly in the west, state park development has lagged because of the large national park or forest holdings therein. Some states with small federal acreage have developed their state parks more extensively. Statewide planning, where practiced, generally provides for state or federal areas within reasonable driving distances of large population centers.

More than 400 million people visit state parks annually. These visitors participate in a wide variety of activities—sightseeing, picnicking, hiking, riding, swimming, boating, camping, and studying natural and historical features. Because parks are in most cases reasonably close to the homes of the users, a large part of their use is for one-day visits, although many parks contain hotel, cabin, and camping accommodations.

State parks are valuable resources for outdoor education. In most cases complete protection to plants and animals is given within their borders, and the natural environment is preserved. They are therefore excellent spots in which to observe and study natural life. Their topographical, geological, and archeological formations, relatively undisturbed by human activities, are also of interest to students. Some of the state parks contain historic sites, usually of importance in state history but in some cases, such as Valley Forge, of great national interest.

Many states, among them California, New York, Indiana, Washington, Minnesota, and Missouri, offer park interpretive services. In these states naturalists or historians conduct field trips, give lectures, prepare bulletins, and give information to visitors throughout the summer season. Various types of specialized facilities are maintained to enhance the program. Among them are trailside museums, displays, bulletin boards, and self-guided nature trails. Many hiking trails lead to points of interest and provide opportunities for visitors to get away from congested areas of the park.

Special services for children are often available. In some cases visiting school groups are provided with naturalist services, which may consist of explanations by the naturalist of displays in a nature center or museum, followed by trips led by the naturalist or teacher.

Approximately 400 organized camp facilities are on state park land. In some parks, such as in Michigan, many of these camps have been winterized and are used for school outdoor education purposes. This relationship between parks and schools is desirable from all points of view—the park-owned facilities are used on a year-round basis, and the schools can take advantage of the educational resources of the parks.

In some states the park naturalist staff gives special attention to the summer camp groups, conducting field trips, discussions based on outdoor interests, and campfire programs, as well as helping with programs in conservation and outdoor crafts.

Though there are many excellent state park programs, the educational potentialities of state parks in general have hardly been touched. Lack of funds has in some cases prevented adequate interpretive services. School use of parks needs to be expanded to help school children attain a firsthand understanding and appreciation of the resources of their own states. It is important for school and park authorities to consider jointly ways in which parks could extend their educational programs.

STATE FORESTS

Like the federal government, the various states own and manage forests. These were established largely for economic reasons.

The first state forestry commission was established in New York in 1885, to assume responsibility for the Adirondack State Forest. California, Colorado, and Ohio also created forestry departments in the same year, and other states gradually began programs. Today there are approximately twenty million acres in state forests.

These lands are used to varying degrees. In most states development for public use has been limited, since the primary function has been the protection of timber. Parks, rather than forests, have as a general rule provided the state-owned developments for public use, although picnicking, camping, fishing, boating, hunting, and hiking have taken place in the forests.

In addition to land holding, state forest agencies carry on important conservation functions. In some states they provide technical services and advice to owners of private forests. They also encourage the establishment of forests on private lands and make available tree seeds and seedlings at little or no cost. They provide forest fire protection on both public and private lands.

Forest personnel are available in some states as consultants to educational groups and may conduct field trips, particularly if problems of forest conservation are involved.

STATE DEPARTMENTS OF FISH AND GAME

Wildlife within a state is considered to belong to the state and is under its jurisdiction. Migratory wildlife is under federal control. The following are some of the functions generally performed by state departments of fish and game:

Improvement of wildlife habitats. Refuges and sanctuaries may be set aside. Plantings, development of farm ponds, improvement of streams and lakes, and establishment of refuges may be encouraged on private property.

Propagation of fish and game. Most states engage in programs for restocking fish and game. Funds for these programs are derived largely from fishing and hunting licenses. Game farms and fish hatcheries are maintained.

Management of hunting and fishing areas. A large number of public hunting and fishing areas are maintained.

Enforcement of hunting and fishing laws. Each state sets up its own laws for the protection of wildlife. Complete legal protection is given to many birds and animals, while others may be taken at any time or in accordance with seasonal restrictions or regulations on bag limits, hours of hunting, and methods of taking. Licenses are required for hunting and fishing in all fifty states. Age requirements and costs of licenses are determined by each state, which also sets up its own system for enforcement of its laws.

Research. Research into wildlife problems is an important aspect of the work of fish and game departments.

Conservation education. Conservation education programs usually include cooperation with schools, publishing materials for public education, and providing audio-visual materials and speakers. Some states have organized extensive adult and youth clubs and in a few cases have conducted youth conservation camps. The purpose of conservation education in fish and game agencies is to acquaint citizens with wildlife problems and enlist their support in conservation policies.

The resources of fish and game agencies may be utilized in many ways for outdoor education, including visits to wildlife areas, fish hatcheries, and game farms. The publications of each state agency are of particular value in that state and may give information unavailable elsewhere regarding local areas. Staff members often assist groups by preparing demonstrations, giving talks, advising on the management of outdoor areas, conducting field trips, and in some cases making wildlife available for study and observation.

state colleges and universities

The place of state colleges and universities in training leaders for outdoor education is discussed in Chapter 12. However, these state institutions render services to outdoor education in additional ways. Laboratory and demonstration schools often take the initiative in developing experimental programs and providing opportunities for future teachers to observe programs in operation. Many colleges and universities conduct their own outdoor education centers which serve both to train leaders and to provide learning experiences for college students. Research is carried on by faculty and graduate students, and publications are prepared relative to outdoor education. In some cases colleges and universities, through field consultation, assist communities in developing or improving their outdoor education programs.

outdoor recreation divisions

The establishment of the federal Bureau of Outdoor Recreation has resulted in the creation in many states of a state outdoor recreation division, usually in the department of natural resources. Several functions, usually including the following, are carried on by these divisions.

1. Developing a state plan for outdoor recreation.
2. Recommending and administering allocations of funds under the federal Land and Water Conservation Act.
3. Giving technical assistance to political subdivisions within the state.
4. Coordinating and serving as a clearinghouse for outdoor recreation functions of the state government.

state interagency councils for recreation

One of the most significant developments in state recreation services relating to outdoor education is the establishment of state interagency councils for recreation. A number of states have such councils.

The council plan represents a trend in state government wherein combined efforts of departments having responsibility for recreation mobilize their efforts to provide more effective services to the state. The council type of coordination is sound because it streamlines state government services and makes the best use of existing resources in meeting the recreation needs of the state. Some of the state agencies represented in the various inter-agency councils include education, health, mental health, conservation, parks and recreation, social welfare, economic development, state police, administration, library, historical commission, tourist council, highway, water resources, and civil service.

This mechanized age with its prospect of increased leisure demands comprehensive planning for recreation. No single agency or arm of state government can claim the responsibility for giving leadership and service in the area of recreation. This responsibility must be assumed by the many public, private, and voluntary agencies that have a legitimate role in the field of recreation.

The potential for recreational services in a state is unlimited. A close examination of the departments of state reveals that many existing arms of state government have certain functions and duties to perform in the field of recreation. However, the quality and extent of these services on the state level depends upon effective coordination of the services.

There are a number of structures for state interagency councils or committees. These varied patterns are due to the differences in structure and function of state agencies. Existing patterns include:

1. A voluntary interagency council or committee with a separate budget appropriated by the state legislature for coordinating services.
2. An interagency council or committee with leadership and funds provided by a state department or agency.
3. A voluntary interagency council or committee without a separate budget, but operating on the basis that each member agency will share the responsibilities.
4. An interagency council or committee appointed by executive order of the Governor.

Principles of organization of interagency councils. A council is composed of the heads or other representatives of state agencies and official organizations that have a responsibility for recreation. Each state should design its own cooperative pattern of operation fitting the needs, resources, and structure of its government. A council may be created by the governor or the legislature. The services of a full- or part-time executive secretary are essential to achieve maximum efficiency of operation.

Nature of an interagency council for recreation. The council is a coordinating body which utilizes a large staff of specialists drawn from member departments and cooperating agencies. It makes the maximum and most economical use of the programs and services of existing agencies that are responsible for recreation. Active support is given to member departments in providing recreation services and in obtaining adequate budgets.

Functions of interagency councils for recreation. A council serves as a clearinghouse for information, and channels and refers requests for services to appropriate agencies. Team operations are thus developed through a better understanding of the functions and services of member agencies. The council gives appropriate recreation services exceeding those which communities should provide for themselves. It serves in an advisory and consultative role to communities and assists them in studying the need for, and availability of, other services. A good council operation sets the stage for interested recreation groups to help themselves through in-service education and training. State-wide, regional, and local planning for total community needs is stimulated to provide adequate recreation opportunities for all the people. An effective interagency council brings into focus the recreation services of all local, state, and federal agencies, public and private, as resources for communities and takes a forward look at statewide needs for recreation.

An interagency council for recreation has significant implications for outdoor education in a state; it can provide resources, leadership, and services that will expedite local programs and offer opportunities for participation in outdoor activities. Represented on the council are usually the agencies which have the responsibility for education and the management of outdoor resources and facilities. There are many services related to outdoor education that the council can render to local communities. Some of them include:

1. Providing consultant services to help local communities plan facilities and land areas for outdoor education and recreation.
2. Encouraging in-service and pre-service education activities for leadership in outdoor education.
3. Providing state-owned outdoor areas and facilities.
4. Assisting local communities in planning and initiating outdoor education programs.

Several conferences of state interagency councils for recreation were held over a period of years. The conferences were informal organizations designed to provide opportunities for personnel from state agencies to discuss common problems relating to state recreational services. Representatives from federal agencies concerned with recreation, and leaders of professional organizations such as the National Recreation and Park Association and the American Association for Health, Physical Education and Recreation, participated in the conferences, which have been held in Michigan, Ohio, Virginia, Missouri, Washington, D. C., and New York.

other state agencies concerned with outdoor education

There are many other individual state agencies that have contributions to make to outdoor education, including libraries, recreation agencies and commissions, planning boards, youth commissions, social welfare departments, and health, highway, and planning departments.

In recent years a large number of federal and state agencies have been established, joining earlier established agencies which have also taken on functions relating to outdoor education and outdoor recreation. Some states which have had constitutional conventions have adopted some changes and revisions reflecting public awareness concerning outdoor resources and needed programs.

Federal and state governments are assuming more responsibility for providing lands, facilities, and leadership for outdoor education and recreation. The role of government in this regard is to provide facilities and services beyond those of local government and communities for increasing numbers who seek outdoor interests beyond the boundaries of their home communities.

SUGGESTIONS FOR FURTHER STUDY AND RESEARCH

1. Determine the extent of federal and state land within fifty miles of your community, and analyze the areas in terms of their possibilities for outdoor education for school groups.
2. Learn what federal or state services are available to contribute to outdoor education in your community.
3. Study the ways in which the federal and state governments cooperate in the field of conservation.
4. Outline a desirable state structure to provide services to local schools in the field of outdoor education.
5. Make a study of the state organizations and services in your state related to forests, parks, and wildlife.

REFERENCES

The Book of the States. Lexington, Ky.: The Council of State Governments, biennial.

Clawson, Marion. *The Federal Lands Since 1956.* Washington, D. C.: Resources for the Future, Inc., 1967. Distributed by The Johns Hopkins Press.

Douglass, Robert W. *Forest Recreation.* New York: Pergamon Press, 1969.

Jensen, Clayne R. *Outdoor Recreation in America.* Minneapolis, Minnesota: Burgess Publishing Company, 1970.

National Conference on State Parks. *1967 State Park Statistics.* Washington, D. C.: National Recreation and Park Association, 1968.

National Recreation and Park Association. *Recreation and Park Yearbook.* Washington, D. C.: McGregor & Werner, 1967.

Outdoor Recreation Resources Review Commission. *Outdoor Recreation for America.* Washington, D. C.: U. S. Government Printing Office, January 1962.

The President's Council on Recreation and Natural Beauty. *From Sea to Shining Sea.* Washington, D. C.: U. S. Government Printing Office, 1968.

Public Land Law Review Commission. *One Third of the Nation's Land.* Washington, D. C.: U. S. Government Printing Office, June, 1970.

Smith, Frank E. *Land Between the Lakes.* Lexington, Ky.: University Press of Kentucky, 1971.

Tilden, Freeman. *Interpreting Our Heritage.* Chapel Hill: University of North Carolina Press, 1967.

_____. *The National Parks.* New York: Knopf, 1955.

_____. *The State Parks.* New York: Knopf, 1962.

U. S. Department of Agriculture. *Outdoor Recreation in the National Forest.* Agriculture Information Bulletin No. 301. Washington, D. C.: U. S. Department of Agriculture, Forest Service, September, 1965.

U. S. Department of Agriculture. *Outdoors USA.* Washington, D. C.: U. S. Government Printing Office, 1967.

U. S. Department of the Interior. *Conservation Yearbook Series: #1—Quest for Quality,* 1965; *#2—The Population Challenge,* 1966; *#3—The Third Wave,* 1967; *#4—Man—an Endangered Species?* 1968; *#5—The Grassroots Conservation Story,* 1969; *#6—River of Life,* 1970. Washington, D. C.: The U. S. Government Printing Office, annually.

9

outdoor education through voluntary, private, and professional agencies

Education has so often been equated with schooling that one must be reminded that education is a process which takes place in every situation. In our social structure, a variety of agencies and organizations share common objectives with schools. In many cases their programs complement those of schools by providing experiences of great value but which are often not considered a responsibility of schools.

Voluntary and private agencies are particularly well equipped to carry on outdoor projects. Not bound by the rigid time and place requirements of school, they are usually more free to take groups outdoors for both short and extended stays.

To these agencies our schools owe a debt for pioneering and experimenting with programs which, once their worth was proven, were subsequently included in school curricula. Courses in adult education, home economics, and physical education owe their origin largely to the work of these organizations. The excellent work in science and conservation offered through such organizations as the Boy Scouts has undoubtedly influenced school curricula in these studies, as has the work of garden clubs, conservation organizations, and similar groups with special interests. The efforts of organizations which work with particular groups, such as handicapped children or the foreign-born, have resulted in the provision of special services for these groups in the schools.

Schools often cooperate with private and voluntary groups in programs which have strong community support. These co-curricular programs include Scout groups, Hi-Y, 4-H, Junior Red Cross, YMCA, and YWCA. Students are encouraged to participate in the programs of voluntary agencies. Facilities are made available, and school leadership is often provided to assist in these important community activities. Some groups have a religious emphasis; and, although the United States is committed to the separation of church and state, schools frequently encourage children to participate in programs of their own faith groups.

Because of their significance in the education of children, a small number of organizations especially concerned with outdoor education are considered below.

THE VOLUNTARY YOUTH-SERVING AGENCIES

The voluntary youth-serving agencies are exemplified by the Boy Scouts, the Girl Scouts, the Camp Fire Girls, the Young Men's Christian Association, the Young Women's Christian Association, Boys' Clubs, Girls' Clubs, and the 4-H. The 4-H organization does receive tax support, but because most of its leadership is voluntary and since its functions are similar to those of the other organizations, it is included here. There are, of course, other organizations, but these are the largest, and are nationwide in their constituency.

These agencies have several similar characteristics. Their purposes are educational, and their programs are based on learning through doing, generally through recreational activities. The adjective *character-building* has often been applied to these groups, inasmuch as they consider their responsibility to be the development of the individual rather than the acquisition of special skills or knowledge.

The term *voluntary* applies to these groups because (1) their membership and leadership are voluntary, (2) financial support comes largely through voluntary contributions, and (3) they are governed through boards and committees made up of citizens who wish to serve their communities in this manner.

Because membership is voluntary and because their programs stress direct participation, these organizations have a powerful influence on their members. All of the eight organizations conduct outdoor-related programs. The Boy Scouts, Girl Scouts, and Camp Fire Girls make outdoor activities a very important part of their year-round program. Not only outdoor skills but also knowledge about outdoor science and conservation are stressed. In recent years these organizations have given special emphasis to the wise use of natural resources and the development of conservation attitudes, understandings, and practices.

The 4-H clubs are directed toward rural problems; many of the projects of 4-H youth are related to agriculture, outdoor science, and conservation.

The programs of the Young Men's Christian Association, Young Women's Christian Association, and Boys' Clubs are generally less outdoor-related than those of the other organizations, but they, too, carry on various activities related to the out-of-doors through their hobby groups, trips, and excursions.

All of these organizations sponsor extensive camping programs. In addition to resident and day camping, there are numerous overnight camps, trips, and nature-related excursions. Some of the organizations consider camping an integral part of their total program for children.

ORGANIZED CAMPING

Organized camps are conducted by a multitude of organizations. Sponsors are of four main types: voluntary agencies, religious groups, private groups and individuals, and public agencies. The voluntary agencies carry on the most extensive camping in terms of the number of camper days. Religious groups—Catholic, Protestant, and Jewish— also maintain camps. In fact, church camping has been one of the most rapidly developing segments of camping in recent years. Private camps are generally of longer duration than other camps. There are at least 2,800 of them in the United States. The public camps are operated by recreation departments, schools and, in a few cases, welfare departments.

Organized camps may be categorized as resident camps, day camps, troop (group) camps, or travel camps. All are characterized by adult leadership, a more or less planned program, and educational objectives.

With so many kinds of groups conducting camps, there is great variation in leadership and effectiveness. The American Camping Association unifies these diverse groups and helps to raise the general level of their operations. By formulating standards and making adherence to them a membership requirement, the American Camping

Association is instrumental in improving camping practices. Conferences, workshops, study groups, and publications are additional services of the Association. Its many committees working on legislation, leadership training, standards, ethical practices, and other matters are significant influences in organized camping.

The following are objectives commonly accepted by leaders in organized camping:

1. The development of a sense of being at home in the natural world.
2. The development of skills for outdoor living.
3. Education for safe and healthful living.
4. Education for the constructive use of leisure.
5. Contribution to personality development.
6. Education for democratic group and community living.
7. The development of spiritual values.

These general objectives are not essentially different from those of schools, except in their greater emphasis on the outdoors and personal and social qualities. While objectives are similar, methods in organized camping differ from those of traditional classrooms. Camping places major emphasis on learning through participation in adventurous, interesting, and recreational experiences.

The standards of the American Camping Association include desirable practices in the following areas: personnel; program; camp sites, facilities and equipment; administration; health; sanitation; safety; and transportation. These standards have been based upon years of experience of camps operated by many public, voluntary, religious, and private groups.

growth of camping

At least eight million children attend about 12,000 camps in the United States each summer. Camp attendance has been growing at a rate somewhat more rapid than the rate of increase of children in our population.

There are certain segments of camping that have grown especially rapidly. Day camping has expanded in the past twenty years; today there are almost as many day campers as resident campers. Camping by religious organizations has also experienced phenomenal growth. All three major faith groups now carry on extensive programs. There has also been a rapid development of special-purpose camps, such as those for handicapped children or children with emotional or behavior problems. Work camps and special-interest camps (such as riding, music, or sports) also have increased in number.

leadership

Because of the close and informal relationships between counselor and camper, the counselor is extremely important to the success of the camp. Most counselors are temporary employees drawn from the ranks of teachers and college students who are available for summer work.

Giant strides have been made in recent years in upgrading camp leadership. Over 200 colleges and universities now give camp leadership courses. In addition, many camping organizations and private camp operators conduct their own pre-camp training. The standards of the youth-serving agencies which conduct camps, and of the American Camping Association, have helped raise the qualifications of camp counselors. A national training program and certification system for camp directors is conducted by the American Camping Association. Certification is dependent upon general education, special camp leadership training, and experience.

Association standards specify that counselors in resident camps should be at least 19 years of age and should have two years of college training or the equivalent in experience significant for camping. The standards also prescribe at least one adult counselor for each eight campers eight years of age and over, and one for each six campers under eight years of age. The camp staff should, of course, include some mature individuals beyond college age.

Salaries at camp are usually much less than can be earned elsewhere. It is to the credit of the camping movement that many excellent and dedicated counselors nonetheless spend their summers in camps. Many counselors are college students who are planning careers in youth work and education; for them the camp experience is one of the most fruitful forms of preparation.

In general, camps need counselors with an understanding of children, an ability to lead in a democratic fashion, and the background for carrying on outdoor-related programs.

structure

Functioning through small groups rather than mass meetings has been basic from the beginning of organized camping. The unit is the small group living with the camp counselor. However, the living unit does not necessarily constitute the program unit, as there are varied approaches to program structure. The large camp is generally broken into units of 18 to 30 campers, with the cabin group or even smaller living group functioning within this unit. The Boy Scouts have increased their program of troop camping, in which, under the direction of the year-round troop leader, the troops assume all responsibilities for their outdoor living.

facilities

There are contradictory currents in facility development in camps today. While some camps have become more comfortable and elaborate, an opposite trend toward simplicity and real outdoor living is evident elsewhere. The demand for winter use is one of the factors resulting in the elaborate camp. When a camp is planned, consideration is often given to its possible use by schools during spring, fall, and winter; as a result, buildings are erected which are more substantial than those needed for summer use only.

Most camps now are being constructed on the unit, small camp, or troop camp basis. Informal structures that adapt to the setting predominate. The rising standards in health, safety, and sanitation have added to construction costs.

As buildings become more elaborate, more ingenuity on the part of the staff becomes necessary to make the camp experience one of real outdoor living.

program

The organized camp is continually tempted to include city-type programs and facilities. However, the preponderance of camp leaders feel that camp should offer experiences different from those of the city and should make the most of its unique opportunities in outdoor living. The general purposes of the camp in regard to personality development and socialization may, in most cases, be realized best through the indigenous program. It is for these reasons that there is a trend toward unit camps or small camps with programs related to the natural environment, and an increase in troop camping such as the Boy Scouts emphasize.

Camps in general are improving their provisions for campers to do their own planning and make their own choices. The very nature of the camp program provides occasions for the practice of democratic procedures. Though there are areas where decisions must be made by the administrators, the needs and interests of campers and counselors are taken into consideration in program planning.

health and safety

Increased emphasis has been given to the health and safety of the individual camper and to the development of practices and attitudes conducive to health and safety. Care in the handling of food, planning of menus, construction of facilities, and development of water resources reflects the concern for health. Medical and nursing services and well-managed health centers are considered necessities in camp. Safety procedures in the conduct of program activities have been developed. The teaching of safe techniques of performance, as well as supervision of the activity, is stressed.

Camping for children should be healthful living in the best sense, with a balance of rest and activity, good diet, and sound personal health practices as part of an accepted mode of living.

legislation

State legislation affecting camping has been more stringent in recent years. Laws and regulations seek to safeguard the health and safety of the camper. Most of the states now have special regulatory legislation pertaining to summer camps. Other states use the regulatory provisions pertaining to child care centers, resorts, and the like, as the basis for their control of camps. Several states, including New York, California, Michigan, and Ohio, require camps to be licensed. Most regulatory legislation is concerned with such items as safe water, milk, waste disposal, food management, and safety of facilities.

In many states, the state sections of the American Camping Association have worked cooperatively with the state boards of health to develop suitable controls to protect the health and safety of campers.

camping and environmental education

It has long been recognized that a good camp provides an almost ideal setting for developing outdoor understandings, appreciations, and skills. The potential of camps has not generally been realized.

In recent years leaders in the American Camping Association have renewed efforts to improve outdoor education by expanding leadership education programs, workshops, and publications. No single pattern of outdoor programs is envisaged; rather, each camp is encouraged to make its contribution in the light of its own natural area, leadership, and resources.

YOUTH HOSTELS

Hosteling offers a unique program for youth. The use of hostels in outdoor education is not as extensive in the United States as in Europe. The youth hostel movement had its origin in Germany about 1910 and has developed in Europe into a major youth-serving movement. The original intent of the hostels was to provide accommodations for school children as a part of an outdoor travel program. The movement later took on an international aspect; today's hostels provide means whereby young people from many lands enjoy living and traveling at a modest cost. In the United States the hostel movement has been more limited in its extent. About 150 hostels are affiliated with the national organization, American Youth Hostels, Inc.

In addition to its programs in the United States, the AYH sponsors trips to various parts of the world. Many local AYH groups carry on program activities, such as hikes, campfires, and lectures, for their members.

Youth hostels in the United States could be used more frequently for outdoor education and outdoor recreation. Youth groups traveling under leadership might well stop at hostels. Also, school groups, like European school groups, might employ the hostels in their outdoor education programs, staying at the same hostel several days while studying a particular place, or moving from hostel to hostel. Such programs would make possible a longer season of hostel use, present use being limited largely to the school vacation months. To accommodate such groups, more hostels would have to be established in suitable sites.

In most youth hostels here and in Europe, only hikers and cyclists are accepted as hostelers. However, the vast distances in the United States and the lack of hiking and cycling trails have made it more appropriate to allow groups traveling by car or bus to use the hostels.

NATIONAL CONSERVATION AND OUTDOOR EDUCATION ORGANIZATIONS

With the increased public interest in the environment, organizations involved in environmental protection and outdoor education have taken on new vigor and, in some cases, new functions. Some of them have a broad ecological approach, while others emphasize protection of particular aspects of the environment, such as national parks, natural areas, or forests. Members of organizations are usually active in promoting conservation on local, state, and national levels. The organizations publish materials of considerable value to the outdoor educator; in some cases they provide consultants to various programs. Many of the publications are specifically directed toward the field of education, with audio-visual materials of high quality often available. Some of the organizations themselves conduct educational programs for children and adults and have made outstanding contributions in the field training of teachers and youth leaders.

As a rule these organizations are quick to rush to the defense of the environment when threats to natural resources arise. Because of their large citizen membership, they have been extremely influential in swaying popular opinion and securing conservation legislation.

Prominent among the organizations that have raised their voices in times of crisis are the Audubon Society, the National Parks Association, the Sierra Club, the National Wildlife Federation, the Izaak Walton League, the Wilderness Society, Nature Conservancy, and various local and regional groups that spring up when particular areas are threatened.

The following descriptions include some of the major national organizations that serve in the field of outdoor education and conservation. Because of their complex and often interrelated functions, the organizations are not categorized here.

The National Wildlife Federation, often considered a sportsman's organization, has in recent years assumed a significant role in environmental protection and education. Its *Wildlife Magazine* and *Ranger Rick* have had wide acceptance. *Ranger Rick* is one of the few efforts to reach children through a national publication directed toward the conservation of natural resources. The Federation, through its conferences and workshops, wields great influence. Its *Index of Environmental Quality* provides up-to-date information on the status of air, water, soil, forests, wildlife, and minerals. Its publications, *Conservation News* and *Conservation Report*, constitute two of the best sources of information regarding current programs and legislation.

The National Audubon Society, founded in 1905, is among the oldest and largest organizations of its kind in the United States. Many people think it is devoted only to the study and protection of birds, but it is committed to the broad field of conservation and outdoor education. Its purpose is "to advance public understanding of the value and need of conservation of wildlife, plants, soil, and waters, and the relation of their intelligent treatment and wise use to human progress."

The Society carries on many activities. About eleven million children have used the material in their junior program. Illustrated lectures, using Audubon Wildlife films, are conducted throughout the country by leading naturalists and photographers. Audubon sanctuaries in several areas give protection to rare and diminishing species of birds. Tours of these areas offer educational opportunities to visitors. Also, Audubon Camps, which give outdoor education training to teachers and other adult youth leaders, are conducted during the summer in four places—Maine, Connecticut, California, and Wisconsin. These camps give both field experience and instruction in nature and conservation. The Society is particularly active in research to save and restore species of animals threatened with extinction. Its Nature Centers Division offers technical services to local groups interested in establishing centers or in widening the educational use of their properties as centers for nature appreciation. The official publication is the *Audubon Magazine.* Many pamphlets, leaflets, and bulletins are also distributed, and the Society maintains a photo and film service. Members of local groups of the Society participate in meetings, projects, and field trips that not only afford satisfaction to members but also render services to the communities.

The Izaak Walton League of America has been, since its founding in 1922, a potent force for conservation. Its major purpose is to work for the restoration of soil, woods, water, and wildlife. One of its principal emphases is the protection of our water resources. Its fight against water pollution has promoted the enactment of *clean water* legislation in many states. The League has also encouraged conservation education in schools and voluntary agencies. It has supported conservation measures related to parks, forests, and wildlife.

The Wilderness Society, organized in 1935, is dedicated to the preservation of our dwindling wilderness as a national resource. It seeks nationwide cooperation in resisting the invasion of wilderness by civilization. The Society enlists the cooperation of other organizations and individuals and endeavors to develop public support. It encourages the protection of wilderness values by public land-holding agencies and tries to influence legislation. The Wilderness Bill, developed and supported in large measure by the Society, is an illustration of the organization's importance in helping to secure needed outdoor areas.

Keep America Beautiful, Inc., the national anti-litter organization, through its conferences, publications, and publicity, maintains a constant effort to prevent the desecration of places of natural beauty. Several of its publications are designed for classroom use and are available to teachers.

The name *Sierra Club* has become synonymous with vigorous struggles to conserve our retreating wilderness. Founded by John Muir originally to protect the Sierra Nevada Mountains of California, it is now a national organization that attacks environmental problems of all kinds. It is particularly forceful in its stand for the protection of natural areas and in its attempts to secure conservation legislation. The *Sierra Club Bulletin* and the many books and pamphlets published by the organization are concerned with open space, natural beauty, and outdoor recreation areas.

Since its organization in 1946, Nature Conservancy has been committed to the protection of natural areas in the United States. It functions largely through local and state groups that locate natural areas worthy of protection and then acquire funds for their purchase. The Nature Conservancy then finds a way of securing permanent protection by turning the areas over to public or private agencies. The organization has shown interest in acquiring and protecting school nature areas for educational purposes.

The American Forestry Association has as its particular focus the forests of America. Its interests, however, extend into total conservation. *American Forests Magazine* not only concerns itself with forestry but also with general natural science, outdoor recreation, and outdoor education.

Some of the organizations which are devoted to the conservation of outdoor resources serve as nongovernmental adjuncts to governmental agencies, carrying on promotional work which the governmental agencies are unable to do for themselves. For example, the National Parks Association, founded in 1919, is a private group concerned with the maintenance of high standards of national park acquisition and operation. In the years since its organization it has striven to maintain the original concept of preservation in national park areas. As an independent organization, it is able to arouse public opinion, influence Congress, and even bring pressure to bear on the National Park Service when it feels that park developments are not in harmony with the purposes of the parks. Its official publication, *National Parks Magazine*, emphasizes the scenic, scientific, and historical values of the national park areas.

PROFESSIONAL AND SERVICE ORGANIZATIONS RELATED TO OUTDOOR EDUCATION

The programs and organizations that have a relation to outdoor education are numerous and varied. Many professional groups, such as the American Association of Biology Teachers, the American Nature Study Society, or the Association of Elementary Science Teachers have long been advocates of the use of the outdoors for educational purposes. The School Garden Association, which has promoted school gardening for many years, should also be included.

Some of the organizations described here are not concerned with formal education but have an important relation to outdoor education.

Professional organizations have several important functions related to outdoor education:

1. They bring like-minded workers together and provide a focal point for their efforts.
2. They sponsor meetings, workshops, and conferences that produce an exchange of ideas and stimulate planning.
3. They develop and distribute publications that pertain to their special interests.
4. They sometimes provide consultant services for the improvement or establishment of outdoor programs.
5. They may work for legislation.
6. They may carry on public interpretation programs.
7. They sometimes conduct or sponsor leadership education programs for teachers.
8. They may sponsor or conduct research programs.

The National Recreation and Park Association emerged from the union of five national organizations: the American Institute of Park Executives, the National Recreation Association, the American Recreation Society, the American Zoological Society, and the National Conference on State Parks. All of these earlier organizations had been engaged to some extent in interpretation and outdoor education. The NRPA offers field services to communities and states in the improvement of park and recreation programs and resources. The many publications of the organization, including the magazine, *Parks and Recreation*, contain materials about conservation, outdoor education, and outdoor environmental planning.

The Natural Science for Youth Foundation offers science experiences to youth through nature centers and other community programs. Its national conference brings together many of the leaders in science education. The Foundation provides field service to help communities develop nature center programs.

The Conservation Education Association, composed largely of college and university leaders in conservation education and state conservation authorities, has worked for several years for the establishment of outdoor teacher training centers and the expansion and improvement of conservation education at all levels of education.

The American Association for Health, Physical Education, and

Recreation, a national affiliate of the National Education Association, has a major concern for outdoor education, both in program development and leadership preparation. Various aspects are given emphasis through the Council on Outdoor Education and Camping and other Association structures, and through district and state associations. The *Journal of Health, Physical Education and Recreation* carries articles on this subject. The Association also has a number of publications on outdoor education. The Outdoor Education Project of the AAHPER gives a special emphasis to outdoor-related sports and skills. The Project is discussed in more detail in Chapter 12.

In many sections of the country, state or regional teachers' conventions give consideration to outdoor education. Some places have organized special sections of teachers' associations. The Association for Outdoor Education in California is an organization of teachers coming principally from schools operating school camp proograms. This group has stimulated the expansion of outdoor education in California by publishing materials for teachers, conducting leadership workshops and conferences, and working cooperatively with other educational groups.

The Outdoor Education Association, Inc. is a national organization which evolved out of the work of the late L. B. Sharp and the National Camps conducted under his auspices. It is designed to further outdoor education through publications, workshops, conferences, and consultant services. The headquarters for the Association is at Carbondale, Illinois.

The Association of Interpretive Naturalists, organized in 1960, sprang from the Workshop on Interpretation which had met annually for six years at Bradford Woods under the sponsorship of the National Conference of State Parks, the American Institute of Park Executives, and Indiana University. The purposes of the Association are the improvement and expansion of interpretive services in public and private areas, the exchange of information, and the development of standards for services and training of personnel.

Its early membership came primarily from professional interpretive staffs of public park and recreation agencies. The rapidly growing membership now includes many people professionally engaged in outdoor programs with schools and voluntary agencies. The AIN annual conference has become a significant meeting for those with varied outdoor interpretive interests.

The American Camping Association, discussed earlier in this chapter, serves as a national voice of organized camping. Its members include private, agency, religious, and tax-supported camps. It publishes *Camping Magazine*, books, and pamphlets. One of its national committees is concerned with school camping and ways in which organized camps can cooperate with schools in developing outdoor schools in camp settings.

The organizations discussed above are a very small portion of those related to outdoor education. State, regional, and local groups are found in great numbers. Hiking and mountaineering clubs such as the Appalachian Trail Conference, the Sierra Club of California, and the Colorado Mountain Club, all have active outdoor programs including conservation education. In many cases the mountain clubs assume stewardship of a particular region. Their services go far beyond their members and include efforts to educate the general public and to influence legislation.

Garden clubs—national, state, and local—are often potent influences in outdoor education. They often endeavor to influence legislation and build public support for conservation. Local and state groups sometimes support children's garden programs, school conservation projects, and local park expansion. They may also provide financial support, including scholarships, for attendance at teacher conservation workshops.

Tremendous numbers of hobby clubs with outdoor interests exist in the United States. They range from bird clubs and conservation clubs to sportsmen's groups. Many of these groups devote their energies exclusively to their own members, but they often have programs and materials of value to school groups.

Outdoor education is of importance to many groups which have great potential for providing outdoor experiences for increasing numbers of children and adults. Some of the organizations have a long and rich history of service in this connection, and by using the resources and materials which are available, outdoor education experiences can be greatly extended and improved.

SUGGESTIONS FOR FURTHER STUDY AND RESEARCH

1. Compare the purposes, program content, methods, and leadership of the major voluntary youth-serving organizations with those of the public schools.

2. Survey your own community to determine what outdoor education activities are provided by private and voluntary organizations and associations, and to what extent the youth and adults participate.

3. Determine the adequacy of the summer camp opportunities in your

community. Evaluate the camp facilities in terms of their possible use during the school year by school groups.

4. It has been said that the good summer camp is one of the most important settings for influencing the behavior patterns of youth. Examine the validity of this statement.

5. Make a study of the youth hostel movement, both in Europe and in the Americas. How could the hostels be utilized more effectively by schools in their outdoor education programs?

6. Make a collection of resource materials and bibliographies from the various national conservation, park, and recreation agencies.

ADDRESSES OF ORGANIZATIONS MENTIONED IN THIS CHAPTER

Note: Literature describing the programs of organizations mentioned in this chapter is obtainable directly from the organizations.

American Association for Health, Physical Education, and Recreation, 1201 Sixteenth Street, N.W., Washington, D.C. 20036 (Council on Outdoor Education and Camping).

American Camping Association, Bradford Woods, Martinsville, Indiana 46151.

American Forestry Association, 919 Seventeenth Street, N.W., Washington, D.C. 20006.

American National Red Cross, 17th and D Streets, N.W., Washington, D.C. 20006.

American Nature Study Society, Milewood Rd., Verbank, New York 12585.

American Youth Hostels, Inc., 20 W. 17th Street, New York, N.Y. 10011.

Appalachian Trail Conference, 1718 N. Street, N.W., Washington, D.C. 20036.

Association of Interpretive Naturalists, 1251 E. Broad Street, Columbus, Ohio 43205.

Boy Scouts of America, New Brunswick, New Jersey 08903.

Boys' Clubs of America, 771 First Avenue, New York, N.Y., 10017.

Camp Fire Girls, Inc., 65 Worth Street, New York, N.Y. 10013.

Conservation Education Association, 1250 Connecticut Avenue, N.W., Washington, D.C. 20036.

Girl Scouts of the U.S.A., 830 Third Avenue, New York, N.Y. 10022.

Girls' Clubs of America, 133 East 62nd Street, New York, N.Y. 10021.

Izaak Walton League of America, 1326 Waukegan Road, Glenview, Illinois 60025.

Keep America Beautiful, Inc., 99 Park Avenue, New York, N.Y. 10016.

National Audubon Society, 1130 Fifth Avenue, New York, N.Y. 10028.

National Conference on State Parks, 1700 Pennsylvania Ave., N.W., Washington, D.C. 20006.

National Parks Association, 1701 Eighteenth Street, N.W., Washington, D.C. 20009.

National Recreation and Park Association, 1700 Pennsylvania Avenue, N.W., Washington, D.C. 20006.

National Wildlife Federation, 1412 Sixteenth Street, N.W., Washington, D.C. 20036.

Natural Science for Youth Foundation, 763 Silvermine Road, New Canaan Connecticut 06840.

Nature Conservancy, 1522 K. Street, N.W., Washington, D.C. 20005.

Outdoor Education Association, Inc., 606½ South Marion Street, Carbondale, Illinois 62901.

Sierra Club, 1050 Mills Tower, San Francisco, California 94104.

Wilderness Society, 729 Fifteenth Street, N.W., Washington, D.C. 20005.

Young Men's Christian Association, 291 Broadway, New York, N.Y. 10007.

Young Women's Christian Association, 600 Lexington Avenue, New York, N.Y. 10022.

REFERENCES

Carlson, Reynold E.; Deppe, Theodore R.; and MacLean, Janet R. *Recreation in American Life.* 2d ed. Belmont, Calif.: Wadsworth Publishing, 1971.

Dimock, Hedley S. *Administration of the Modern Camp.* New York: Association Press, 1958.

Hammett, Catherine T., and Musselman, Virginia. *The Camp Program Book.* New York: Association Press, 1954.

Hanson, Robert F., and Carlson, Reynold E. *Organizations for Children and Youth.* Englewood Cliffs, N. J.: Prentice-Hall, 1972.

Lurie, Harry L., ed. *Encyclopaedia of Social Work*. New York: National Association of Social Workers, 1965.

Mitchell, Viola A., and Crawford, Ida B. *Camp Counseling*. 5th ed. Philadelphia, Pa.: W. B. Saunders, 1970.

Shivers, Jay. *Camping: Administration, Counseling, Programming*. New York: Appleton-Century-Crofts, 1971.

IV

resources and leadership for outdoor education

10

land and facilities
for outdoor education

Since outdoor education is primarily concerned with direct learning in the outdoors, it is evident that the natural environment has a major influence on the quality of the learning opportunities. Whether in understanding principles of conservation, studying some aspect of science, becoming acquainted with problems of agriculture, or developing outdoor living skills, the natural resources are of paramount importance.

Facilities are developed primarily as an adjunct to the land for the purpose of making the use of the land more effective. They are not ends in themselves, but rather devices either for the comfort and convenience of the users or for enhancement of understanding and appreciation of the natural environment.

Lands rich in plant and animal life, with varied topography and high aesthetic values, inspire learning in the outdoors. However, an outdoor area has many more possibilities for learning than is generally recognized, and lack of an ideal spot need not deter development of an outdoor education program. An eroded hillside or an abandoned farm may teach lessons that cannot be observed in a well-managed location. Problem lands often stimulate projects that would offer little challenge elsewhere. One of the objectives of outdoor education is to make students aware of problems involved in the wise use of the natural environment, not only areas abundant with many resources, but any lands—the school grounds, the home neighborhood, or the larger community.

Jean Henri Fabre, the French naturalist, conducted much of his research in a worn-out, infertile field; and yet he was able to bring to the science of entomology new knowledge and insight into insect life that had escaped those with far more adequate resources. If there is perceptive leadership, the possibilities for good outdoor education are unlimited in almost any situation.

BACKGROUND OF OUR NATIONAL LAND PROBLEMS

One cannot understand the present situation in regard to natural resources without some knowledge of the background of our national land use policies and the conflicts which, through the years, have militated against a consistent application of conservation principles.

Our forefathers found a country unbelievably rich in soil, wildlife, water, and timber. The first settlers wrested their living chiefly from the land, learning from the Indians many of the lessons necessary for survival. The gun, the axe, and the plow quickly changed the character of a land which the small Indian population had scarcely affected.

The wildest dreams of the early settlers could not have envisioned today's large population and resource needs. However, even in those remote days, there were forebodings of problems to come. In 1641 the Massachusetts Bay Colony by ordinance provided that "great ponds" (ten acres or over) "of fresh water should be forever open to the public for fishing and fowling." This law is, as far as we know, the first public act in what is now the United States for the protection of the public interest in wildlife. Many of the early cities of our eastern seaboard laid out public parks, and some New England communities established community forests. A few early acts indicated concern for timber and wildlife. There was, however, no widespread interest in the protection of wild lands nor in provision for their use by the general public.

Following the War for Independence, the vast territory from the Appalachians to the Mississippi River became available for settlement. The Land Ordinance of 1785 provided for the survey of lands in the west and for their disposal to the public. This act led to the township system and the policies of land sale that resulted in the transfer to private ownership of practically all of the land east of the Mississippi River.

The Timber and Stone Act and the grants made to railroads for western development continued the disposal of public lands. More than a billion acres of public land were distributed through various sales, grants to states, homesteads, military bounties, and railroad grants.

The nineteenth century may well be termed the century of uninhibited exploitation of natural resources. This was the period of serious loss of soil, with millions of acres of land despoiled and deserted. Land that should never have been cleared of its forest was plowed, farmed, and abandoned. Wasteful lumbering practices, accentuated by fierce competition, led to the depletion of major timber resources, particularly in the eastern half of the continent. Fires often completed the desolation left by man. Wildlife, once deemed inexhaustible, dwindled. Some species disappeared entirely; others were reduced to pitiful remnants. Water resources, once lightly regarded, became a major concern. Pollution by human and industrial wastes began to destroy the quality of the waters. The destruction of timber on watersheds resulted in serious land erosion and further impaired the waterways. Heavy inroads were made on our mineral wealth, although it remained for the twentieth century to exploit these to their utmost. We are today paying the price of misuse through polluted rivers, eroded lands, and depleted wildlife.

Except for a few isolated instances, there was little attempt until the twentieth century to save the nation's scenic, scientific, historical, and recreational resources. A small beginning was made by the federal government in 1832, when Congress set aside for public use four sections of land in Arkansas as the Hot Springs Reservation. In 1864 the state of California created the first state park, and in 1872 Congress created the first national park.

LAND NEEDS TODAY

The twentieth century witnessed the beginnings of a strenuous conservation effort. Much remains to be done, however, if the needs of future generations are to be met. Resources will be needed, not only to feed and clothe our people and to provide fuel and other materials for industry, but also to afford education, inspiration, and enjoyment.

Land for the growing of food will, of course, always take precedence over any other land needs. Although we find ourselves today with a food surplus and no immediate danger of scarcity, a continued growth in population may some day necessitate the utilization of a larger percentage of land for agriculture. The value of agricultural land for educational purposes should not be overlooked, although natural areas are usually associated with outdoor education.

There is considerable conflict of opinion between those who wish to preserve the aesthetic and scientific values of land and those who are interested in the economic values, such as lumbering, mining, or grazing. There is also conflict between those who wish to preserve recreational lands in their unspoiled natural state and those who wish to expand roads, accommodations, utilities, and artificial developments. The concept of multiple use has also divided the proponents of land preservation. Some lands certainly can be used simultaneously for several purposes, such as timber cutting, recreation, and education, while other lands may best serve educational or recreational functions exclusively.

The automobile has created problems in land use. There are more than 90 million automobiles in the United States, and this number is increasing annually. Travel in the future has significant implications for outdoor education. The expanding automobile highway system not only eats up tremendous acreage, but also adds to the pressures on formerly isolated lands by making them readily accessible to vacationists. The automobile has also been in part responsible for the so-called *urban sprawl*. Housing developments spread farther and farther into the country, gobbling up farms and forests and eliminating open spaces which should be preserved.

Increased leisure and income of the American people, along with increased mobility, make it possible for ever greater numbers to visit open land at the very time that land is dwindling. It is estimated that the demand for outdoor recreation will treble or quadruple by the year 2000. There will be heavy pressures on areas close to centers of population.

PLANNING FOR TOMORROW

The surge to the outdoors and the resultant pressures on land call for adequate outdoor education in our schools. The rising generation of young people must be able to use the outdoors with regard for others and yet with personal satisfactions. They must understand problems relative to resources and their wise use. If present population trends continue, there will be at least 310 million people in the United States by the year 2000, and immediate planning for future needs is urgent.

Areas for tomorrow's outdoor education purposes must be reserved today. With the competition for land for agriculture, home sites, airports, roads, and industries, it becomes more difficult yearly to find or acquire suitable sites. Lands held by local, county, state, or federal government may frequently be used for outdoor education; but even on public land demands for various uses often result in a loss for outdoor education purposes. It is important to remember, however, that public lands belong to all the people and should be developed to serve the best interests of the people.

In view of present conditions and trends, planning for land needs for outdoor education should follow a pattern of logical growth and development. One cannot foresee the future with certainty because technological, political, and social upheavals affect living patterns unpredictably. However, there must be careful planning, based on research, for the days to come. A master plan is not a fixed blueprint, but a guide that may be altered as conditions require.

Good planning today must transcend municipal, county, and state boundaries. Although planning on a municipal basis needs to be done, more success in acquiring adequate areas can be accomplished on a regional basis. More cooperation between governmental units than heretofore, and more consideration of the resources held by voluntary agencies and private groups, are essential to success.

Schools, particularly, need to work with park and recreation agencies. Authorities have generally recommended the provision of one acre of local park and recreation land for every 100 persons. This standard must be interpreted in terms of the distribution of the land and the extent of its protection and development, as well as probable future population growth. There are no generally accepted standards for state park acreage. However, many states attempt to establish state parks within fifty miles of the homes of all residents.

Surveys in communities, as well as in schools, should give attention to the acquisition and development of land for various types of outdoor education, under various sponsorships and involving all age groups. The accessibility of land must be borne in mind. A wide variety of areas sufficiently rich in resources to make outdoor education significant should be provided.

PROVIDING FOR THE RESIDENT OUTDOOR SCHOOL

In the years ahead, many schools will wish to develop their own outdoor areas and camp facilities. In many instances, it is advisable to utilize the resources of other agencies, public, private, and voluntary.

In the United States at present, thousands of summer camp facilities are located on the more than a million acres of land held by camping agencies. Most organized camps for children operate only during the summer, and some facilities, if they are partially or wholly winterized, are available for school use during the remainder of the year.

Some schools use private camps through the school year. The camp owners might provide meal service, thereby freeing the school system to devote its energies to the educational program.

School use usually requires modification of the summer camp facility. Inclement weather in many parts of the United States makes it necessary to provide insulation and heat for the buildings. School use may also necessitate indoor space for work and study which the summer camp does not require. Moreover, accommodations for sleeping and eating should be planned with special consideration for class groups.

Certain standards for land and facilities have been developed by the American Camping Association. In addition, there are other important considerations such as:

1. A minimum of one acre of land per camper.
2. Facilities located and constructed so as to provide a sense of isolation and a feeling of living in the woods.
3. A safe and sufficient water supply, approved and inspected by the State Board of Health.
4. Living quarters constructed for small group living (usually not over eight persons to a room).
5. Forty square feet of living space for each bed, with beds so arranged that there is a distance of six or more feet between the heads of sleepers.
6. Screening and protection from weather.

CAMPS FOR SCHOOL USE

Although it may be desirable for schools to use camp facilities that have been developed by other groups, many school systems will establish their own facilities as the outdoor education program grows. In northern Europe many individual schools have set up their own outdoor centers. In the United States it is more common for a large school system or several small school districts to operate a camp facility for outdoor programs.

If a school system plans to develop a camp facility, a number of factors should be considered. Careful planning is essential, involving the classroom teachers, administrators, and specialists in outdoor education. Technical help is available and should be sought, since there are many problems in outdoor facilities that are different from those in the central school plant. The vast experience gained by private individuals and organizations in building thousands of camps should be appropriately utilized. A carefully selected planning committee should consider all resources in order to develop the best possible outdoor center, and should allot time to visit and study good camp facilities before acquiring land or beginning construction.

The following outline suggests a few of the many factors that should be considered in establishing a camp for school outdoor education purposes:

the camp area

1. An area with rich and diversified natural resources and varied topography is desirable.

2. There are advantages in being within fifteen to thirty miles of the school because of ease of transportation and the potential for a broad use of the facility for many educational activities. However, the quality of an outdoor area should not be sacrificed, since modern transportation makes more remote facilities accessible.

3. An ideal setting is one with good roads, but with sufficient distance from major highways and other developments to give a sense of being in the woods and away from the city.

4. One acre per camper is generally considered desirable to provide a sense of isolation and to protect the area from future encroachments.

5. Adequate pure water resources for domestic and program purposes should be available.

6. The area chosen should have good building sites and possibilities for future expansion.

More detailed information may be found in materials prepared by authorities in organized camping and specialists in parks and recreation. A helpful chapter will be found in a publication of the Athletic Institute.[1]

---

[1] The Athletic Institute and the American Association for Health, Physical Education, and Recreation, *Planning Areas and Facilities for Health, Physical Education, and Recreation* (Chicago, Ill.: The Athletic Institute, 1965).

developments

1. *Planning.* In all instances, the uses planned for the property should determine the types of developments. A careful analysis of future needs and uses should be made. A few of the many considerations are:

Age of campers
Size and numbers of groups
Length of stay
Types of program activities
Leadership available

Seasons of use—if the camp is used by school classes during the school year and by other groups during the summer, plans for construction must consider the differing numbers, ages, and program requirements of the campers.

2. *Living facilities.* It is generally desirable, in organized camping, to plan for boys and girls to live in separate buildings. For schools, however, a most satisfactory arrangement is the cottage that would accommodate a number of children equivalent to a classroom, plus at least two adults. Each cottage may be divided into two or more rooms, ideally, with eight or ten in a single room. Teachers and counselors should be provided with separate rooms. Heating should be adequate for the coldest weather in which the buildings will be used. Toilet and shower facilities should be located within the building. A day room, preferably with a fireplace, should be provided. This room should be large enough to accommodate all children in the cottage for meetings or leisure use. Provision of locker space makes neatness possible in the cottages.

3. *Dining hall and lodge.* Because of the problem of cold-weather heating, it is often desirable to provide a building that will care for dining needs, meetings of the total camp, and program activities that at times must be carried on indoors. Because of early darkness and cold weather, evening activities may have to be carried on indoors during the winter.

A typical dining hall may accommodate two classes with the camp staff during the winter, a total of about 80 people. The same dining hall, during the summer, may need to care for 120 people.

Some of the program facilities described below may be included in a combination dining area and lodge.

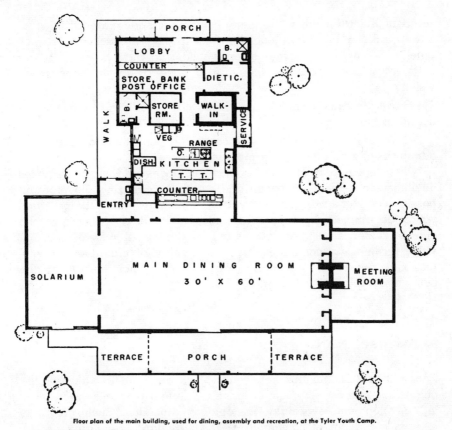

Floor plan of the main building, used for dining, assembly and recreation, at the Tyler Youth Camp.

4. *Program facilities.* Some of the program facilities that should be considered are:

Indoor work rooms for projects in science and arts and crafts
Library and study rooms
Trading post
Storage space for tools, cookout equipment, and other outdoor equipment
Campfire circle
Nature trails
Science displays
Outdoor cooking spots
Space for demonstration science projects

5. *Staff and guest housing.* Provision must be made for housing the program staff and others who cannot be accommodated in the

campers' living facilities. Too many centers lack adequate facilities for these purposes. If student teachers are expected to observe or participate in the program, rather extensive housing may be required for them. Most school centers should also have overnight housing for visitors.

6. *Health center.* Each camp should have facilities to care for the health of the campers.

7. *Administrative office.* If the camp is a year-round operation, an administrative unit should be provided.

By consulting many of the excellent books and other resources dealing with outdoor education and carefully analyzing the program possibilities of the site, a planning committee may evolve the program, which determines the type of facilities to be developed. Since the outdoor center is an instructional unit for the school system, and provides facilities for community use, the quality of planning and professional assistance should be equal to the other phases of the educational plant.

PARK-SCHOOL PLANS

Cooperative relationships between schools and public parks for the acquisition and development of lands for mutual purposes is a promising development, especially for outdoor education. Such programs exist in a number of communities. The park lands generally lie adjacent to the schools and serve both as adjuncts to the schools and as community parks.

One of the best-known school-park cooperative developments is in Glencoe, Illinois. Here, park lands adjacent to schools provide meeting places outdoors and space for various types of field trips and other outdoor projects. The Glencoe plan also includes cooperation in plant propagation in the park greenhouses and in many of the plantings on school grounds, parks, and streets of the city. This program thus provides a ready outdoor resource for the schools as well as parks for children and adults in the community.

The following features might be included in a school-park:

Meeting spots for school groups

Horticultural plantings

Water areas—swamp gardens, ponds, lakes, running streams, or ocean shore

Camping and day camping sites

Picnic and outdoor cooking spots

Outdoor amphitheatres

Trails for hiking, horseback riding, and cycling

Nature trails

Area for such outdoor sports as casting and archery

Wildlife displays

Arboretums

Children's gardens

Nature centers

Shelter houses

Natural undisturbed areas

SCHOOL SITES

Even the most limited school grounds—including those in inner cities—have some possibilities for outdoor education. Trees, lawns, and shrubs, even if few in number, are outdoor resources. Cracks in sidewalks and concrete surfaces often have persistent plants and insects that live in limited spaces.

Many older schools have inadequate space. New schools often have larger acreages and include specific provisions for outdoor education. The high cost of property often prohibits the acquisition of desirable land, but school building authorities now advocate the construction of new schools in areas where population growth is anticipated but where open land can still be secured at a reasonable price.

Of course the size of the school affects land needs; but in general it is recommended that elementary schools have, if possible, a minimum of 10 acres; junior high schools, from 10 to 20 acres; and high schools, from 20 to 40 acres. Many of the newer sites are much larger, ranging from 20 to 100 acres. Land for buildings, parking, physical education, and recreation is essential, but a substantial part of the site should serve outdoor education purposes. Some schools have acquired large natural areas adjacent to their grounds, where developments such as those of the park-school are possible.

The Worthington, Ohio, Public School District has an 80-acre plot on which are located a junior high school and a senior high school. The major part of the property is used as an outdoor education laboratory, available not only to the two schools, but to the elementary schools of the community as well. There is space for field trips, gardening, conservation projects, tree planting, and outings. Nature trails,

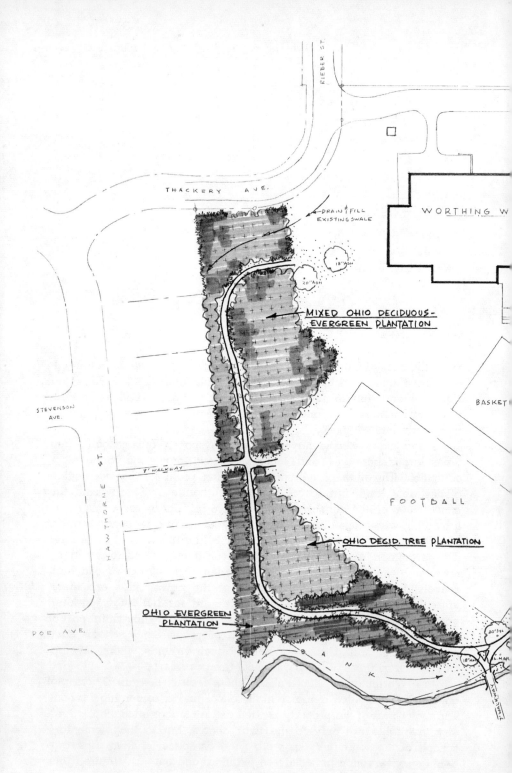

RIEBER ST.

THACKERY AVE.

WORTHING W

DRAIN & FILL
EXISTING SWALE

18" ASH

20" ASH

MIXED OHIO DECIDUOUS-
EVERGREEN PLANTATION

BASKET

STEVENSON
AVE.

THORNE ST.

T' WALKWAY

FOOTBALL

OHIO DECID. TREE PLANTATION

OHIO EVERGREEN
PLANTATION

DOE AVE.

B A N K

20" SYC.

18" HA

L. MAPL.

T' WALKWAY

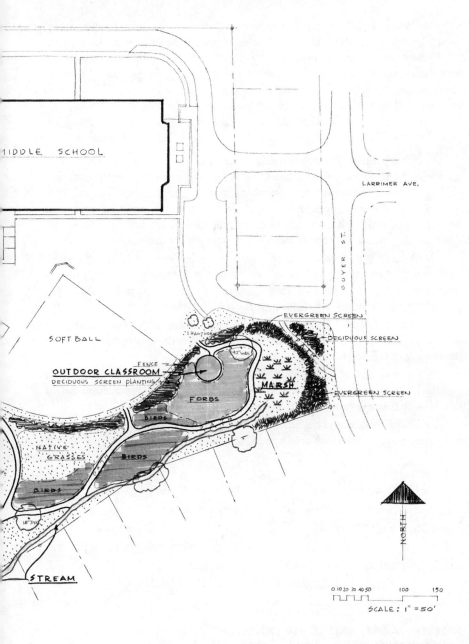

MIDDLE SCHOOL

LARRIMER AVE.

GUYER ST.

SOFTBALL

EVERGREEN SCREEN

DECIDUOUS SCREEN

2 HAWTHORN

42" WALL

OUTDOOR CLASSROOM
FENCE
DECIDUOUS SCREEN PLANTING

FORBS

MARSH

EVERGREEN SCREEN

BIRDS

NATIVE GRASSES

BIRDS

BIRDS

18" SYC.

STREAM

NORTH

0 10 20 30 40 50   100   150

SCALE : 1" = 50'

TRI-DISTRICT OUTDOOR EDUCATION FACILITIES
WORTHINGWAY MIDDLE SCHOOL
WORTHINGTON, OHIO

LANDSCAPE ARCHITECT
1645 MERRICK RD., COL'S
8-4-69

wildlife area, school garden plots, a wildflower garden, observatory, shelter house, cookout site, and picnic areas have been developed. With the cooperation of community and state organizations, this property has become not only a distinctive educational project, but also a community resource of great value. It serves the school system at all grade levels as a laboratory for outdoor study.

Every school ground is different, and each has its own program possibilities. The following should not, however, be overlooked.

1. *Horticultural areas.* Lawns and plantings for beautification may serve educational functions as well. By assisting with planting and care, young people may develop the skills and knowledge that will help them maintain home gardens. Observation can acquaint students not only with the kinds of plants and plant families but with their requirements for continued growth and reproduction.

2. *Woods.* The woods may range from a few shade trees to natural woodlands. Even a few trees make it possible to become acquainted with principles of tree growth. Woods of considerable size provide opportunities for nature trails and forestry projects.

3. *Water areas.* Streams, ponds, and bogs may sometimes be found or developed on school grounds, affording opportunities to observe water life, both plant and animal.

4. *Garden areas.* Plots where individuals may plant their own gardens, horticultural demonstration areas, or farm crop demonstration areas are all possible on suitable land.

5. *Other outdoor education developments.* While some of the following require considerable space, others demand but little:

Nature trails	Picnic site
Astronomy observatory	Woodcraft area
Outdoor classroom	Day camp area
Outdoor amphitheatre	Fish pond or small lake
Trailside museum	Turtle pond
Weather station	Greenhouse

Bird feeding stations; bird houses; bird baths

FORESTS, FARMS, AND OTHER OUTDOOR LABORATORIES

School forests, farms, and other outdoor laboratories have been discussed in Chapter 4. Their importance will increase as population grows and American culture continues to be more and more urbanized.

AN EXAMPLE OF A SCHOOL SITE-PLAN.

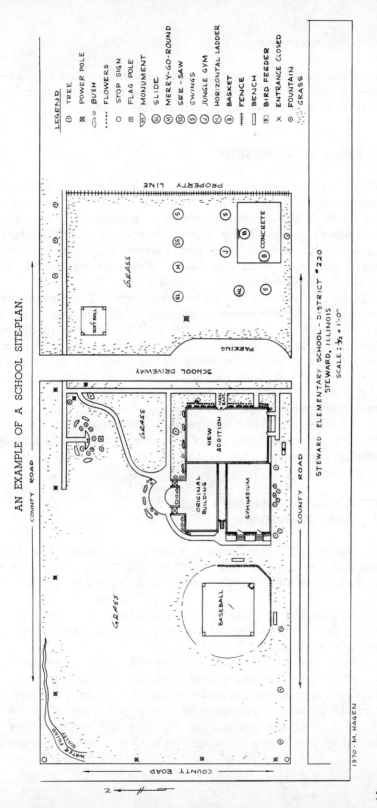

LEGEND

- TREE
- POWER POLE
- BUSH
- FLOWERS
- STOP SIGN
- FLAG POLE
- MONUMENT
- SLIDE
- MERRY-GO-ROUND
- SEE - SAW
- SWINGS
- JUNGLE GYM
- HORIZONTAL LADDER
- BASKET
- FENCE
- BENCH
- BIRD FEEDER
- ENTRANCE CLOSED
- FOUNTAIN
- GRASS

STEWARD ELEMENTARY SCHOOL - DISTRICT #220
STEWARD, ILLINOIS
SCALE : $\frac{3}{32}$ = 1'-0"

1970 - M. HAGEN

The combined resources of schools, other public agencies, and private agencies need to be mobilized for acquisition and development of these laboratories before open land becomes unattainable.

COLLEGES AND UNIVERSITIES

Colleges and universities have for many years operated various types of outdoor education areas. In recent years these have been expanded not only to provide education for college students, but also programs for children's groups. Many institutions of higher learning maintain biological field stations, geological camps, general natural science centers, and field campuses, which give field experience college credit as an adjunct to classroom work.

Some colleges and universities also operate field centers for out-door leadership in education and recreation, maintaining at the same time children's programs which are used by the college classes for observation and practice leadership. In some instances, the college simply makes the facility available for school use and uses this type of program for field experiences.

A number of colleges and universities operate camps and other outdoor recreation areas. They may serve student groups or alumni and their families. Other colleges and universities that do not hold their own properties make use of private or public lands for outdoor education purposes.

NATURE CENTERS, CHILDREN'S MUSEUMS, AND TRAILSIDE MUSEUMS

The programs of nature centers, children's museums, and trailside museums have been discussed in Chapter 4. The facilities themselves and the land on which they function are the particular concern of this section.

The purposes of a center should determine the character of its development. Outdoor education is the primary concern of most of the centers developed in the United States.

A center may range from a department in an adult museum of a crowded city to a development in a natural outdoor area, where the out-of-doors is the principal resource and the facilities are developed as an aid in its use. Centers vary also in the types of groups they serve. Some serve school groups primarily and are developed and financed as part of the school program. Others serve a membership clientele and offer programs of clubs, classes, field trips, lectures, and work activities. Service to youth groups is often an important part of the program. Still other centers, such as those in national and state parks, serve the transient public and are commonly designated as *trailside museums* or *visitor centers.*

Nature centers generally may be divided into three types: first, those that are located at some distance from the homes of the participants so that transportation is a major consideration; second, those that are located in natural areas within walking distance or easy transportation of the homes of large numbers of participants; and third, the large-city centers that lack outdoor areas, so that the program is largely conducted indoors.

land requirements

In city areas where space is not available, the designation *children's museum* or *junior museum* is more appropriate than *nature center*. More emphasis must be placed on the buildings, the exhibits, and provisions for indoor work.

In a nature center, several hundred acres of land are desirable; and the more varied and natural the area, the greater the interest and value of the center. Abundant plant and animal life, significant geological features, and water areas such as ponds, streams, and lakes, contribute to the success of the center.

The centers surrounded by large natural areas are often found in state and county parks and forests and in outlying city-owned reservations and parks. In some cases private lands serve as the outdoor resources.

outdoor developments

Each area has its unique story of natural science and human history, and plans for any development should center around the ways in which this story may be best interpreted.

Trails suitable for use for field trips and explorations are needed. Self-guiding nature trails are desirable, particularly if an area is to be used by groups without specially trained leaders. Trailside displays and displays-in-place may be used to call attention to particular features.

Outdoor meeting places are extremely desirable. A small amphitheatre, a council ring, or merely a comfortable seating spot for group discussions may be provided.

Photographic blinds are generally helpful. Elevated walkways may be provided in pond or marsh lands. An observation tower, garden, and nursery can add program possibilities.

Because users may come from a considerable distance and may plan to spend full days at the centers, certain types of accommodations may be needed that are not required in city centers, where visits may be brief. Parking spaces are essential. Places for picnics, cookouts, and campcraft activities may be desirable; these activities should be so located that they will not impinge upon the natural areas and contribute to their destruction.

nature center buildings

Nature center buildings differ widely in size and purpose. The following rooms are typical of a building located in a large natural area; the building is used during the school year by classes coming by bus with their teachers, and during the summer by organized youth groups from agencies and camps. Such a center also serves as a visitation center for adults and children.

Display room. Although the principal attraction of the building usually does not lie in its displays, nevertheless they are an important part of the development. Habitat cases, maps, and other types of displays are generally included.

Meeting room. Many centers need space for informal talks and for the presentation of audio-visual materials. If school groups and other organized groups use the center, there must be adequate space to accommodate them when inclement weather makes it impossible to use the out-of-doors. In some buildings meeting space may be provided in display rooms, although it is generally desirable to have separate rooms.

Work room. A room where exhibits may be prepared and studies made is needed. In addition to staff space a place where visitors may work is desirable.

Other rooms. An office, library, toilets, and storage space are additional necessities.

SCHOOL AND COMMUNITY GARDENS

Modern urban living denies to many the opportunity to grow plants and to participate in the learning and pleasure that come from gardening. In any plan for land for outdoor education, consideration should be given to gardening, both for its educational values and for the satisfactions it gives children and young people. When acquiring and developing sites, schools should try to provide garden space. Park and recreation agencies should attempt to make such space available if it is not provided by schools. Where cooperative school-park programs exist, space for gardens should be considered.

In general, it might be said that the more crowded the urban situation the greater the need for garden experiences for children, but, unfortunately, the greater the difficulty in finding adequate land. Garden space preferably should be located close to both the schools and the homes of participants, as the garden program takes place all year round.

Desirable garden land is not always easily located. If land with good soil is not available, it can sometimes be improved over a period of years through planting and fertilization. It is better not to initiate a school garden until land is of sufficiently high quality to make garden experiences successful.

Leadership, as well as space, is the key to good gardening. Those who expect to operate a new program should have the opportunity to visit several of the successful garden programs now in existence. Materials available from garden projects such as those of Cleveland or the Brooklyn Botanic Garden are of great help. In addition, there are people in every community qualified to give advice and assistance.

types of gardens

There are three types of children's gardens that have had widespread success: (1) the home garden, which is intended for those who have adequate space in their own homes and who, through participation in an organized program, may be encouraged to establish and maintain a garden at home; (2) the group production garden, in which a class or other group participates in planting, caring for, and harvesting the products of the garden; and (3) the tract garden, with individual plots, which is the most common type of school or community garden and one in which individuals are responsible for the care and management of their own plots.

The group production garden. The land requirements for a group production garden are not great. A group of younger children may require only 20 to 50 square feet in which to plant flowers and a few vegetables. A class of older children may require a garden of several hundred square feet in which flowers and vegetables are planted and later, when harvested, divided among the gardeners.

A school site might contain land which can provide several such gardens. A community park department might also make land available for a group project.

A group production garden may vary greatly both in size and in plantings. In many cases it serves as a means of practical application of class garden instruction. It may also serve as a teaching center for children with home gardens, in which case it becomes a demonstration plot.

The tract garden.   Tract gardens are generally the most popular type of children's gardens. Individual plots are the responsibility of individual children, and there is a natural human response to having something of one's own for which to care. The success of the individual garden rests directly on the shoulders of the individual child, and results depend upon knowledge, industry, and perseverance. It is possible in the tract for one child to compare his results with others, and this comparison often provides incentives to accomplishment.

The tract garden provides a setting for instruction and supervision and makes possible the provision of tools, fertilizer, and equipment at minimum cost.

It is generally necessary to have at least one-third of an acre to justify the development of a tract garden. In the elementary grades, approximately 150 to 180 children might be accommodated on an acre of land.

A tract garden should be located close to the homes of users. During the summer, children should not be expected to travel much more than a quarter of a mile to participate. It is also desirable for it to be near school grounds so that it may be used during school time or just after school. Probably the most desirable setting is the elementary school grounds. The modern trend to larger school sites should make possible land for gardens. In some cities special gardens have been acquired close to elementary schools to serve children on a neighborhood basis.

Good gardens are planned gardens, and effective planning necessitates a site that can be used on a more or less permanent basis. If the soil is not of the best quality, it may take years to improve it. Continuing use of the same property is necessary so that other improvements may also be made, such as developing an irrigation system or constructing facilities for meetings of children, for tool storage, or for propagation of plants indoors.

The following are some of the considerations in developing a tract garden.

1. The size is dependent on present and future usage. Individual plots may vary in size from four by eight feet for very young children, to sixteen by twenty feet for older elementary school children, or twenty by fifty feet for older youth. If an area is to be used by high school students, there should be demonstration plots for instruction in landscaping principles.
2. Ready access to water is important. In many areas it is desirable to provide for irrigation.
3. A tool storage area is essential.
4. A spot should be provided for a compost heap and for the disposal of waste materials.
5. The total area should be made attractive through some landscaping.
6. A building large enough for group meetings and for indoor work during bad weather is an asset to the program.
7. A greenhouse is desirable for a large garden.
8. Adequate pathways should be provided.
9. In most gardens, fencing is needed for protection from vandalism.

Further discussion of children's gardens will be found in Chapter 4.

NATURAL AREAS

There has been growing interest in recent years in the utilization of small natural areas for outdoor education. These areas might range from a few to hundreds of acres, and their primary purpose would be to provide settings for studying natural processes where man's interference is minimal. Nature Conservancy has been active in promoting the preservation of such areas. Educational institutions at all levels have acquired some areas, but most are held by private or public park agencies, including park departments and natural resource departments.

THE IMPORTANCE OF OUTDOOR RESOURCES

The mounting problems accompanying the growth of population, urban sprawl, and the disappearance of much natural landscape make particularly important the immediate consideration of preserving land of the right kind for outdoor education. In the midst of the pressures of the atomic age, we need to be reminded that we, as human beings, belong to the biological world and are dependent upon the world of nature.

Every community needs to give serious thought to preserving natural features and developing facilities that will make outdoor learning and outdoor enjoyment possible. Community agencies should work together to find the best possible approach for the acquisition, protection, and use of outdoor resources.

SUGGESTIONS FOR FURTHER STUDY AND RESEARCH

1. Prepare a plan for the grounds of a new junior high school. Assume that there are 20 acres of land. Include a variety of outdoor education developments.

2. Visit a country school. Analyze the school grounds and the surrounding property in terms of outdoor education opportunities. Include possibilities for conservation projects, beautification projects, gardening experiences, or field trips.

3. Draw up plans for a facility to be used during the summer as a camp for a voluntary youth-serving agency and during the winter as a school outdoor education center.

4. Develop plans for a nature center for a community of about one hundred thousand people. Map the land area and locate desirable outdoor developments. Draw a floor plan for the nature center building.

5. Prepare a plan for a school garden for a particular community that will be used by several schools.

6. Examine critically a citywide plan to determine what provisions have been made for outdoor education areas and facilities. Add to the plan your own recommendations for outdoor education areas and facilities.

7. Locate the natural areas adjacent to your community and describe the special resources of each area.

REFERENCES

Ashbaugh, Byron L. *Planning a Nature Center.* New York: National Audubon Society, 1963.

————. *Trail Planning and Layout*. New York: National Audubon Society, 1965.

Athletic Institute and American Association for Health, Physical Education, and Recreation. *Planning Areas and Facilities for Health, Physical Education, and Recreation*. Chicago, Ill.: The Athletic Institute, 1965.

Bone, Maurice D., ed. *Site Selection and Development*. Philadelphia, Pa.: United Church Press, 1965.

Douglas, Robert W. *Forest Recreation*. New York: Pergamon Press, 1970.

Ezersky, Eugene M. *City to Country*. New York: Educational Facilities Laboratory, Inc., 1969.

Goodrich, Lois. *Decentralized Camping*. New York: Association Press, 1959.

Johnson, Verna. *Natural Areas for Schools*. Sacramento, Calif.: Office of Conservation Education, n.d.

Marsh, Norman F. *Outdoor Education on Your School Grounds*. Sacramento, Calif.: Office of Conservation Education, 1967.

National Association of Biology Teachers. *Manual for Outdoor Laboratories*, ed. Richard L. Weaver. Danville, Ill.: Interstate Printers and Publishers, Inc., 1959.

Resident Camp Standards. Rev. ed. Martinsville, Ind.: American Camping Association, 1969.

Shomon, Joseph J. *Manual of Outdoor Conservation Education*. New York: National Audubon Society, 1964.

————. *A Nature Center for Your Community*. Information-Education Bulletin no. 1. New York: National Audubon Society, 1962.

U.S. Department of Agriculture. *The Community School Site*. Lincoln, Neb.: USDA, Midwest Regional Technical Service Center, 1968. (Originally published by Michigan Department of Public Instruction as Bulletin no. 314.)

11

personnel and resources
for outdoor education

The amount, type, and nature of leadership necessary for outdoor education depend on the nature of the agency or organization involved. Since outdoor education is interdisciplinary in character and applies to all the learning activities that are related to the use of the outdoors, the question of personnel must be approached accordingly. As suggested in previous chapters, the teacher or leader in outdoor education will be attached to the agency or organization involved. Indeed, it may be fairly stated that the major task of program development is one of staff development. Before considering the personnel for specific situations, there are some basic premises which should be kept in mind.

1. Some learning activities can be achieved or enriched through the use of an outdoor setting.
2. Opportunities for learning outdoor sports or activities should be provided in schools, colleges, and community agencies.
3. All personnel employed by schools, colleges, and other community agencies whose programs can be enhanced by outdoor education should be competent to teach in outdoor settings.

4. All local resources, such as areas and facilities, should be used in community education.

The application of the above to personnel for outdoor education can be described by observing the following characteristics of leadership preparation needed for those engaged in outdoor education, particularly in situations involving children and youth.

1. An understanding of the values of outdoor education;
2. An understanding of the relationship of outdoor education to the school curriculum;
3. Skills in planning for outdoor experiences and in working with children in the outdoors;
4. An appreciation of the values of living in a peer community, having daily living tasks and work experiences;
5. The concept that the teacher should be concerned with development of the total child.[1]

In discussing specific responsibilities of personnel in outdoor education, it is necessary to deal with each of several categories of teacher and leadership positions.

SCHOOLS

Reference has been made to the responsibility of the classroom teacher. The classroom teacher should be the central figure in the outdoor classroom. Ideally, the well-prepared classroom teacher would be able to use the outdoors as effectively as the classroom or the library or any other facility for instruction. Modern teaching methods and the required preparation in subject matter should equip teachers to teach wherever the environment is most conducive to the learning objectives in question. The outdoors is free from the usual classroom props and traditional procedures. Skillful teaching should take place in the community laboratory as well as in the classroom. Too often teacher preparation and pre-service experiences have been related largely to the classroom and the teaching of abstractions. Adequate preparation is described in Chapter 12.

One difficulty in comparing teaching competency in the outdoors

[1] George W. Donaldson and Oswald H. Goering, *Outdoor Education: A Synthesis* (Las Cruces, N.M.: Education Information Resources Center, Clearinghouse on Rural Education and Small Schools, New Mexico State University, March 1970), p. 11.

with that of the classroom is the fact that classroom procedures and their results are often taken for granted. They should receive the same analysis and evaluation as that given to instruction in newer and more unusual circumstances, such as the outdoor settings described in this book.

If the classroom teacher is the central figure in outdoor classroom activities, what are other personnel needs? First, there needs to be involvement of all school staff who have responsibility for objectives included in the planned outdoor experiences. The entire teaching staff, or appropriate segments of it, are being involved more and more in the curriculum of today's schools. This trend is reflected in core courses, unified studies, block plans, teaching teams, and a variety of other patterns designed to make learning more effective and continuous, and to achieve wholeness instead of fragmentation.

Outdoor education provides excellent opportunities to coordinate the efforts of a school staff and to make greater use of the abilities and interests of all teaching personnel. A few examples will illustrate.

use of outdoor laboratories for field experiences

One of the first steps in using available community outdoor areas and facilities is to conduct a systematic inventory. An outdoor education committee for the school system or a group of interested teachers may, through such a survey, inform the staff of the outdoor resources that could be used by the entire school system, grades K through 12. The survey team, which should represent a wide range of interests and subject matter areas, would be an example of the interdepartmental approach which might result in cooperative action in the use of the available facility. There would be no better way to relate the interest of the science teacher to the elementary classroom, to involve the biology teacher in a conservation field trip, or to join the efforts of the physical education instructor who teaches outdoor skills with the appropriate phases of science or social studies. Much of the hope for competent school personnel for outdoor education lies in the possibilities of a coordinated approach in the entire school system.

outdoor classrooms

The plan employed by most schools conducting programs in camps is to supplement the leadership of the classroom teacher with that of others in the system, such as other interested classroom teachers, members of the staff who teach related areas, and specialists in physical education, art, music, shop, homemaking, and library. This plan offers an excellent opportunity for relating a wide variety of learning experiences. It also establishes cooperation in other school activities as well as in the program at camp. Other resource personnel from the community, from schools and colleges, and from state and federal agencies supplement staff services. In elementary programs, particularly, parents with special abilities can assist in the program.

In schools that have extensive year-round programs, the central camp staff employed to assist the classroom teachers usually represents a variety of interests, training, and backgrounds such as science, conservation, physical education, recreation, health education, guidance, social studies, arts and crafts, and nursing. In this way, the staff members serve as resources to each other and constitute an effective team. Schools operating in this manner employ certified teachers who are regular members of the school staff.

The question is often asked as to what type of person should direct the program and what should be the nature of his training and experience. It has been said that the director of the outdoor classroom program must be a Jack-of-all-trades, ranging from a maintenance engineer of the facility to a social psychologist. In the larger school systems, the director usually has the status of a principal or supervisor, and may have the title of Director, Coordinator, or Supervisor of Outdoor Education or the Outdoor School.

As a matter of practice, a school administrator will select a person best qualified to perform a variety of functions in administration, curriculum, guidance, buildings and grounds, finance, and public relations. It is interesting to note that those now employed in school systems came from many fields, with large numbers from science, physical education, and elementary education. As in other plans for selecting personnel, experience and personality are large factors. In most instances a central staff has had experience in some type of camping.

outdoor sports

Usually the teaching of sports and games is part of physical education and recreation in schools and colleges. In elementary schools the teacher is often assisted by a specialist in physical education. In too many instances, physical education and recreation leaders have had little or no experience or training in many of the outdoor sports. It is important to select teachers, both men and women, who have an interest in such activities as casting, shooting, boating, water sports, camping, and winter activities, and who are anxious to broaden the offerings in physical education to include the lifetime outdoor skills in the list of class activities. Fortunately, with the increasing interest in outdoor education, more teachers are becoming qualified to teach outdoor skills. There is need for cooperation and coordination with other areas of the curriculum, such as shop, science, and homemaking.

the specialist in outdoor education

While outdoor education is largely the responsibility of the classroom teacher, there is a need for leaders with special training. In many situations there will be several specialists on the staff, such as in science, physical education, and recreation. Depending on the breadth of the school's efforts in outdoor education, and the nature of the activities and the facilities, an administrator may be needed to help coordinate and implement the whole program. Some types of outdoor education experiences, such as outdoor classrooms and excursions, require much planning since students may be away from home for one or more days and will need to be transported to distant locations. There may also be a need for special equipment, a knowledge of the local and state facilities, information about laws, and other pertinent facts that will help make the venture a success. It is important in such instances that competent staff be employed to assist the classroom teachers and to help interpret the program to the parents and the community.

COLLEGES AND UNIVERSITIES

The arrangements for personnel in colleges and universities somewhat parallel those in the public schools, except that there is more specialization. Traditionally camping and outdoor activities have been offerings of departments of health, physical education and recreation, while science and conservation were related to the physical sciences, fisheries and wildlife, or natural resources. More recently, there have been significant developments in colleges and universities in an interdisciplinary approach.

RESOURCE LEADERS

Reference has been made to the use of resource leaders in outdoor education. It is probable that no phase of the educational curriculum has more qualified resource leaders than outdoor education. They will be found in every community—they may be staff members in local, state, and national agencies; specialists in state and federal governments and departments; members of local outdoor organizations; or parents and citizens, high school and college students who have outdoor hobbies, interests, and skills. In planning local programs, an inventory of leadership should be developed and much thought should be given to ways of using their services effectively. In some states, conservation agencies have special consultants and administrative procedures for assisting schools in the various phases of outdoor education. One of the difficulties in using resource personnel is in relating the diverse interests in the outdoors to the program objectives. Following are some suggestions for effective use of personnel.

1. Analyze the instructional unit or program carefully to determine the need for resource personnel.

2. If lists of local and state consultant services are available, select the person who seems best qualified to provide the specific assistance needed. If such lists have not been compiled for school use, a community inventory should be made to determine the interests, hobbies, and talents of local citizens who might be potential resource leaders. State lists are often available from state agencies, colleges, and professional associations.

3. Communicate with the prospective resource leader as to his availability to assist with the assignment. Full details on the type of service needed, instructional procedures, time, place, and remuneration, if any, should be given by the administrator or the person in charge of the program.

4. Whenever possible or feasible, the resource leader should participate in a planning session, especially when a field experience in a new setting is involved.

5. The resource leader's function is usually of two general types: (a) to provide information needed to supplement the classroom project; or (b) to assist the teacher or leader with procedures or teaching methods, specific information on the subject, or materials needed for conducting the learning experience. In most instances, resource personnel should assist the teacher, rather than supplant him. An ultimate result of good consultant service is to increase the competency of the teacher or leader.

6. Train high school and college students who have abilities and interests in outdoor education and who can work with staff members and adult leaders.

7. Following the use of resource personnel, the experience should be evaluated by the group in order to improve the quality of instruc-

tion and increase the competency of the resource leader and teacher for a similar future occasion.

COMMUNITY AGENCIES

The concerns relative to personnel for outdoor education in community agencies are comparable to those in schools and colleges, except for the wide use of volunteer leadership, especially in youth agencies. Much of the training and experience for professional leaders in recreation departments, camps, voluntary youth organizations, and other such agencies should be comparable to that required for teachers. Leaders in community agencies and teachers serve children and youth of like ages, backgrounds, and community environment; the only difference is in the nature and purposes of the organization involved. Consequently, trained agency personnel should have preparation in such areas as child growth and development, psychology, leadership techniques, outdoor skills, and a knowledge of the outdoor environment. Too often there is a feeling that leaders in community agencies need training entirely different from that of teachers. But careful analysis of the job to be achieved will indicate that very little separate training is needed. This is particularly true of recreation leaders. As in schools, there is a need for the team approach of specialists and nonspecialists, and for using all the resources and facilities of the community.

The most important trend in the in-service preparation of agency personnel for outdoor education is cooperative planning, sharing facilities and resources. The community school is in a strategic position to stimulate cooperative endeavors for supplying well-qualified personnel for outdoor education. While schools should provide the basic instruction for grades K through 12 and adult education, the community agencies can supply additional opportunites for participation for all members of the community. Wasteful duplication of personnel, programs, and facilities makes it difficult to provide adequate opportunities in outdoor education. Through the careful selection and training of leaders, and through cooperative community planning, it would be possible to provide the personnel necessary to meet the leadership needs in providing outdoor education for all.

RESOURCES AND MATERIALS FOR OUTDOOR EDUCATION

In addition to a wealth of leadership in outdoor education, there are abundant resources and materials available to many local communities at the present time. Some of these are made available by national, state, and local organizations and agencies. Among the many organizations actively involved in outdoor education are the following.

National

1. American Association for Health, Physical Education and Recreation, 1201 Sixteenth Street, N.W., Washington, D. C. 20036
2. American Camping Association, Bradford Woods, Martinsville, Indiana 46151
3. American Canoe Association, 83 Warren Street, Ramsey, New Jersey 07446
4. American Casting Association, P. O. Box 51, Nashville, Tennessee 37202
5. American Fishing Tackle Manufacturers Association, 20 North Wacker Drive, Chicago, Illinois 60606
6. American Forestry Association, 919 Seventeenth Street, N. W., Washington, D. C. 20036
7. American Friends Service Committee, 20 South 12th Street, Philadelphia, Pennsylvania 19107
8. American National Red Cross, 17th and D Streets, N. W., Washington, D. C. 20006
9. American Nature Association, 1214 Sixteenth Street, N. W., Washington, D. C. 20036
10. American Youth Hostels, 20 West 17th Street, New York, New York 10011
11. Association of Private Camps, 55 West 42nd Street, New York, New York 10036
12. The Athletic Institute, 805 Merchandise Mart, Chicago, Illinois 60654
13. Boy Scouts of America, New Brunswick, New Jersey 08903
14. Camp Fire Girls, Inc., 65 Worth Street, New York, New York 10013
15. Conservation Education Association (no permanent address)

16. Girl Scouts of the USA, 830 Third Avenue, New York, New York 10022

17. Izaak Walton League of America, 1326 Waukegan Road, Glenview, Illinois 60025

18. National Archery Association, Box 48, Ronks, Pennsylvania 17572

19. National Association of Engine and Boat Manufacturers, 420 Lexington Avenue, New York, New York 10017

20. National Association of Secondary School Principals, 1201 Sixteenth Street, N. W., Washington, D. C. 20036

21. National Audubon Society, 1130 Fifth Avenue, New York, New York 10028

22. National Congress of Parents and Teachers, 700 North Rush Street, Chicago, Illinois 60611

23. National Council of Catholic Youth, 1312 Massachusetts Avenue, N. W., Washington, D. C. 20005

24. National Council of Churches of Christ in America, 475 Riverside Drive, New York, New York 10027

25. National Education Association (and many of its affiliates), 1201 Sixteenth Street, N. W., Washington, D. C. 20036

26. National Field Archery Association, Route 2, Box 514, Redlands, California 92373

27. National Jewish Welfare Board, 145 East 32nd Street, New York, New York 10016

28. National Recreation and Park Association, 1700 Pennsylvania Avenue, N. W., Washington, D. C. 20006

29. National Rifle Association, 1600 Rhode Island Avenue, N. W., Washington, D. C. 20036

30. National Shooting Sports Foundation, Inc., 1075 Post Road, Riverside, Connecticut 06878

31. National Wildlife Federation, 1412 Sixteenth Street, N. W., Washington, D. C. 20036

32. Outboard Boating Club of America, 333 North Michigan Avenue, Chicago, Illinois 60601

33. Resources for the Future, 1755 Massachusetts Avenue, N. W., Washington, D. C. 20036

34. Sport Fishing Institute, 719 Thirteenth Street, N. W., Washington, D. C. 20005

35. Sporting Arms and Ammunition Manufacturers' Institute, 420 Lexington Avenue, New York, New York 10017

36. Young Men's Christian Association, 291 Broadway, New York, New York 10007

Federal

1. Bureau of Outdoor Recreation, U. S. Department of the Interior, Washington, D. C. 20240

2. ERIC Document Reproduction Service, 4936 Fairmont Avenue, Bethesda, Maryland 20014

3. Fish and Wildlife Service, U. S. Department of the Interior, Washington, D. C. 20240

4. Forest Service, U. S. Department of Agriculture, Washington, D. C. 20250

5. Geological Survey, U. S. Department of the Interior, Washington, D. C. 20242

6. National Park Service, U. S. Department of the Interior, Washington, D. C. 20240

7. Office of Education, U. S. Department of Health, Education, and Welfare, Washington, D. C. 20202

8. President's Council on Physical Fitness and Sports, Washington, D. C. 20201

9. Superintendent of Documents, U. S. Government Printing Office, Washington, D. C. 20402

10. U. S. Army Corps of Engineers, Washington, D. C.

State

1. State Beach Commission
2. State Camping Association
3. Board of Commerce and Trade
4. Department of Conservation or Department of Natural Resources
5. State Department of Economic Development.
6. State Forest Department or Commission
7. State Game and Fish Department or Commission
8. State Health Department
9. State Association for Health, Physical Education and Recreation
10. State Highway Department
11. State Historical Commission
12. State Inter-Agency Council for Recreation
13. Inter-State Waterways Commission
14. State Land Use Committee

15. State Library
16. State Park Department or Commission
17. State Police or Highway Patrol
18. State Office or Department of Public Instruction
19. State Recreation Department or Commission
20. Soil Conservation Service
21. State University and State College Extension Departments

Local

1. American Red Cross
2. Catholic Youth Organization
3. Citizens' Development Committee
4. Civic and Service Clubs
5. County Sanitarian or Health Department
6. 4-H Clubs
7. Garden Clubs
8. The Grange
9. Historical Societies
10. Jewish Youth Organization
11. Metropolitan or County Park Authorities
12. PTA
13. Sheriff and Police Departments
14. Sportsmen's Clubs
15. YMCA and YWCA

It would be impossible to identify by name and source the leadership, equipment, and materials that relate to the broad area of outdoor education. The best procedure is for those interested to assemble information from agencies by obtaining reports, directories, and catalogs which describe the offerings. Some find it helpful to categorize the information according to consultant services, equipment, publications, and audio-visual resources. These may be further divided according to discipline or field, such as science, conservation, physical education, recreation, arts and crafts, and outdoor sports.

SUGGESTIONS FOR FURTHER STUDY AND RESEARCH

1. What competencies should a classroom teacher or recreation leader have in order to participate in an outdoor education program?
2. In what types of situations would a school or recreation department need a specialist in outdoor education to administer or supervise a program?
3. Identify some of the resource personnel that would be available for assisting in the initiation and development of outdoor education programs for the schools or agencies of a community with which you are familiar.

REFERENCES

American Association for Health, Physical Education and Recreation. *Leisure and the Schools*, Chapter 4. Washington, D.C.: AAHPER, 1961.

Corbin, H. Dan. *Recreation Leadership*. 2d ed. Englewood Cliffs, N.J.: Prentice-Hall, 1959.

U.S. Department of Agriculture. *Outdoors USA*. 1967 Yearbook. Washington, D.C.: U.S. Government Printing Office.

U.S. Department of the Interior. *Federal Outdoor Recreation Programs*. Washington, D.C.: U.S. Government Printing Office, 1970.

12

teacher and leadership preparation

The thesis set forth in this book is that outdoor education is an emphasis in education and a way of learning. This principle makes it necessary to study all phases of teacher and leadership preparation that are in any way related to outdoor education. To make any significant contribution to the improvement of leadership in outdoor education, there are two possible approaches to be considered: (1) to include appropriate courses, activities, and adaptations to existing offerings in one department; and (2) to follow an interdisciplinary approach. It is the opinion of the authors that the interdisciplinary approach to teacher and leadership preparation for outdoor education is the most effective, if not the only, way to assure that outdoor education will become an integral part of the educative process. If the major responsibility for preparing teachers and leaders for outdoor education should rest with one department, there still should be cooperation with other departments that have related interests lest the program be limited and segmented.

In view of the apparent advantages of the interdisciplinary approach it seems appropriate to elaborate further on procedures necessary to develop an adequate program. Unlike most phases of education, teacher and leadership preparation in outdoor education will require little by way of new courses and activities, but much in adjustment within the existing curriculum. Even more effort will be needed in securing cooperation and coordination of all departments and schools that have a concern in outdoor education.

The most basic problem is to provide adequate preparation for all classroom teachers who may in any way be involved in using the outdoors as a laboratory or in teaching outdoor skills and activities. One of the basic premises is that all teachers and leaders in outdoor education should be competent to teach wherever the learning environment is best, including the outdoors. In addition to the preparation needed for all teachers, consideration must be given to special areas and to the administration and coordination of outdoor education programs. Leadership preparation will involve both in-service and pre-service training at the graduate and undergraduate levels.

THE PROBLEM

Since modern life and education tend to be moving farther away from experiences close to nature, any change in the educational system to include outdoor education must be accompanied, if not preceded, by teacher and leadership preparation. The problem in improving this preparation in colleges and universities is similar in many respects to that encountered in initiating a program of outdoor education at the local level. The college classrooms, like those in schools, too often consist of barren walls; and the schedules and routines on a crowded campus make field work extremely difficult. Such difficulties can be and are being offset now by some institutions which have secured field campuses and larger blocks of time for field experiences.

For the most part, educational institutions now have, and will have in the future, most of the resources in leadership and facilities necessary for adequate preparation of leadership in outdoor education. The major problem will be an all-campus approach to provide the necessary experiences in the appropriate departments, courses, and activities. Among the criteria to be considered in analyzing courses and activities with respect to their potential for outdoor education are:

1. Do they offer opportunities to understand children, human growth and development, and the nature of learning?
2. Will they give insights as to what potential learning situations are encountered in an outdoor setting?
3. Will there be opportunities to gain competency in the interpreta-

tion of the outdoors in all seasons and in all types of topography, such as a woodland, swamps, and water areas?

4. Does the institution offer opportunities for field experience in courses and activities such as science, social studies, physical education and recreation?

5. Are teaching techniques and methods for outdoor experiences used and taught in teacher and leadership preparation?

6. Are there provisions for student teaching and intern experiences in outdoor programs where there are opportunities to work with children?

7. After analyzing the existing offerings of an institution, what new courses need to be added to constitute a complete program of preparation for outdoor education?

8. Are there adequate facilities and land areas available to the institution that may be used as outdoor laboratories?

THE INTERDISCIPLINARY APPROACH

Since outdoor education cannot be regarded as a subject matter area, but rather as an interpretation of many subjects and disciplines through the use of the outdoors, teacher and leadership preparation must be concerned with many areas in higher education institutions. This means that professional preparation cannot be provided within a single department or college, and flexibility should be comparable to that found in local programs.

All appropriate resources in the college or university should be utilized to provide a broad background for the many patterns of outdoor education. Some of the subject matter areas include botany, biology, astronomy, zoology, geology, anthropology, psychology, education, physical education, recreation, conservation, fisheries and wildlife, sociology, and arts and crafts. The major advantages of this approach are that the existing resources of all departments involved will be effectively utilized, thus avoiding duplication; students with many interests and backgrounds may get preparation in outdoor education through the department in which they have chosen a major; each department can make the necessary adaptations, to include outdoor education; and departments can serve each other, keeping courses in their proper settings and making necessary adjustments to meet students' interests and needs.

To make the interdisciplinary approach function, the creation of an interdepartmental council or coordinating committee is desirable.

Each department concerned should be represented. One department which has major responsibility for outdoor education may be selected to house one or more staff members to serve the council and to facilitate the campus-wide participation in the development of effective programs for teacher and leadership preparation. Some of the functions of the council include: inventory the resources of the college or university for outdoor education and assist in the development of the interdisciplinary plan for the institution; assist the individual departments in analyzing their own offerings and in developing appropriate courses and activities to fit into the all-campus plan; facilitate the development of relationships with the field for consultant services, off-campus courses, and in-service education; and acquire and develop any such facilities as field campuses, camps, or outdoor laboratories. If a department to house the leadership for the interdisciplinary plan has not been selected prior to the formation of the council, an important function of the council then would be to help decide this matter. In many instances, cooperative enterprises of this type have been stifled by the aggression of departments seeking to build empires. It is very important in outdoor education that all departments have opportunities to make their unique contributions.

Traditionally, health, physical education, and recreation departments have had a major role in outdoor skills and sports, while the physical sciences have had more concern with the outdoors as a laboratory and with the conservation implications of outdoor education. Social studies, arts and crafts, and music have peculiar roles related to all phases of outdoor education. It is important that the selection of the department with the coordinating function be made with the consent of those involved, and that each seek to make its unique contribution to the students and to serve the other departments that are involved in the campus plan for cooperative action.

A PLAN FOR TEACHER PREPARATION IN OUTDOOR EDUCATION THROUGH THE INTERDISCIPLINARY APPROACH

The experience of the University of Northern Colorado at Greeley in establishing a program for teacher education and leadership training in outdoor education will illustrate some of the major considerations and procedures that may be employed through the interdisciplinary approach. The institution has a record for being sensitive to the needs in teacher education, and when interest in outdoor education began to develop, steps were taken to move forward in the preparation of

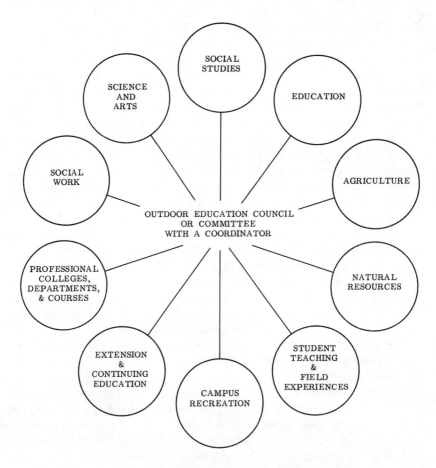

OUTDOOR EDUCATION IN COLLEGES AND UNIVERSITIES

An Interdisciplinary Approach

for Teacher and Leadership Preparation

teachers and leaders for schools and agencies. Interested staff members had participated in a regional Outdoor Education Workshop sponsored by the Outdoor Education Project of the AAHPER, and in conference with other members of the faculty discussed the matter with the administration. Subsequently, a committee was appointed to study the matter and make recommendations for a course of action. One of the first important steps was a workshop of deans, department heads, and other staff members having a major concern in outdoor education. The implications of outdoor education for existing courses and activities were discussed, which helped interpret the broad nature of outdoor education and identify the contributions of the various disciplines and departments. One faculty member was given time to work with the staff committee, prepare materials, and help implement the recommendations of the faculty as approved by the president.

A ten-day workshop in outdoor education was conducted at the beginning of the summer session, involving the departments of health, physical education and recreation, science, and others. This workshop helped determine the needs of teachers in the various fields and explored ways of relating subject matter to learning in the outdoors.

From the beginning, the faculty felt that a location or "home base" for spearheading outdoor education should be in a department having a major concern in education, such as the College of Education. The introduction of outdoor education into the general education program, as well as in the professional education program, could be realized with greater ease than in one of the more specialized subject matter fields. The subject matter areas were not excluded from the emphasis on outdoor education in the education program. Their inclusion drew attention to the fact that the approach in outdoor education is interdisciplinary in nature. Many subject matter areas have a body of materials or information which are significant to outdoor education. This approach verified the idea that outdoor education cuts across all subject matter lines. It further verified the principle that subject matter should be taught where it can best be taught, whether it be indoors or outdoors or in science, art, music, physical education, humanities, or any other discipline.

Attention was turned to specific suggestions for curriculum modification of the teacher education program for elementary, junior high, and high school teachers. Some of the suggestions for the purpose of increasing the use of the out-of-doors as a resource in teaching were:

1. Consider what is known about child growth and development and apply it to teaching. Modify teaching methods to use the out-of-doors when it is most effective in learning.
2. Recognize that the out-of-doors constitutes a laboratory for teaching where there is a living body of subject matter, and that it should be used.
3. Recognize that the method of using the out-of-doors in teaching is more real and meaningful than using abstractions and vicarious experiences.
4. Use the subject matter contained within books in conjunction with the resources found out-of-doors.

5. Consider the basic outdoor skills that are characteristic of the age group and that will be essential for the prospective teacher. Provide, through the various departments, some experiences that will help the teacher to achieve the broad general background necessary to offer important outdoor skills.

6. Provide, through the various departments, elective courses, such as group dynamics, social studies, and ecology, that will contribute to a broad general background for the teacher. This will probably be more important than mastery of skills. An interested, competent person with a good background of experience will soon develop basic skills.

7. If possible, provide a natural outdoor area which can be used by the sciences, arts, physical education, and other subject matter fields so that outdoor experiences may be provided during the training period of the prospective teacher.

8. Encourage students, through clubs and organizations, to spend as much time as possible learning about the outdoor environment in which they could effectively teach.

9. Use the out-of-doors to teach skills for leisure-time pursuits.

The identification of existing or possible activities having implications for outdoor education is a detailed process, but a few examples will illustrate some that were listed by the committee.

arts

The Division of the Arts has a significant contribution to make to the broad area of outdoor education:

1. Lapidary activities—rock collecting, identification, cutting and polishing.

2. Woodcraft—use of native materials in woodcraft; identification of trees, showing the relationship between trees in their native state and their use as craft and building material; survival skills relative to woodcraft.

3. Art as a recreational activity.

4. Outdoor cooking and campfire cooking—with the increased activity in outdoor living, family camping, and outdoor cooking, home economics has a distinct contribution to make; survival cooking is also important.

health and physical education

Health, like the arts, needs to be a part of every subject and there are many specific courses already offered in the curriculum. The field of physical education has much to offer:

1. Life saving and water safety
2. Orienteering
3. Canoeing, boating, motor boating
4. Shooting
5. Casting
6. Archery
7. Camping
8. Skiing
9. Dancing—square and folk
10. Survival skills

The courses listed above can be offered on either a service course basis for one-hour credit, or two or three activities could be combined as a two- or three-hour course. Many of these skills can be better conducted outside a classroom or gymnasium, thus making the activity more feasible and less expensive to the institution.

humanities

The area of humanities has an excellent opportunity to provide instruction which is pertinent to outdoor education, and many important outdoor-related activities can be effectively conducted under the leadership of the teachers of the humanities. This area can provide experiences emphasizing the relationship of the out-of-doors to literature and poetry. Suggested activities include:

1. Creative writing—about outdoor experiences or about the out-of-doors in general.
2. Interpreting the significance of the out-of-doors as revealed in poetry.
3. Storytelling—tall tales and folklore.

sciences

The science area has much to offer in teaching prospective teachers about the out-of-doors. Suggested courses:

1. Botany
2. Biology
3. Zoology
4. Geology
5. Entomology
6. Ornithology
7. Conservation—land, trees, water, and wildlife

Within these courses there are many specific experiences that may be used to apply the field of science to a study of the outdoors:

1. Nature trail study
2. Rock collections
3. Leaf collections
4. Insect collections
5. Weather study—study of cloud formations
6. Survival activities—a study of edible plants and animals; purification of water; protection from animals, insects, and the elements
7. Map and compass activity
8. Orienteering

music

The following are some examples of music activities that can be related to the outdoors:

1. Campfire singing—reflecting different periods in our history
2. Nature songs—appreciation of nature through music
3. Camp bands—using improvised instruments
4. Action singing—using motions to describe the words being sung

social studies

The social studies division has a distinct contribution to make to outdoor education. Most activities in outdoor education have an intangible relationship to the social studies. The human interrelationships that occur in outdoor settings are of extreme significance to outdoor education.

1. Group dynamics
2. Anthropology
3. History of the area—local, state, or regional

After considering the contributions of the various subject areas to teacher and leadership preparation in outdoor education, the committee determined the needs for additional experiences and recommended the addition of only a few courses, largely for orientation in the outdoors. These were placed in the departments of health, physical education and recreation, and science.

As time went on, necessary modifications and additions have been made. The experience of this institution is significant because the interdisciplinary approach to outdoor education was employed from the beginning, thus avoiding contention and duplication of efforts by faculty members and departments.

GRADUATE PREPARATION IN OUTDOOR EDUCATION

An undergraduate program of teacher and leadership preparation should make it possible for all elementary and many secondary school teachers to have some experiences in outdoor education. Graduate work should provide opportunities for more extensive and intensive preparation for those in positions of administrative leadership in outdoor education in schools and colleges.

The essentials in a program for the preparation of leadership should include: a greater understanding of human growth and the learning process; the ability to use the outdoors as a learning laboratory; techniques and understanding needed for teaching in informal outdoor settings; skills and appreciations for enjoying the outdoors; and a knowledge of curriculum instruction and school administration. The courses and experiences needed to achieve these essential qualities would involve education, the physical and social sciences, conservation, sociology, and social work. At the graduate level, especially, it is most desirable to tailor the offerings in outdoor education in accordance with the previous training and experience of the individual.

An example of this approach will be found at Michigan State University, where outdoor education is considered an area of emphasis. The course work and activities related to outdoor education are interwoven into the candidate's major field. For example, a student with an undergraduate background in science would need more of his graduate experiences in education, such as educational psychology, child growth and development, and physical education. Similarly, a student majoring in the field of physical education would require more work in science, conservation, and general education courses. All would need field experiences in resident outdoor education programs and other outdoor settings. A few special courses, preferably of a workshop nature, combining an interpretation of the outdoors, teaching techniques, and patterns of outdoor education should be provided. Such is the case at Michigan State University where the College of Education conducts off-campus courses in outdoor education and a two-week summer workshop for pre-service and in-service preparation of teachers and leaders.

The interdisciplinary pattern for outdoor education, therefore, implies that all the appropriate offerings on a campus should be included in planning a series of experiences that will help all teachers and others interested to make the best use of the outdoors for learning. Wherever possible, existing courses in the various disciplines can be adapted to meet the growing trend for teacher preparation for outdoor education. A minimum number of new courses should be added, as needed, by the appropriate departments.

This pattern for graduate education for outdoor education presupposes that a single prescribed course of study cannot be established, nor should outdoor education be regarded as a major curriculum. Flexibility makes it possible for several established major areas to include outdoor education as an area of emphasis. Usually, the required dissertation would be on some aspect of outdoor education, thereby giving additional opportunity for the candidate to pursue more intensive study in a particular phase of the field.

FIELD EXPERIENCES IN OUTDOOR EDUCATION

Innovations in teacher and leadership preparation may be needed in the field experiences provided in undergraduate and graduate education. Such opportunities may include: field trips in all appropriate courses, such as educational methods, physical sciences, and those related to outdoor interpretation; student teaching in centers where there are outdoor education programs; field experience off campus for recreation and youth leaders; and internships.

field investigations in college courses

One of the major difficulties in applying subject matter to teaching situations is the lack of field experience. Not only do prospective teachers and leaders need more assistance in using subject matter in the problem-solving approach, they should participate in direct experiences under the supervision of skillful college teachers. Too often the adage "Teachers teach first as they are taught last" is true of those who have been subjected to poor teaching in the college or university. Field courses in science, conservation, and environmental studies, particularly, are needed to help teachers interpret the outdoors to elementary and secondary school students. The same is true of educational methods and curriculum courses that need to be extended to life situations where children are learning in an outdoor setting. Not only do prospective teachers gain information about how learning takes place, they see children in quite a different perspective in a camp or on a field trip. Likewise, outdoor skills and sports courses should provide maximum opportunities for participation. There is little chance that a teacher will be competent or enthusiastic about outdoor education unless there has been some learning experience in the outdoors during the pre-service education.

Colleges and universities have used the outdoors to varying degrees for many years as instructional laboratories and for conducting educational activities. Outdoor experiences of these kinds have been used in subject areas such as science and social studies in regular college courses, and in the preparation of teachers and leaders for specific fields such as science, elementary and secondary education, physical education, camp counseling, and recreation.

The kinds of outdoor experiences associated with the curricula of colleges and universities may be classified generally as follows: (1) the use of the outdoors as a laboratory for subject courses such as science and social studies; (2) field experiences in camps, biological stations, and other outdoor facilities as prerequisites to professional study in forestry, fisheries and wildlife, park management, and others; (3) instruction in outdoor skills and recreational activities through the use of outdoor areas in physical education, outdoor education, and recreation classes; and (4) campus recreation.

Many prospective teachers and leaders get some educational experiences in the outdoors through one or more of the above categories. Whether the major purpose of the outdoor venture is to gain intimate knowledge of flora and fauna, to gain skills related to the outdoors, or for recreational purposes only, it is axiomatic that lasting interests in the outdoors are developed and cultivated. A general description of the nature of courses and activities that involve the outdoors, with specific examples, willl illustrate the great potential for the preparation of teachers and leaders for outdoor education.

THE USE OF THE OUTDOORS FOR LABORATORY COURSES

Laboratory experiences are usually conducted through short field trips, excursions, and mobile classrooms. A wide variety of outdoor areas are used, depending on the nature and purposes of the trip and the outdoor resources available. The range and nature of the studies are illustrated by the following samples: cruises for the study of marine biology; science study of bogs, forests, and agricultural areas; geological explorations; ecology and land management; surveys of soil; game management; field work in entomology; ornithology; landscaping; art; surveying; and numerous other special areas of investigation.

Outdoor experiences of this type are usually well planned and closely related to the subject matter involved. Frequently trips include camping experiences in national and state parks and forests, and other opportunities for outdoor recreation activities.

FIELD EXPERIENCES IN CAMPS, BIOLOGICAL STATIONS, AND OTHER OUTDOOR FACILITIES, AS A PART OF THE PROFESSIONAL PREPARATION FOR TEACHERS AND LEADERS IN OUTDOOR EDUCATION AND RELATED FIELDS

An increasing number of colleges and universities are now acquiring outdoor areas in which to conduct required courses and field experiences in the biological sciences, natural resources, park management, teacher education, and other fields. These land areas and facilities constitute field campuses and in some instances are so designated. Usually students are in residence for periods ranging from one to twelve weeks. In addition to the technical studies and intensive field work, opportunities are offered in outdoor sports, individual outdoor interests, and hobbies.

The facilities used for this type of field experiences fall into several categories, such as biological stations, camps, outdoor centers, environmental studies areas, field campuses, and conservation schools. These field and off-campus experiences include formal credit courses, workshops, individual and group research projects, and extension courses. A brief description of the nature of the educational experiences will illustrate the diversity of the outdoor knowledge and skills involved.

Biological stations. The major purpose of a biological station is to provide appropriate settings in which study, field work, and research in the biological sciences may be combined. They are usually operated during the summer months for periods of six to twelve weeks and often house 50 to 100 college students in residence. Such course offerings as the following are usually available: botany, ecology, taxonomy, field entomology, limnology, research in fisheries and wildlife, geography, parasitology, microbiology, teaching methods in science, ornithology, zoology, and ichthyology.

Camps, outdoor centers, and field campuses. There has been a rapid increase in the number of colleges and universities that have acquired camps, outdoor centers, field campuses, and other outdoor facilities to be used for field work, research, and outdoor living activities. The trend is toward the more extensive use of such facilities by all disciplines and departments in institutions of higher education. In New York State, for example, most of the Colleges of the State University have camps or other outdoor areas.

Conservation schools. Several colleges and universities cooperate with state conservation departments in offering credit and noncredit courses and in-service education activities in science and conservation. A number of states conduct summer conservation laboratories for teachers, which offer broad opportunities to develop outdoor skills and interests.

instruction in outdoor skills and recreational activities in health, physical education, and recreation

This category of outdoor learning opportunities in colleges and universities is most directly related to outdoor recreation and has a significant impact on the increased use of outdoor resources for the future. More than 600 colleges and universities offer professional preparation in health, physical education, and recreation, and most of the remaining 1,500 or more colleges and universities have offerings in these areas as required service courses or as electives. It is estimated that camping and outdoor education courses are available in most of the institutions that have majors in health, physical education, and recreation, and many of the others provide opportunities for camp counselor training. A majority of the 600 colleges and universities have access to or own camps or other outdoor facilities, which are used for field experiences in the outdoors and outdoor recreational activities. One of the usual patterns is to require all physical education and recreation majors to have a resident experience in camp. In addition, field trips, outings, and weekend trips are available in a large number of colleges and universities.

The nature of the outdoor-related activities associated with health, physical education, and recreation is broad and diverse. Some of the more common outdoor sports are usually taught—small craft and water activities, casting and angling, shooting and firearms safety, skiing, and archery. Other camping and outdoor skills are offered depending on the section of the country and the availability of resources and facilities. Some of these offerings include camp crafts and nature lore, use of map and compass, lapidary activities, mountain climbing, riding, skin and scuba diving, packing, and caravan camping.

Many colleges and universities in recent years have established graduate and undergraduate summer outdoor education workshops which are usually held in college or publicly owned camps. These are designed largely for in-service education and are available to teachers and youth leaders who are interested in the development of outdoor activities in their own institutions.

CAMPUS RECREATION

Colleges and universities are now giving much more attention to recreational opportunities for students on campus. The programs are often administered by intramural departments or college unions; in a number of instances staff members are assigned to give leadership to campus recreation. Student services departments, religious centers, fraternities, sororities, and youth agencies also are providing opportunities for student participation in recreational activities. Outdoor pursuits are prominent and popular with students in these programs. Many institutions have outing clubs which provide a wide range of activities for students, including hiking, boating, shooting, mountain climbing, and winter sports. Some of the outdoor resources and facilities described above are used for campus recreation as well as for instruction.

It is believed that campus recreation will become increasingly available and that outdoor recreation will constitute an important part of this type of program.

student teaching

In recent years, student teaching has undergone some much needed changes, resulting in more meaningful and effective experiences for prospective teachers and leaders. One significant change is a plan whereby those planning to teach spend a term or semester in a community. In addition to student teaching, the student participates in school and civic life as a resident of the community and under the supervision of a college staff member who usually holds a formal appointment with the college and the local school system. If the school system involved has a good outdoor education program in which the student teacher can participate, this is near ideal in preparing for future teaching. Such is the case in Battle Creek, Michigan —Michigan State University students assigned to the student teaching center spend a week at the Battle Creek Outdoor Education Center participating in the resident outdoor education experience. Another plan is for the student teacher to spend a short time in a resident program or comparable activity in addition to the regular student teaching assignment. A number of colleges and universities now have plans of this general type.

An example of a Department of Outdoor Teacher Education is at Northern Illinois University where students majoring in elementary education have successive outdoor education experiences at the University's Lorado Taft Field Campus. A block plan in which students meet with one instructor from two to four hours a day makes it possible for them to spend considerable time in planning classes and preparing for the experiences at the Field Campus.

The first part of this field plan takes place during the sophomore year, when the students spend a two-and-a-half-day period at the Field Campus studying the use of the outdoors as a laboratory for learning. There is an attempt to develop an awareness of the outdoors as an extension of the classroom. The major focus is on analyzing the nature of the learning process by having students examine their own reactions when involved in learning in an outdoor setting.

The second phase of the program is for elementary education majors in their junior year. Three days are spent at the Field Campus investigating subject areas of the elementary curriculum and supplementing these content subjects with firsthand observations and direct experiences. This is done in cooperation with the resident outdoor education program in operation at the Field Campus. The final experience occurs in the senior year, when the seniors spend a week in the camp, living with and teaching a class of elementary pupils from a school which uses the Field Campus for an outdoor classroom experience.

Prior to the third experience, the prospective elementary teachers spend time setting up objectives, becoming familiar with the operation of outdoor classrooms, and preparing for their teaching in the outdoor laboratory. Many of the college students have the additional experience of visiting in advance the classroom with which they will work in the camp setting. During the week with the children at camp, the college students live through all the experiences—eating, sleeping, and a wide variety of program activities. They participate with the children in the evaluation of the learning that takes place and often keep anecdotal records and do sociometric studies. The final important activity is a visit to the class after the return to the school in order to see the follow-up activities and observe tangible results of the outdoor classroom experience.

These three related experiences go far in helping teachers use the outdoors as an effective learning situation.

internship in outdoor education

The internship is beginning to have wide use in the preparation of teachers and administrators. Such a plan has significance for outdoor education because it provides a longer period of training in an established program. There are internships for graduate and undergraduate students in a number of institutions. The periods usually are for a term or semester, except for administration, which are often longer.

IN-SERVICE EDUCATION

In-service education is an immediate answer for schools, colleges, and agencies that desire to initiate outdoor education programs. Since any new outdoor activities will be a part of, or related to, existing courses and programs, much of the leadership must come from staff members and personnel already employed in the school or agency. Much is being done in in-service education at all levels—local, state, and national. Some general and specific patterns and programs are described that will illustrate some of the effective in-service education programs.

local

Local schools and organizations can do much to prepare teachers and leaders for outdoor education. Some of the more common patterns include:

1. *Study committees.* These may be voluntary or appointed by an administrator. The committees collect information and materials, gather data, inventory available community resources, and recommend procedures. Some schools and organizations have outdoor education committees representative of administrators, teachers, community leaders, and students, which are effective in interpreting, planning and formulating programs.

2. *Local workshops and clinics.* It is very important for those who

are to be involved in outdoor education activities to have firsthand experiences in an outdoor setting. Well-planned workshops and clinics in camps, parks, and other types of outdoor areas are effective in identifying learning opportunities and in creating confidence and interest in the outdoor laboratory. Well-chosen consultants and resource leaders can be of great assistance in exploring the local opportunities for outdoor education and developing competencies on the part of teachers and leaders. Field trips, outdoor cooking, native arts and crafts, and skills clinics lend much to the interest and enthusiasm of a staff.

3. *Off-campus courses and summer workshops.* Many colleges and universities in cooperation with state departments of education and conservation agencies and other organizations concerned with outdoor education, now offer opportunities for local teachers and agency leaders to gain information and competencies related to outdoor learning and living. Such in-service education opportunities may be offered in local communities, camp and park facilities, or in outdoor centers operated by institutions and agencies. Several universities now provide these opportunities upon the request of school systems or communities.

state and regional

An increasing number of in-service training workshops and conferences are conducted on a state, area, or regional basis by colleges and universities. Some are for short periods, while others are more extensive and offer credit. A number of state conservation departments conduct summer laboratories and workshops, many of which have scholarships available for selected teachers and leaders. Camping and recreation agencies and professional education organizations also conduct workshops, clinics, and conferences dealing with programing and facilities.

national

Each year more opportunities for in-service education are available through professional organizations, private associations, and governmental agencies. There are many special emphases, such as conservation, parks and recreation, camping, science, and outdoor sports. Many of these are held in outdoor areas with excellent facilities—state parks, conservation training schools, biological stations, ranches, and mountain lodges. Nationally known consultants and specialists assist in "on-the-ground" experience. Several well-known programs are briefly described.

Michigan State University Summer Outdoor Education Workshop. The workshop is sponsored by MSU in cooperation with the Outdoor Education Project of the American Association for Health, Physical Education, and Recreation, and is held at an outdoor center or camp. It has become national in character, with many states represented each summer. The workshop offers graduate credit, and is one of the few workshops that encompass all aspects of outdoor education, including outdoor interpretation, resident outdoor education programs, conservation and environmental studies activities, and outdoor skills. School and college administrators and teachers, state department of education personnel, conservationists, and recreation and youth leaders attend the workshop. The major purpose is to assist the participants in planning outdoor education programs for their own institutions and agencies and in preparing curriculum materials for courses and activities.

Bradford Woods Summer Session, Indiana University. At Bradford Woods, a variety of outdoor education, recreation, and conservation courses are offered which attract leaders from many states. The facility and area, with several camps operating during the summer, provide a wide range of opportunities for study, field trips, and observations in many aspects of outdoor education.

Audubon Camp. The National Audubon Society conducts several regional camps during the summer months for teachers, youth leaders, and others with a professional or avocational interest in nature and conservation. The camps are in Maine, Connecticut, Wisconsin, and California.

American Camping Association. From time to time, the Association has sponsored national or regional workshops and consultation conferences for camp leaders and others interested in the outdoors. Workshops have been held on conservation in camping, facilities, arts and crafts, and other special interests.

The Outdoor Education Project of the AAHPER. This Project, national in scope, represents one of the most extensive efforts in outdoor education. Prompted by the need for better leadership in teaching skills, attitudes, and appreciations for a better use and understanding of the outdoors for modern living, the AAHPER initiated the Outdoor Education Project in 1955. Following the effective pattern in cooperative programs by business-industry-education, some of the trade associations and industries concerned with the manufacture of outing and outdoor sports equipment made grants of funds available to carry forward the venture.

The Outdoor Education Project has been a cooperative enterprise from the beginning. In additon to industry groups that make grants, many other organizations have worked with the Association in achieving the Project's objectives. They include other departments and affiliates of the National Education Association, the National Rifle Association, the American Casting Association, state departments of education, conservation agencies, and schools and colleges. A National Advisory Committee, widely representative of school and college administrators and groups interested in outdoor education, helped guide the efforts of the project in the early years. The major activities of the Project may be categorized as follows.

1. **Leadership training.** Workshops and clinics are conducted in nearly all the regions of the United States for school, college, and agency leaders interested in developing outdoor education activities in their own institutions and organizations. The workshops are planned by state and regional committees working cooperatively with the Project staff. State agencies (such as departments of education and conservation), professional organizations, schools, colleges and universities, and interested individuals have joined in the planning and execution of the workshops. The three-day sessions feature discussions, clinics, and demonstrations covering the broad areas of outdoor education, with special emphasis on the leading outdoor pursuits.

2. **Interpretation and program development.** Through conferences, visitations, and materials, the nature and scope of outdoor education is interpreted to school and college administrators and teachers, and to leaders of community and youth agencies. Assistance is given in the initiation and development of outdoor education programs.

3. **Instructional materials.** Available materials in outdoor education are distributed by the AAHPER and many resource agencies. New publications are developed and distributed by the AAHPER. Some of the major ones include **Casting and Angling** (1958); **Shooting and Hunting** (1960); **Marksmanship for Young Shooters** (1960); and **Archery** (1972).

Evaluation of the Project's efforts indicate that educational programs throughout the nation have been expanded and enriched through outdoor education. It is a timely and sound venture because outdoor activities which are stressed find their appropriate places in the curriculum and contribute toward the accepted objectives of education.

Reference is made in other chapters to in-service and pre-service training in relation to specific outdoor activities. With respect to leadership in outdoor education, it appears that developments, particularly in in-service education, are keeping pace with the needs and demands of the time.

SUGGESTIONS FOR FURTHER STUDY AND RESEARCH

1. Suggest the essentials in a graduate program of study for preparing an outdoor education specialist, using the multidisciplinary approach.
2. What type of courses and activities would be appropriate at the undergraduate level in helping to prepare elementary teachers for outdoor education in the area of physical education? Recreation? Science?
3. Outline an in-service education program in outdoor education for a school (grades K through 12), and for a recreation department.

REFERENCES

American Association for Health, Physical Education and Recreation, *Leisure and the Schools.* Washington, D.C.: AAHPER, 1961.

————, *Outdoor Education for American Youth*, Chapter IV. Washington, D.C.: AAHPER, 1957.

————, Report of the Conference on Professional Preparation for Health, Physical Education and Recreation, 1962.

Combs, Arthur W., *The Professional Education of Teachers.* Boston: Allyn and Bacon, 1965.

Corbin, H. Dan, *Recreation Leadership*, 2nd ed. Englewood Cliffs, N.J.: Prentice-Hall, Inc., 1959.

Cyphers, Vincent A., "A Study to Determine the Significant Outdoor Experiences for Elementary Teachers." Unpublished Ed. D. dissertation, Colorado State College, 1961.

Hug, John Wallace, "Analysis of the Factors Which Influence Elementary Teachers in the Utilization of Outdoor Instructional Activities." Unpublished D.Re. dissertation, Indiana University, 1964.

V

planning for
outdoor education

13

plans for action

The initiation of outdoor education activities and programs in a community is a phase of the broader process of curriculum improvement and community development. Since outdoor education relates to all the learning experiences in and for the outdoors and cuts across disciplines, departments, and a myriad of community agencies, the usual procedure in modifying, adapting, or enriching any phase of the curriculum program should be followed. When a community plans for action in outdoor education, programing should be done in terms of those to be served—children, youth, or adults. A program plan should be made for the community with continuous adjustments to suit the individuals or groups involved.

PLANNING FOR OUTDOOR EDUCATION PROGRAMS

Program planning for outdoor education should be consistent with good curriculum practice and program development, as in any other phase of an educational enterprise. Planning must occur prior to and during the initiation of a new program and should involve all those persons directly affected with the program that is being designed. In the school curriculum for grades K-12, for example, students of the various grade levels, teachers, administrators, parents, and laymen should be represented on planning committees or councils for outdoor education. Such planning bodies should be given appropriate responsibilities to make decisions and to help guide the development of the program. Some of the essential steps in planning include:

1. Identification of specific needs, problems, and interests of the children and adults in the community for which the outdoor education program is designed.
2. Inventory of the resources in the community by way of leadership, facilities, and materials that are already available.
3. Study and investigations of similar developments in outdoor education which will include on-site visitations of innovative programs, assembling a library of publications and audio-visual resources pertaining to the various aspects of outdoor education.
4. Design and propose a plan for an outdoor education program, immediate and long range, based on needs, resources available, and appropriately related to and consistent with general educational objectives and the curriculum design of the school.
5. Develop a plan to inform and persuade those in formal and informal positions of leadership, including opinion leaders in the school system and community, of the worth of an outdoor education program. The legitimization and sanction by such leaders are important phases of the change process in the adoption of a new program.
6. Select for pilot efforts one or more classrooms or schools in the district where there is already interest and readiness on the part of students, teachers and parents. This is another important phase of the change process and should precede the full-scale operation of an extensive program, particularly when major changes in the administrative structure of the school are involved.
7. Set the stage for interpretation and evaluation of the pilot efforts for formulating the long range plan of action to be submitted to the policy determining and administrative groups.
8. Plan for an effective in-service education program of the school staff and resource leaders who will be involved in the program. In-service education should be a continuous process prior to and during the operation of a new program. Some of the ingredients of a good in-service education program include:

a. A study by committees and through staff sessions of the potentials of outdoor education in the subject areas and activities of existing school programs. This procedure helps give the teacher a "stake" in outdoor education.

b. On-site workshops and conferences at the locations to be used in the various outdoor education activities.

c. Staff visitations to good programs that are under way.

d. Participation in outdoor education workshops that are conducted by colleges and universities, state departments of education, professional education organizations, and other agencies.

e. In-service education and institutes sponsored by one or more interested school districts in cooperation with colleges, universities, and other agencies.

f. Attendance by teachers at state and national workshops and conferences concerned with outdoor education and related areas.

g. Graduate work with outdoor education as an area of emphasis.

Sustained and thorough planning together with continuous evaluation will assure quality outdoor education as an integral part of the comprehensive educational program.

COMMUNITY IMPROVEMENT

The benefits and values of outdoor education at any age level, in any educational organization can be achieved most effectively through a community action program seeking to improve learning and the quality of the environment for those who live within its boundaries. If learning and living experiences in the outdoors are to be made possible for all who seek them, the cooperation of all community agencies, public and private, is essential in order to provide the learning activities, the opportunities for participation, and the facilities.

The community school, referred to in preceding chapters, is often the agency that gives impulse to a planned program of community development. Whether the stimulus comes from the school, another community agency, or through a cooperative and coordinated effort of several organizations, the community school has an important role in the process.

Community development for outdoor education is particularly significant now because of the increasing difficulty in securing adequate lands for parks and outdoor facilities. Many new schools are being constructed which require larger sites, and it is important that the need for space be considered by both public and voluntary agencies. A park-school plan, for example, would be an effective, economically sound development in many communities. In a park-school, the school district and municipality join together in the purchase of land suitable for a school site and a park. The board of education may purchase only enough land for buildings, leaving the remaining acreage for a park which would be maintained by the park commission of the municipality or township, but used by the schools and public. Another possible park-school plan is that the municipality would own the entire acreage and give the board of education a long-term lease of a sufficient acreage for the buildings. Under this arrangement, the school buildings are designed to serve the park area by providing dressing rooms, equipment storage, and toilet facilities. The park commission usually maintains the entire site, while the board of education is responsible for the buildings. Grand Rapids, Michigan, has a successful park-school arrangement in several sections of the city. It began in the early 1950s under the leadership of Frederick C. See, Superintendent of Parks, who cited the following advantages of the plan:

1. The school board can have more funds available to spend for its buildings and include facilities for community recreation because of reduced land requirements. The school can be located in, or adjacent to, areas belonging to the park or other city-owned departments where only a few acres will have to be acquired to add to existing city-owned land in order to obtain the desirable ten acres for a park-school. In certain sections of the city the park department will have to acquire properties to satisfy the need for playgrounds and play fields, and if these locations coincide with the need for a school it is possible to save capital in the acquisition of land by buying separately and developing these areas jointly. Neither party will have to acquire as much as would be needed for separate individual departments.

2. The park department does not have to build field or community houses and can spend its funds on . . . ground improvements.

3. With the school maintaining the buildings and the park authorities maintaining the grounds, there is no duplication of maintenance crews or equipment, thereby reducing annual corporate expenses. These savings can be used for improved services and facilities.

4. Assessed valuations in the immediate vicinity of park-schools

are not affected adversely to the same degree as property values near a school having a small school yard. Surveys indicate that property values adjacent to schools depreciate considerably. Existing valuations in the immediate vicinity of park-schools can be stabilized and in many instances actually increased.

5. From the recreation point of view, the transition from school to play is negligible. The association between education and recreation among children and adults is unified.

6. The park-school area does much to focus the center of public interest on a single area and enables the park authorities, schools, and recreation department to present a larger, more attractive, and more efficient unit to the community, thereby reducing tax requirements and also taxpayers' objections to taxes for essential facilities and services.[1]

The advantages of a park-school to a community outdoor education program are many. A sufficient acreage of land, part of which can be used as an outdoor laboratory for the schools, recreation department, and community agencies, is an important first step toward such a program. A school and community garden might also be possible, depending on the soil and location of the site.

COMMUNITY CAMPUS

The near-ideal for a community outdoor education program would be a long-range development of what might be termed a *community campus*. Such a plan is based on the premise that a floor of common facilities can and should be provided by the public agencies and supplemented by the voluntary organizations which receive community support. This plan can become a reality only when a community, through a representative group such as a council, determines the educational and recreational needs and designs an economically sound plan for meeting them.

One of the most important steps in the development of a community campus is to plan facilities to avoid duplication and waste and to provide for maximum use by many agencies. For example, there should be clusters of public buildings on adequate sites which would serve the program needs of schools, recreation and park departments, and voluntary agencies. This would make it possible for

[1] From a "Report on Park-Schools," by Frederick C. See, Superintendent of Parks, April 1951. (Mimeographed.)

each to have its own identity in programming, but share many facilities such as gymnasiums, swimming pools, recreation rooms, auditoriums, play areas, arts and crafts studios, outdoor laboratories, camps, farms, and forests.

In a large city, the central cluster would contain the buildings for common use and headquarter offices for the community organizations and agencies. For example, a well-designed building near the center of the city would serve as a school and a community center with all of the indoor facilities needed for the functioning of both (such as some of those listed above); the offices of the board of education, park department, voluntary agencies (such as the YMCA, YWCA, Scouts, Boys' Club) could have their own individual offices in a single or in separate buildings depending on the size of the governmental unit. Other common facilities would be dispersed in various parts of the city, such as neighborhood schools, skating rinks, and parks. On the outer perimeter would be the larger land areas and facilities, many of which could have multiple uses. Camps, parks, recreation areas, forests, museums, zoos, lakes, ponds, streams, and ski slopes would serve the needs of the entire community. There would be only a minimum number of facilities for the sole use and under the control of one agency, and usually these would be for special purposes not conducive to broad use. Beyond the limits of the community are the state and federally owned outdoor areas, such as parks, preserves, reservoirs, group camps, and recreation areas, which can serve the needs of many local units of government.

Most of the nation's communities could have a network of lands and facilities, supplemented by state and federal resources, which could provide for the educational and leisure-time needs of large segments of the population. An effective plan of community development complemented by equally effective planning for schools and community agencies would insure a comprehensive program of outdoor education. All of the varied activities described in this book would be possible with well-prepared teachers and leaders. In fact, many of them could be and are being conducted with limited facilities. It will be only through a well-integrated community plan, however, that all the citizens, young and old, will have maximum opportunities to learn and participate in lifelong activities of their own choosing. There are many communities that have accomplished much in certain phases of outdoor education, but few have undertaken a long-range program for a large area which includes all of the community agencies and organizations. The need for community planning cannot be overemphasized. While segments of a program can be undertaken and conducted successfully, the only way to insure efficiency and economy is to have a master plan in which each segment fits into the pattern.

PILOT PROGRAMS

As has been previously mentioned, the logical, natural approach to initiating a program, small or large, is through pilot or experimental ventures. This is particularly true in public education, which does not have the structure or financial reserve for large-scale experimental operation by individual school districts to test untried methods and procedures.

Pilot efforts in outdoor education, whether funded by federal programs or conducted through local or state resources, have been unusually successful. For example, a large school system, with hundreds of children in one grade level, could seldom find it possible or feasible to undertake a large school program that would encompass the whole grade or grades the first year: it would be difficult to find sufficient facilities and virtually impossible to interpret the value and advantages of such a venture to the parents and the community. Most of the more extensive outdoor classroom developments in school districts have followed a pilot plan, extending it as the need and community support warrant until it becomes an integral and functioning phase of an instructional program. Usually there are facilities to accommodate at least a small pilot effort, making it unnecessary for the school district to expend funds in renting or constructing facilities until there is need and support. Pilot efforts are possible and desirable in most outdoor education patterns, particularly when eventual adoption will require additional staff, equipment, and facilities.

The Elementary and Secondary Education Act of 1965, which funded innovative and exemplary programs, served a pilot function in several areas of the country. A substantial number of the ESEA programs were related to outdoor education and the records indicate that a significant number were continued with local financing after federal funds were discontinued.

An *action-research* program is equally effective and desirable in state and national efforts, particularly when conducted by professional organizations and agencies. In this connection, grants for action-research are often available through public and private sources. An example of an early state project was the experimental outdoor education program conducted by the Michigan Department of Public Instruction and the Department of Conservation, in cooperation with the W. K. Kellogg Foundation. This effort gave impetus to a more rapid development of outdoor education in Michigan. An example at the national level is the Outdoor Education Project of the American Association for Health, Physical Education and Recreation, a cooperative business-industry-education venture described in Chapter 12.

ADMINISTRATION AND FINANCE FOR
OUTDOOR EDUCATION

In planning for outdoor education, as in all other aspects of the curriculum, careful study and planning need to be given to those parts of the program that will require additional funds for operating costs and capital outlay. Some kinds of outdoor learning, such as the use of outdoor resources in and out of the classroom that require no transportation of students, special equipment or additional staff, will involve little if any extra cost. The exception might be in-service education of teachers and in some instances a few additional instructional materials. The use of outdoor areas as laboratories beyond walking distance of the classroom will require some provision for transportation, usually the school buses. Some schools have fleets of buses and are able to absorb usual transportation costs through the regular budget, the same as is done for excursions, athletic events, and other similar activities. Some schools, colleges, and recreation departments have purchased special buses for such purposes, while others make arrangements for common carriers.

To date, most school districts have not needed to buy land and build facilities for outdoor education because of the availability of parks, camps, outdoor centers, recreation areas, and other public lands and facilities which may be used at no cost or for a minimum fee. In most types of outdoor education, most of the needed equipment, supplies and instructional materials are already available in the various instructional programs such as science, physical education, school shops, and the library.

Like all other aspects of an educational program, additional personnel, if needed, would require the greatest expenditure of funds. Other than resident outdoor education, additional personnel is not usually employed except in larger school districts with extensive programs that may need a part-time or full-time coordinator or director and part-time resource personnel. In many systems, especially in the beginning stages of a program, some responsibility for outdoor education has been given to existing personnel in physical education, science, and other specialties.

Resident outdoor education usually requires more additional financing than other kinds of programs. Consideration was given to the general principles of financing resident programs in Chapter 5. Many school districts and communities have been able to initiate pilot outdoor education programs with little or no additional cost. Others have secured funds through state, federal, and community agencies until such time as outdoor education has been included in the regular budget.

It is impossible to provide accurate information on finances for outdoor education since there are too many variables involved in the many types and sizes of school districts, colleges, and agencies. The best source of information would be active outdoor education programs that are comparable to the program being planned. Hovever, there are a few general principles regarding administration and finance which should be considered when public school outdoor education programs are being designed. Since outdoor education is an integral part of the curriculum, the established school policies relating to professional personnel, transportation, health and safety, equipment, liability, and the like, should pertain to outdoor education. These guidelines are suggested:

1. Personnel: Teachers and administrators, certified by the state, should be responsible for instruction, assisted by resource leaders and paraprofessionals in accordance with school policy.
2. Transportation: The school district should provide the transportation to outdoor areas and facilities; advance arrangements must be made with those responsible for the property to be used.
3. Health and safety: Established school health and safety policies should apply to outdoor education with regard to the services of the school nurses, physical examinations, use of information on health records, and availability of first aid.
4. Land and facilities: Land and facilities needed for outdoor education should be acquired in accordance with school policies relating to the purchase of sites and the construction of other school plant structures with long-range planning for multiple use. If outdoor centers or camps are needed the sites purchased should be, if possible, adjacent to or near public parks and recreation areas which may be used for educational purposes. Outdoor areas and facilities should be designed for year-round use by the community.
5. Organizational patterns: Multi-school district outdoor education programs requiring outdoor areas and facilities should be considered, especially in resident outdoor education. More adequate leadership, programs, and facilities can be provided through a cooperative arrangement with several school districts. With the probable development of the extended school year, an outdoor education center with larger acreage could serve a variety of programs such as field study, resident outdoor education, outdoor

sports and skills, in-service education, continuing education, and recreation.

EVALUATION

Because outdoor education is an integral part of the learning experiences of the various curriculum areas and activities, and since it contributes to the attainment of many of the school program's objectives, evaluation in outdoor education should be consistent with and a part of the general evaluation practices of the school. It is often difficult to isolate the "outdoor" part of the school program and to measure it independently from what occurs in the regular classroom. The spotlight of evaluation should not simply be turned on short field trips or on a resident outdoor school experience, for example, without considering both the pre-planning for these activities which takes place before the actual time students and teachers spend in the outdoors, and the events that follow the outdoor experience.

Evaluation in outdoor education is further complicated by the fact that many of the outcomes of outdoor education are not only in the cognitive and motor performance domains, but also in the affective domain which is more difficult to measure.

These problems and limitations of evaluation of outdoor education experiences do not imply that planned and continuous evaluation of such programs in school systems should be ignored or avoided. By carefully stating program objectives, along with procedures to be followed to attain those goals, and then by using a variety of measuring devices, such as motor skill tests, attitude measurements, parent surveys, anecdotal records, standardized examinations, teacher-made instruments, student participation records, sociograms, and other methods appropriate to specific activities, worthwhile evaluation of the various patterns of outdoor education can be accomplished. The following are suggested as elements of a good evaluation design:

1. **Program objectives.** State specific objectives for each outdoor education program. They should be identified in the cognitive, affective, or psychomotor (motor skills) domains and written so that they can be measured.

2. **Procedures or activities.** Determine the specific procedures or activities which will be used to obtain each program objective. Several activities may be planned to attain one objective, and, conversely, more than one objective might be achieved by a single activity.

3. **Evaluation techniques.** Identify a variety of evaluation instruments which will aid in collecting data and analyzing the degree of achievement of the program objectives.

Some schools have devised "opinionnaire" type instruments for evaluation of outdoor education activities. Such an instrument might be given to students, teachers, and parents to evaluate a resident outdoor school experience, for example. A sample of this type of evaluation form is included in a publication of the Michigan Department of Education entitled *Outdoor Education in Michigan Schools.*[2]

Some research in outdoor education has been accomplished through doctoral studies, a number of which serve as evaluation aids for various aspects of outdoor education. A summary of doctoral dissertations in outdoor education written since the early 1930s has been prepared for the AAHPER Outdoor Education Project.[3]

There are enough extensive and continuous outdoor education programs under way to warrant some needed longitudinal studies. Several resident outdoor schools have been in operation for many years and data could be collected that would provide significant findings concerning outcomes of outdoor education experiences. Careful measuring and recording of data about children and teachers participating in a program over a period of years should be conducted. New programs of outdoor education should "build in" this kind of long-term evaluation design.

Some of the contributions of outdoor learning experiences to the education of children that need to be investigated include:

1. change of behavior and attitudes in the realm of human relations
2. alteration of self concepts
3. solution of conservation and environmental quality problems
4. acquisition of outdoor skills and interests for leisure time
5. vitalization of learning in the out-of-doors as compared to indoor classroom performance
6. changes in teacher attitudes and in teaching skills that accrue through outdoor teaching experiences.

[2] Michigan Department of Education, *Outdoor Education in Michigan Schools* (Lansing, Mich.: Michigan Department of Education, 1970).
[3] Donald R. Hammerman, William D. Stark, and Malcolm D. Swan, *Research in Outdoor Education* (Washington, D.C.: Outdoor Education Project, AAHPER, 1969).

SUGGESTIONS FOR FURTHER STUDY AND RESEARCH

1. If you were asked to propose a plan for initiating a complete program of outdoor education in a school or recreation department or agency, how would you proceed?
2. Sketch a plan for a community campus for a city of 50,000.

REFERENCES

Athletic Institute and American Association for Health, Physical Education, and Recreation. *College and University Facilities Guide for Health, Physical Education, Recreation and Athletics.* Athletic Institute and AAHPER, 1968.
_____. *Planning Areas and Facilities for Health, Physical Education, and Recreation.* Athletic Institute and AAHPER, 1965.
Seay, Maurice F., and Crawford, Ferris N. *The Community School and Community Self Improvement.* Lansing, Mich.: Clair L. Taylor, Superintendent of Public Instruction, 1954.

14

outdoor education
and the future

A view of the current scene indicates that the need for outdoor education will become increasingly acute as the interest of people in the outdoors grows at an accelerated rate. The search for satisfying and creative activities caused by industrialization and the accompanying free time shows no sign of abating, but rather will be stimulated and intensified by the expanding population.

This book has given much attention to the need for understanding the outdoor environment and for developing the attitudes and skills that will lead to its wise use and protection. We should, in this context, remember that most people in the United States in the years ahead will be city dwellers and that their primary contact with the natural environment will occur during leisure activity. The argument is sometimes heard that the city dweller has little use for knowledge about the outdoors because he lives and works in an urban setting. He needs, of course, to comprehend the environmental problems of the city. However, evidence indicates that great masses of city dwellers, even those from its crowded heart, seek the outdoors during weekends and vacations. If, in the future, the problems of poverty in our cities are alleviated, even more city residents can be expected to use the outdoors during their leisure time. Some estimates today indicate that as much as 80 percent of our population is even now involved in some type of outdoor recreation. It is vitally important that these growing numbers understand the natural environment, both so that they may help to protect it and so that they may derive the fullest satisfaction from their outdoor experiences.

Never before has there been such an awareness of, and concern for, environmental conditions. People have begun to realize the interrelationships of all living things within the environment, and now that they have defiled and partially destroyed this environment, they feel an urgency to improve and conserve it through immediate action. There is a growing recognition that perhaps the very existence of the human race depends upon concerted, cooperative effort toward alleviation of destructive forces and initiation of improvement and renewal measures. These present conditions have strong implications for outdoor education and recreation.

At one time the environment was considered as merely a supplement to enhance the educational process; outdoor education, under the best conditions, played a secondary role to most other educational programs. But now that the environment has become a focus of attention and of great concern to education, the importance of outdoor education will increase perceptibly on all educational levels. Moreover, since education in general will concern itself with an approach to the problems of the total environment, then outdoor education will, of necessity, widen its scope accordingly.

The environment has always dictated the course of man's actions, though in a subtle way. In the future, however, its direction of man's course will be obvious to most people. Therefore, individuals, private groups, communities, state governments, and the federal government will comprise a web of relationships to deal with environmental problems and to plan for the future. Outdoor education will be an important member of the cooperative forces with but one goal—man's survival, and perhaps, ultimately, a humanistic society upholding a quality life for all men. Beginning now, the continuing task of outdoor recreation and outdoor education will be to provide opportunities for worthwhile outdoor recreation experiences for *all* people, and guidance toward man's better understanding of nature. The task appears to be formidable, but it must not be considered hopeless.

In the early history of our country outdoor education and recreation were of little concern to most people. Long hours of hard work were necessary to make a living, and there was not much leisure time. Survival was possible primarily by dint of hard work, dependence on native wit, and use of natural resources. The pioneers lived on the land and made their living from it. Often, in pursuit of supplementary food, they hunted and fished. From living so closely with their environment, they had an inherent nature sense, based on firsthand experience. In addition, an understanding of nature was handed down from one generation to the next by parents and other members of the society. In this early period there was no concern for conservation of natural resources and no recognizable need for such concern. The land was vast, and the population was small and widely dispersed. Resources appeared inexhaustible. The people could not have foreseen the environmental conditions existing today.

Today, in contrast, about three-fourths of our people are concentrated in urban areas. Since so many of our people know only urban areas, they do not have the old feeling for the land—they do not possess a nature sense. These city people, however, are perhaps the greatest users of our natural resources, and recognizing that natural resources are not inexhaustible, they will control, through their influence and votes, resource conservation in the future. For these reasons outdoor education programs and outdoor recreation will, of necessity, be expanded in the future.

THE FUTURE CLIMATE FOR OUTDOOR EDUCATION AND RECREATION

The current setting for outdoor education and recreation was described at some length in Chapter 1. By way of review here, the major factors having implications for outdoor education and recreation deserve some mention before we go on to discuss specific conditions relative to both. The following statements of conditions and projections are based on research.

Increase in population. By the year 2000 the population may reach 265–322 million, at the present rate of increase.[1] In terms of this factor, in conjunction with the following factors, the demand for outdoor recreation can hardly do anything but increase, and the stage is set for an increase in outdoor education.

Increase in leisure time. The work week by the year 2000 will approach 30 hours.[2] In the immediate future more time will be available for outdoor recreation.

[1] Council on Environmental Quality, *Environmental Quality: The First Annual Report of the Council.* Washington, D.C.: U.S. Government Printing Office, 1970.

[2] Outdoor Recreation Resources Review Commission, *Projections to the Years 1976 and 2000: Economic Growth, Population, Labor Force and Leisure, and Transportation,* Study Report 23, 1962.

Increase in disposable income. The upward trend in real income per capita is likely to be 2 per cent annually, and this will lead to an approximate doubling by 2000; a larger portion of this income will be spent for recreation of all kinds.[3]

Increase in mobility of people. By 2000 the average personal travel may well have more than doubled—to 9,000 miles annually, and an increasingly large proportion of this increased travel will be for recreation.[4] Auto travel, especially, will be more adapted for travel to outdoor areas with improvement of vehicles designed for this kind of use.[5]

Increased urbanization. Three-quarters of our people live in urban areas, and, if the present trend continues, most of them in the future will live in a few mammoth urban concentrations.[6] Recreation will increase to provide elements of continuity in the midst of social upheaval and to serve as an antidote to modular living.

A deteriorating environment. It is estimated that the people of our country are using up 40 per cent of the world's scarce or nonrenewable resources; they are destroying or degrading much of the natural resources in their own country. Outdoor education and recreation will increase efforts to help people to gain an understanding of their environment and man's place in it.

Diminishing land space. Open space for urban man continues to dwindle, and few cities have kept up with the need for park lands. Only 5 per cent of our total land acreage is in refuges, parks, and public institutions for recreation, and only 5 per cent is state, county, and city owned.[7] Population growth demands better land use and requires more land for recreation.

More funds for education and recreation. There will be more funds, particularly through government agencies, for education (including outdoor education) and recreation. The federal government has assumed the leadership and coordinating responsibilities for the total effort toward environmental quality and will allocate billions of dollars toward this end. State, county, and city governments will have to cooperate and follow the lead of the federal government and the mandate of the people. From these sources will come more funds for outdoor education and recreation.

---

[3] Marion Clawson and Jack L. Knetsch, *Economics of Outdoor Recreation.* Baltimore, Maryland: The Johns Hopkins Press, 1966.

[4] Ibid.

[5] ORRRC, *Projections to the Years 1976 and 2000: Economic Growth, Population, Labor Force and Leisure, and Transportation,* Study Report 23, 1962.

[6] Council on Environmental Quality, *Environmental Quality: The First Annual Report of the Council.* Washington, D.C.: U.S. Government Printing Office, 1970.

[7] Ibid.

In addition to this brief examination of general conditions having implications for outdoor education and recreation, some attention must now be given to some specific conditions relative to both. Until recently the school systems have conformed to the public's notion of what a school program should be. Practically speaking, that notion has been that all learning should take place within the classroom. Under these conditions, education in and for the out-of-doors has had no priority position in the curriculum comparable to the three R's. With this notion, and with teacher preparation as it has been, outdoor education even to meet current demands has had short shrift; provisions to meet future demands have been wholly inadequate.

Up to this time, relatively few educational institutions have acquired land sites for outdoor education. When land could have been purchased at a reasonable price, purchase was postponed or was preempted by the demands of more traditional programs. Often, too, educational institutions were losers to competitors such as land developers, airports, highways, and private industry.

Until recently, only a few institutions of higher learning have offered courses in outdoor education; still fewer have offered interdisciplinary programs. As for ecology, a discipline that has suddenly come into the limelight, most often no provision was made for it as a part of the outdoor education program. Also, the social sciences, particularly those concerned with human behavior and motivation, played no great part in the programs either. Thus, possibilities for developing outdoor leadership personnel with sound backgrounds and in great numbers have been limited. Since outdoor education has had no identity as a separate discipline or subject matter area it has not received its appropriate emphasis in teacher preparation. A few teacher training institutions have made outdoor education an integral part of the total training program or curriculum for teachers as a supplementary or enriching area for exploration.

It was not until the 1960s that a comprehensive survey of outdoor recreation trends and needs was undertaken. When *Outdoor Recreation for America* and the accompanying special reports of the Outdoor Recreation Resources Review Commission (ORRRC Reports) were published under the auspices of the federal government, they were the most important series of publications in the field. They still remain the benchmark for much study and research.

Though a considerable amount of research has been done in outdoor recreation, it has been fragmented and almost purely academic in nature. Research has also been beset with the problems of inadequate methodology and a lack of analytical models into which to fit data. These problems must be resolved before any appreciable amount of reliable results can be realized. Furthermore, prior to its initiation, research for this area of practical problems must have a purpose and must be suitable for practical application.

There is a real need for experimentation which would be concerned with testing and modifying ideas in many facets of outdoor recreation and the development of a body of reliable, basic knowledge. Too little experimentation has been done in comparison with purely academic research.

FUTURE DEVELOPMENTS IN EDUCATION RELATIVE TO OUTDOOR EDUCATION-RECREATION

In addition to the programs described in earlier chapters of this book, there are other developments and possibilities in education which are significant for outdoor education and recreation, and, ultimately, for the partial renewal of the environment sometime in the future.

community school education

Many people are aware that changes must be made in education, but there is little agreement on what the changes must be. In this period of rapid change in our society, and because of the people's desire for immediate action to save our environment, decisions must be made. No matter what concepts are adopted to bring about immediate action, in the long run the underlying concept must be that of a broad educational program that will begin with the nursery school and continue through all educational levels and throughout life.

The community school program, as best conceived and administered in this country, provides one of the most promising ways to help human beings to find their true place in an ecological community. The principles and practices of the community school type of education have already been discussed in Chapter 2.

Many citizens today feel an urgency to become environmentally informed in order to judge issues for themselves. They are beginning to realize that citizens' views can be cogent, and their influence on the legislative process in the future can be substantial. They recognize that people in leadership positions, whether national, state, or local, can no longer ignore their dictates on environmental issues, or other issues, either.

A community school educational program will be able to give help to citizens in the local community—people who want immediate, tangible action where they live. Already they want information on available government assistance for improvement programs and how to get them started. Many communities are especially interested in ways to provide more and better educational opportunities and more recreation possibilities for all citizens. As already stated in Chapter 2, the community school is in a strategic position in relation to the physical environment, and it can serve as a mobilizing force for concerted action on these issues.

The community school, because of its comprehensive nature, will be able to help guide and direct the "youth movement" which is sweeping the country. Since youth will live with this environment longer than the present mature generation, they have a right to a basic understanding of it as a basis for individual or group action. The community school program can give them a basic understanding through an idea-centered, problem-oriented, experience-centered, community-centered, and interdisciplinary approach.

The revival of the "primary social group" within the framework of the community school concept is considered by many people as the long-range solution to the social problems and the environmental problems of today. A conscious design to bring all the people, including youth, into contact with realities and problems and to involve them in serious and exciting work could bring out all their deeper, latent energies. This conscious design will include all the family of agencies serving the common purpose of community improvement. There is no better way for bringing about a sense of community than by face to face associations of groups or agencies.

Outdoor education and recreation are now recognized as enriching components of the educational system. In time they will be accepted as necessities in our efforts to enhance the quality of the environment and to secure the well-being of all our people. In addition to development of skills, then, they will be responsible for more emphasis on environmental understanding and humane values. As a lasting legacy, it will be possible for people to develop skills and attitudes at the same time, and thus help insure a quality environment and a quality life.

Sometime in the near future the public schools throughout the country will operate on a twelve-month basis. Such action will make for more efficient use of plant facilities, greater economic return, and fulfillment of the needs of a greater number of citizens. The extended school year, as a part of a broader use concept, will have very significant implications for outdoor education and recreation.

university and college programs

Although colleges and universities have offered opportunities for leadership preparation for outdoor education and recreation for some time, they have been caught off-guard by the new wave of environmentalists and by the increased demand for outdoor education and recreation. The current conditions are causing some critical self-evaluation by the institutions of higher learning and some serious and determined efforts toward structuring good programs for training leadership and for teacher preparation for a new era.

In the immediate future the institutions of higher learning will provide experiences—both pre-service and in-service—in outdoor education through many disciplines and departments, while utilizing outdoor laboratories for field experiences and requiring student teaching in outdoor settings. They will make provision for special preparation for those who will administer and supervise outdoor education activities.

For some time now, authorities in the field have agreed that no one pattern of education can produce people who can be called professionals in the field. The sort of training required cuts across such a variety of disciplines, and now, in addition, the environmental focus must be taken into consideration. It appears that the interdisciplinary approach may become the most feasible method of training both leadership and teachers in outdoor education in the future.

It is entirely possible that the two-year colleges will assume more of the characteristics of a community college and will offer opportunities for preparation of persons to work on the program level. Many of the jobs in outdoor recreation now held by college graduates can be done effectively by someone with two years of well-planned training.

research, experimentation, and demonstration

Whether working as individual researchers or as a team, people with many types of training and competence will be needed to do research in outdoor education and recreation. With imaginative ideas and concerted energies in this direction, research will increase to meet the demands of the times. Adequate research methodology will evolve from creative minds, as well as analytical models for measuring and evaluating data. Without doubt, there will be a markedly greater amount of research by the federal government, by organizations, by institutions, and by individuals. Without doubt, too, a great deal of it will be team research.

Further, within some organization or institution a central clearinghouse will be established for research materials in outdoor education and recreation. The clearinghouse will provide a comprehensive coverage of ongoing, as well as past, research, and a retrieval, communication, and loan service as a part of its plan. In all likelihood, the clearinghouse will maintain a close relationship with the Environmental Policy Division of the Library of Congress, which was recently designated the depository for proven data and reliable interpretation on environmental issues.

To plan intelligently for outdoor recreation, there must be more extensive experimentation and more extensive demonstration, as well as research. The type needed, on a large scale, is that which would be comparable to some of the experimental and demonstration work in agriculture that has for many years been conducted by land-grant universities. In line with this idea, a general design for what might be termed an outdoor recreation experiment station is suggested.

A SAMPLE DESIGN FOR AN EXPERIMENT STATION FOR OUTDOOR EDUCATION-RECREATION

the nature of the experiment station plan

An outdoor recreation experiment station designed to meet the needs of the American people must be concerned not only with working for people so that they can take advantage of its offerings, but also with involving them in the actual planning and development of the program. Families as well as individuals must be served, and they should be involved as participants, not merely as consumers.

Involvement of participants should be diverse, continuous, and natural and fitted to the individual tempo of living of all those concerned. The limitations of such involvements would be based on the interests, abilities, and skills of the participants, subject to the accepted policies and procedures of the management area. The individual or the family involved should find this co-performing process both emotionally and intellectually satisfying. Conflict can be minimized by a design of this kind set up to include those to be served as co-performers and even co-planners in the total process.

This program might be activated in one of many different areas of publicly owned lands, such as parks, game refuges, or public school grounds. If activated on any publicly owned lands, it would greatly extend the use of the land.

objectives of the experiment station plan

Basic to the program is the development of an adequate statement of its objectives, which should indicate the general scope and range of its content and the methodology to be used. This plan for outdoor recreation experimentation and demonstration has the following objectives:

1. To develop an outdoor recreation program compatible with the ecological demands of the times.
2. To determine the types of recreational use that can be made of the area which tend to establish a harmonious relationship between man and the land.
3. To study the sociological factors involved in the use of the area in such a manner as to contribute to a more effective program for family outdoor education.
4. To determine the ways of involving the family as co-performers in each of the major aspects of the proposed experimental program: experimentation, demonstration, research, and service.
5. To provide the family with opportunities for receiving recognition and rewards for participation in the outdoor recreation program.
6. To devise a comprehensive outdoor recreation program that will serve the needs of both sexes of the widest possible age range on a year-round basis.
7. To carry on a comprehensive program of continuing education in the area of outdoor recreation.
8. To finance, construct, maintain, and operate the necessary physical sites and facilities.

the plan in action

It is recommended that the outdoor recreation plan for the general public be on a year-round basis and that activities be developed for participation by all ages and both sexes.

Participants should be involved as contributors toward the preservation, enrichment, and extension of the area and its resources, and as co-performers in some of the related activities necessary for the continuation of a year-round recreation program.

Under the co-performer idea, individuals or families permitted to work would receive compensation in the form of certificates, which would be honored in any cooperating area, as well as at the station. Under these provisions a family or individual, by contributing a few hours whenever possible, could earn enough credit during the year to finance, with only minimum monetary outlay, a vacation in the area, or other areas, with use of a cabin, a boat, or other recreational equipment.

Employed personnel of the area, in cooperation with advisory committees, would define appropriate short-time terminal jobs for individual or family co-performers. Before engaging in the jobs, the co-performers would be required to take short courses for their own and others' protection and safety.

There should be a centrally located administration unit, with a staff equipped to offer training in the phases of outdoor recreation suited to the area through demonstrations and experiments, short courses, and research activities, and also prepared to give counsel and supervision on projects.

The actual program activities should, by necessity, be scattered over a wide area. For instance, camping facilities would be located at various points. A paramount consideration should be to provide a reasonable amount of privacy for those who desire it as a part of their recreational experience. Privacy could be assured and controlled, not by gates, but by the location of roads and location of the physical facilities themselves, according to a design for the area that would maintain the quality of its native beauty. Appropriate use should be made of the resources peculiar to each special segment of the area, such as lakes, open meadows, fishing streams, and hunting areas.

The five major phases of the recreation plan are:

1. *Experimentation.* This phase of the plan would be concerned with planning and conducting experiments for the purpose of discovering new forms of recreational pursuits. For instance, using all the potential interests—no matter how simple—found on a nature trail might help develop and stimulate new recreational pursuits in the outdoors.

Experimentation may be concerned with the established forms of recreation to discover ways of achieving greater satisfaction for participants. Experimentation may also be concerned with recreational activities for the aging or handicapped. In the past, activities have been developed more in terms of use by normal, healthy youth and active younger adults. For the most part, outdoor recreation has been considered a fair weather pursuit for the summer season. Experimentation in pursuits for the other seasons is needed. No matter what types of experimental work might become a part of the plan, any type would have to be in terms of good ecological principles.

2. *Demonstration.* The program plan would provide for special demonstrations of two kinds: on-site and off-site. On-site demonstrations would be largely for the education and recreation of the consuming public. They would consist of demonstrations in the use of special equipment and various kinds of shelter, and in a variety of recreational activities. There would also be demonstrations in administrative and

management procedures. For instance, the management procedure of pollution control would be demonstrated.

Off-site demonstrations for groups would be on privately owned or other publicly owned areas. Some things to demonstrate might be trailmaking, trail use, and trail maintenance.

3. *Research.* This particular type of research is characterized by its location: it takes place on the recreation site. It may be concerned with the biotic community and man and his relationship to or inter-relationships with other members of the biotic community.

The actual details and design of the many types of research studies and surveys should be under the general direction of the professional staff of a university and the management agency involved in the plan. The management agency will, in turn, solicit assistance from participants who are interested and qualified to engage in some phase of the research.

Those engaged in the fields of behavioral sciences should have the responsibility of devising ways to study the sociological, anthropological, and psychological forces affecting the use of the recreation area. These professional behavioral scientists and the professional staff of the management area should devise ways of studying the recreational interests and needs of the people in terms of the natural resources and the human resources involved in the total recreation program.

4. *Instruction.* There are two parts to an instructional program of this kind. One part is directed toward teaching individuals how to make a contribution to operation and maintenance of the plan in such areas as construction of shelters, elementary forestry, or even simple accounting and record keeping, depending on the knowledge, skills, and interests of the participants.

The second part would involve training individuals and families in outdoor activities suited to the environment at hand. This would consist of systematic instruction, tailored for the beginner and the more advanced learner, and would include imparting knowledge and teaching skills, and establishing socially desirable habits and attitudes, as well as developing an appreciation of and interest in the outdoors.

Instruction may be in the form of short courses at the administrative area or in the field. Some of these courses should be obligatory if the participant wishes to take part in some operational, maintenance, or recreational activity for which he is not demonstrably qualified.

Other instruction would be offered on a voluntary basis, including the teaching of skills such as fishing, swimming, boating, archery, specimen collecting, photography, geology, shooting, hunting, and nature lore.

The instructional program may be conducted by professionals trained at nearby centers of learning, the professional management staff, qualified participants, and specialists who would visit the site at periodic intervals to offer instruction in their particular field or fields. In the latter instance, the specialists would be offered a choice of reimbursement—an honorarium plus expenses, or credit under the co-performer plan.

5. *Service.* In order to achieve the maximum effect in the five-phase program of experimentation, demonstration, research, instruction, and service, the outdoor recreation experiment station should be closely associated with a university. If it is associated with a land-grant institution, it could profit from the institution's experience in similar work with agricultural experiment stations. For many years the farmers of our country have availed themselves, profitably, of the services of agricultural extension.

As far as service is concerned, the outdoor recreation experiment station would be concerned with four groups that comprise the public:

1. The general consuming public, and the range of possibilities and skills and understandings necessary for them to participate effectively in the outdoor recreation program.
2. The producers of outdoor recreation, and the services, types of equipment, programs, facilities, and areas needed.
3. The professionals, including city, county, state, and federal employees, and the types of programs, equipment, and sites necessary to serve the public.
4. The private landowner, under certain conditions, might use idle land to provide a varied and profitable recreation program for the public.

Direct learning experiences are as inseparable from the outdoors as classrooms and libraries have been inseparable from research to increase man's knowledge. It has been adequately demonstrated that the use of the outdoor laboratory is effective in helping relate the individual to the environment. Since the outdoor recreation experiment station would provide direct learning experiences, it could do much toward extending the realm of possibilities for all concerned with the better use of our land and other resources, and toward bringing man into a harmonious relationship with his natural environment.

OUTDOOR EDUCATION AND CURRICULUM
ADAPTABILITY

Specific objectives of outdoor education and the nature of the curriculum are affected by the ebb and flow of national and world conditions. In the future outdoor education, as an integral part of the educational process, will experience changes in curriculum content and in methods just as will all other aspects of education. Future educational opportunities for the learner in outdoor education will be determined by the situations evolving from the interaction of our man-made environment and our natural environment. Therefore, a preconceived, unchanging body of learning experiences will no longer be suitable. The curriculum content and the learning experiences will be created and shaped by leaders, or teachers, and the learners working as a learning team as they deal with changes resulting from the use of our environment.

In contrast to the past's very slowly changing body of curriculum experiences, there is already evidence that "disposable" curriculum materials will emerge. This application of the "disposable" principle as a positive factor rather than as a destructive factor, as was the case when applied to our natural resources, will assure current and applicable materials for use by the learning team.

The process of creating and fashioning relevant curriculum materials and experiences will make heavy demands on the outdoor education leader and teacher. They must have the knowledge and the skills to collect and organize evidence, and to make use of proven data to test their materials. They must then be able to help the learner to determine the nature and the extent of his own involvement. The ultimate outcome should be recognition and acceptance by the learner of the solution to the problem. At the same time, the learner must experience a feeling of successful achievement.

No longer will the teaching of mere facts be the only responsibility of the teacher or leader. Skills, habits, socially acceptable attitudes, interest, and appreciation will be concomitant learning outcomes of concern to the teacher or leader. These aspects of behavior will require both teacher and leader to be deliberate in selecting a broad learning opportunity in order to accomplish all desired behavioral changes.

The acceptance of this procedure will require a method that will encourage experimentation, use of research findings, and formulation of generalizations. It will result in the production of learning materials that will be constantly in a state of revision.

The procedure will require many basic changes in our libraries. The function, facility, organizational procedures, staff, financing, and both nature and scope of the collection must all undergo change. Libraries, no doubt, will be known as "resource centers," or some similar name, and it will be the responsibility of the library to make it easy for all the community to obtain learning materials—as easy as getting a quart of milk from the dairy. The acceptance of this learning procedure will, of course, bring about significant changes in administrative procedures, not only for outdoor education but also for the total educational process.

Before this procedure can be realized, the public must discard the notion that all learning must take place within the classroom. In the future, it is likely that as much or more learning will take place outside the classroom.

"What changes will be made in education during the next ten to fifteen years? We know there should—and will—be many changes, but the nature and direction of those changes can only be determined by the people who live in each community, state and in the nation, and, to some extent, by international developments. The kind and quality of decisions reached—and of changes that are made—may have a significant bearing on the future of the nation and even of humanity." [8]

WHAT OF THE FUTURE—1985 AND BEYOND?

There can be little doubt that the outdoors will beckon increasing numbers of people who search for adventure and relaxation amid the complexity of modern living. The Outdoor Recreation Resources Review Commission reports shed much light on the behavioral patterns and interests of a cross-section of the population as far as outdoor recreation is concerned. Even more important than additional outdoor recreation resources is the need for outdoor education. There is some reason to believe that the discrepancy between the need for and the

[8] Edgar L. Morphet and Charles O. Ryan, eds., *Designing Education for the Future, No. 2: Implications for Education of Prospective Changes in Society* (New York: Citation Press, 1967).

use of outdoor education will be less than in some aspects of education.

The sense of urgency and timeliness in moving forward in the area of outdoor education and recreation is reflected in action by all levels of government, private groups, industry, citizens groups, and the mass media.

The Bureau of Outdoor Recreation provides assistance to states for development of outdoor recreation resources to meet the needs of the people. The President has stated that he proposes that the Department of Interior be given authority to convey surplus real property to state and local governments for park and recreation purposes. Prospects appear extremely good for increased assistance in providing more land for outdoor recreation.

State and local governments are also taking action and are providing more land for outdoor recreation. Many are making or have made provision for outdoor education in the school curriculum and for outdoor laboratories. The Department of Health, Education and Welfare has furnished assistance to many communities, under the Elementary and Secondary Education Act, Title III, in the development of outdoor education programs with outdoor laboratories.

Private groups are furnishing assistance—financial, leadership, and educational—in an effort to fill the gap in recreational resources and outdoor education. Outstanding among these groups are the National Wildlife Federation, the Sierra Club, the National Parks Association, the Izaak Walton League of America, the National Audubon Society, and the Wilderness Society.

Private industry has initiated action toward provision of many more recreation possibilities for the people and provision of much educational material on the outdoors. Power companies have done much in this direction.

Better-informed citizens groups are initiating action on diverse items, including recreation and environmental education; their actions often are being guided by the Citizens Advisory Committee on Environmental Quality. They are now appearing in court to get action on problems pertaining to the preservation of natural areas.

A mass of literature on environmental issues is pouring from the presses, and increasingly more environmental information is being included in commercial T.V. programming. Also, educational T.V., film-makers, magazines, and newspapers are devoting more time and space to environmental subjects.

If present trends foreshadow things to come, then there is reason to believe that the present urgency to improve and to conserve our environment is not a passing fancy. Quite to the contrary, the action begun appears to gain momentum daily, and more people, groups, organizations, and agencies join the ranks. At this rate there is a possibility that eventually the major portion of our population will be concerned with and engaged in the improvement of our environment.

There is no doubt that information and education are the keys to the solution of our problems. It is the task of outdoor education and recreation, then, as a part of the total educational process, to assume some of the responsibility for helping the bulk of our population to improve its understanding of the ecology of our environment and how man's actions affect it.

SUGGESTIONS FOR FURTHER STUDY AND RESEARCH

1. What are the most significant developments of the federal government's program as stated in the report of the Council on Environmental Quality?
2. What are the significant implications of the ORRRC reports for education?
3. Suggest some kinds of research that are needed to help plan programs and facilities for outdoor education-recreation in the future.

REFERENCES

American Association of School Administrators. *Conservation—in the People's Hands.* Washington, D.C.: AASA, 1964.

Carson, Rachel. *Silent Spring.* Boston: Houghton Mifflin, 1962.

Clawson, Marion, and Knetsch, Jack L. *Economics of Outdoor Recreation.* Baltimore, Md.: The Johns Hopkins Press, 1966.

Council on Environmental Quality. *Environmental Quality: The First Annual Report of the Council.* Washington, D.C.: U.S. Government Printing Office, 1970.

Dasmann, Raymond. *The Last Horizon.* New York: The Macmillan Company, 1963.

Ehrlich, Paul R. *The Population Bomb.* New York: Sierra Club and Ballantine Books, 1968.

Fitch, Edwin M., and Shanklin, John E. *The Bureau of Outdoor Recreation.* New York: Praeger, 1970.

Leopold, Aldo. *A Sand County Almanac,* with other essays on Conservation from *Round River.* New York: Oxford University Press, 1966.

Loughmiller, Campbell. *Wilderness Road.* Austin, Texas: The Hogg Foundation for Mental Health, 1965.

McHarg, Ian. *Design with Nature.* Garden City, N.Y.: Natural History Press, 1969.

Mitchell, John G., and Stallings, Constance L., eds. *Ecotactics: The Sierra Club Handbook for Environmental Activists.* New York: Pocket Books, 1970.

Morphet, Edgar L., and Ryan, Charles O., eds. *Designing Education for the Future, No. 2: Implications for Education of Prospective Changes in Society.* New York: Citation Press, 1967.

Outdoor Recreation Resources Review Commission, *Outdoor Education for America.* A Report to the President and to the Congress. Washington, D.C.: U. S. Government Printing Office, 1962.

——, Study Reports 1–27:

1. *Public Outdoor Recreation Areas—Acreage, Use, Potential.*
2. *List of Public Outdoor Recreation Areas—1960.*
3. *Wilderness and Recreation—A Report on Resources, Values, and Problems.*
4. *Shoreline Recreation Resources of the United States.*
5. *The Quality of Outdoor Recreation: As Evidenced by User Satisfaction.*
6. *Hunting in the United States—Its Present and Future Role.*
7. *Sport Fishing—Today and Tomorrow.*
8. *Potential New Sites for Outdoor Recreation in the Northeast.*
9. *Alaska Outdoor Recreation Potential.*
10. *Water for Recreation—Values and Opportunities.*
11. *Private Outdoor Recreation Facilities.*
12. *Financing Public Recreation Facilities.*
13. *Federal Agencies and Outdoor Recreation.*
14. *Directory of State Outdoor Recreation Administration.*
15. *Open Space Action.*
16. *Land Acquisition for Outdoor Recreation—Analysis of Selected Legal Problems.*
17. *Multiple Use of Land and Water Areas.*
18. *A Look Abroad: The Effect of Foreign Travel on Domestic Out-*

door Recreation and a Brief Survey of Outdoor Recreation in Six
Countries.

19. National Recreation Survey.
20. Participation in Outdoor Recreation: Factors Affecting Demand
    Among American Adults.
21. The Future of Outdoor Recreation in Metropolitan Regions of the
    United States.
22. Trends in American Living and Outdoor Recreation.
23. Projections to the Years 1976 and 2000: Economic Growth, Popula-
    tion, Labor Force and Leisure, and Transportation.
24. Economic Studies of Outdoor Recreation.
25. Public Expenditures for Outdoor Recreation.
26. Prospective Demand for Outdoor Recreation.
27. Outdoor Recreation Literature: A Survey.

Owings, Nathan Alexander, *The American Aesthetic*. New York:
Harper and Row, Publishers, 1969.

President's Council on Recreation and Natural Beauty, *From Sea to
Shining Sea*. A Report on the American Environment—Our
Natural Heritage. Washington, D.C.: U.S. Government Printing
Office, 1968.

Shepard, Paul, and McKinley, Daniel, eds., *The Subversive Science:
Essays Toward an Ecology of Man*. Boston: Houghton Mifflin
Company, 1969.

Swift, Ernest F., *A Conservation Saga*. Washington, D.C.: National
Wildlife Federation, 1967.

Toffler, Alvin, *Future Shock*. New York: Random House, 1970.

Udall, Stewart L., *The Quiet Crisis*. New York: Holt, Rinehart & Winston,
1963.

Whyte, William H., *The Last Landscape*. New York: Doubleday and
Company, 1968.

index

329

T

Teaching:
  archery, 153–55
  boating and water activities, 155–57
  casting and angling, 147–50
  interpretive service, 183
  outdoor laboratory, 45
  personnel, 262–66
  preparation, 274–94
  program planning, 123–24
Tennessee Valley Authority, 207
Terrariums, 96
Tract gardens, 72, 257–59
Trails:
  park and recreation agencies, 187, 188
  park-school plan, 248–49
  state parks, 212
Trailside musems, 84–85, 212, 254–56
Travel, 93
Traverse City program, 161–62
Trips, 93 (see also Field trips)
Twelve-month school year, 315
Tyler outdoor education programs, 107,
    111–12, 115
Tyler School Farm, 82

U

Universities (see Colleges and universities)
University of Northern Colorado, 277
Urbanization, 6
U. S. Army Corps of Engineers, 205, 271
U. S. Fish and Wildlife Service, 196, 203–4,
    271
U. S. Forest Service, 196, 200–202, 271
U. S. Geological Survey, 271

V

Vivariums, 65, 96
Vocational education, 19, 71–72, 79–80, 82
Voluntary agencies, 221–27

W

Washington outdoor education programs,
    109–10
Water:
  government programs, 205–6
  outdoor activities, 155–57
  resident outdoor education, 140
  school sites, 252
  sports, 205–6
Weather stations, 67, 96, 124, 129, 142
Western Michigan University, 168–69
Wildlife:
  collections, 65
  government protection, 195, 203–4
  park-school, 249
  projects, 65, 66
  resident outdoor education, 128, 141
  state fish and game departments, 210–12
Winter sports, 157–58, 201
Wipper, Kirk, 161
W. K. Kellogg Foundation, 106, 107, 108,
    109, 110, 111, 112, 115
Woodworking, 94, 125, 129
Work activities, 127–28
Wykoff, Jack, 108

Y

Yellowstone National Park, 197
YMCA, 221, 271
Youth hostels, 227
YWCA, 221

Z

Zahn, D. Willard, 43
Zoology, 57, 90
Zoos, 85, 181, 184–85

Date Due